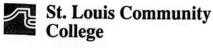

St. Louis Community College

Forest Park
Florissant Valley
Meramec

Instructional Resources
St. Louis, Missouri

ROMANTICISM IN PERSPECTIVE:
TEXTS, CULTURES, HISTORIES

General Editors:
Marilyn Gaull, *Professor of English,*
Temple University/New York University
Stephen Prickett, *Regius Professor of English Language and Literature,*
University of Glasgow

This series aims to offer a fresh assessment of Romanticism by looking at it from a wide variety of perspectives. Both comparative and interdisciplinary, it will bring together cognate themes from architecture, art history, landscape gardening, linguistics, literature, philosophy, politics, science, social and political history and theology to deal with original, contentious or as yet unexplored aspects of Romanticism as a Europe-wide phenomenon.

Titles include:

Toby R. Benis
ROMANTICISM ON THE ROAD: The Marginal Gains of Wordsworth's
Homeless

Richard Cronin (*editor*)
1798: THE YEAR OF THE *LYRICAL BALLADS*

Péter Dávidházi
THE ROMANTIC CULT OF SHAKESPEARE: Literary
Reception in Anthropological Perspective

Charles Donelan
ROMANTICISM AND MALE FANTASY IN BYRON'S *DON JUAN*
A Marketable Vice

Tim Fulford
ROMANTICISM AND MASCULINITY: In the Writings of
Burke, Coleridge, Cobbett, Wordsworth, De Quincey and Hazlitt

David Jasper
THE SACRED AND SECULAR CANON IN ROMANTICISM
Preserving the Sacred Truths

Malcolm Kelsall
JEFFERSON AND THE ICONOGRAPHY OF ROMANTICISM Folk,
Land, Culture and the Romantic Nation

Mark S. Lussier
ROMANTIC DYNAMICS: The Poetics of Physicality

Andrew McCann
CULTURAL POLITICS IN THE 1790s: Literature, Radicalism
and the Public Sphere

Ashton Nichols
THE REVOLUTIONARY 'I': Wordsworth and the Politics of
Self-Presentation

Jeffrey C. Robinson
RECEPTION AND POETICS IN KEATS: 'My Ended Poet'

Anya Taylor
BACCHUS IN ROMANTIC ENGLAND: Writers and Drink, 1780–1830

Michael Wiley
ROMANTIC GEOGRAPHY: Wordsworth and
Anglo-European Spaces

Eric Wilson
EMERSON'S SUBLIME SCIENCE

John Wyatt
WORDSWORTH'S POEMS OF TRAVEL, 1819–42
'Such Sweet Wayfaring'

Romanticism in Perspective
Series Standing Order ISBN 0–333–71490–3
(*outside North America only*)

You can receive future titles in this series as they are published by placing a
standing order. Please contact your bookseller or, in case of difficulty, write to us at
the address below with your name and address, the title of the series and the ISBN
quoted above.

Customer Services Department, Macmillan Distribution Ltd
Houndmills, Basingstoke, Hampshire RG21 6XS, England

Jefferson and the Iconography of Romanticism

Folk, Land, Culture and the Romantic Nation

Malcolm Kelsall

Professor of English
University of Wales
Cardiff

First published in Great Britain 1999 by
MACMILLAN PRESS LTD
Houndmills, Basingstoke, Hampshire RG21 6XS and London
Companies and representatives throughout the world

A catalogue record for this book is available from the British Library.

ISBN 0–333–69824–X

First published in the United States of America 1999 by
ST. MARTIN'S PRESS, INC.,
Scholarly and Reference Division,
175 Fifth Avenue, New York, N.Y. 10010

ISBN 0–312–22252–1

Library of Congress Cataloging-in-Publication Data
Kelsall, M. M. (Malcolm Miles), 1938–
Jefferson and the iconography of romanticism : folk, land,
culture and the romantic nation / Malcolm Kelsall.
p. cm. — (Romanticism in perspective)
Includes bibliographical references and index.
ISBN 0–312–22252–1 (cloth)
1. Jefferson, Thomas, 1743–1826—Influence. 2. Jefferson, Thomas,
1743–1826—Homes and haunts—Virginia. 3. Monticello (Va.)
4. United States—Civilization—1783–1865. 5. Romanticism—United
States—History. 6. Idealism, American—History. 7. National
characteristics, American. I. Title. II. Series.
E332.2.K45 1999
973.4'6'092—dc21   98–53725
                                                                    CIP

This book is printed on paper suitable for recycling and made from fully managed and
sustained forest sources.

10   9   8   7   6   5   4   3   2   1
08   07   06   05   04   03   02   01   00   99

Printed and bound in Great Britain by
Antony Rowe Ltd, Chippenham, Wiltshire

I contend that we are the finest race in the world, and the more of the world we inhabit, the better it is for the human race.

Cecil Rhodes

Contents

List of Plates   viii

Acknowledgements   ix

1.   The Pilgrimage to Monticello   1

2.   Jefferson Seals the Revolution   45

3.   Kennst du das Land? *Notes on the State of Virginia*   69

4.   The Villa on a Hill   105

5.   Writing Monticello   159

Notes   177

Index   200

List of Plates

1. Monticello: the garden front (author's photograph)
2. The University of Virginia: the Jeffersonian campus (engraving by Benjamin Tanner, 1826) (by courtesy of the University of Virginia Library)
3. The Seal of the United States of America (as displayed on the one-dollar bill)
4. Monticello in the Virginian landscape (by courtesy of Monticello/the Thomas Jefferson Memorial Foundation, Inc.)
5. Chiswick Villa, London (from William Watts, *The Seats of the Nobility and Gentry*, 1779)
6. Monticello: the entrance front (by courtesy of Monticello/the Thomas Jefferson Memorial Foundation, Inc.)
7. Monticello: the hall (by courtesy of the Thomas Jefferson Memorial Foundation, Inc.)
8. Houghton Hall, England: the stone hall (from the current guide book) (by courtesy of Lord Cholmondeley)
9. Plan of the ground floor of Monticello
10. Monticello: Jefferson's bedroom (by courtesy of Monticello/ the Thomas Jefferson Memorial Foundation, Inc.)
11. Monticello: the tea-room (by courtesy of Monticello/the Thomas Jefferson Memorial Foundation, Inc.)
12. The Temple of Ancient Virtue, Stowe, England (from Benton Seeley, *Stowe, A Description*, 1797)
13. Monticello: the dome-room (by courtesy of Monticello/the Thomas Jefferson Memorial Foundation, Inc.)
14. The Jefferson Memorial, Washington, DC (author's photograph)
15. Monticello: a staircase (by courtesy of Monticello/the Thomas Jefferson Memorial Foundation, Inc.)

Acknowledgements

I am particularly grateful to Stephen Prickett of the University of Glasgow for his courage in commissioning this book when it was little more than a perplexed reaction to Monticello in the author's mind. While working in Virginia, I owe an immense debt of gratitude both to Kaye and Peter Graham, and Joseph Byron Yount. They drove my wife and myself the length and breadth of the State and overwhelmed us with the richness of their hospitality. I should like to thank also all the staff of the International Center for Jefferson Studies at Monticello for their unfailing and continuous help while I was privileged to be resident at the Center and for responding so promptly, courteously and efficiently to my many transatlantic requests for help. Douglas and Sharon Wilson, in particular, were generous beyond the call of duty. So too, in Charlottesville, were George and Grace Shackelford. More generally, I am grateful to Howard Weinbrot of the University of Madison, Wisconsin, and to the staff and postgraduates who attended my seminars there during my residence in 1996. They first heard my ideas as they took shape, and I am indebted to their perceptive and constructive criticisms.

The British Academy generously funded an extended visit to the United States in 1997 and, with equal generosity, the International Center for Jefferson Studies granted me the status of visiting scholar. Cardiff gave me 15 weeks of study leave to write the book, and our research board supported me with funds which have averaged £40 a year to work in the Bodleian and the British Library.

I gratefully acknowledge permission to reproduce the following plates: 4, 6, 7, 10, 11, 13, 15, Monticello/the Thomas Jefferson Memorial Foundation, Inc.; 2, University of Virginia Library; 8, Lord Cholmondeley. My thanks also to Howard Cheetham of the Graphic Services Department here in Cardiff for his skilled work here and in 1992/93 in *The Great Good Place* (from which, by a regrettable oversight, his name was omitted).

1
The Pilgrimage to Monticello

The day will come...when sublime Germania shall stand on the bronze pedestal of liberty and justice, bearing in one hand the torch of enlightenment, which shall throw the beam of civilization into the remotest corners of the earth....The people will beg her to settle their disputes; those very people who now show us might is right, and kick us with the jackboot of scornful contempt.
Siebenpfeiffer, at the Hambach Festival, 1832.[1]

On Thursday, 4 November 1824 a long procession ascended the hill to Thomas Jefferson's villa at Monticello. The carriage of the guest of honour – the Marquis de La Fayette, 'the Nation's Guest' – was headed by a detachment of cavalry; next came a body of American dignitaries; behind marched the Albemarle Lafayette Guards, and finally a great body of citizens. It was a long and circuitous route to the top of the 'little mountain'. Everywhere, so it was claimed, 'it seemed that thousands of freemen had sprung up from the hills, and woods, and mountains, to hail the arrival' and to express 'a nation's gratitude [in]...one wide, wild spread of enthusiasm'. At Monticello itself a substantial body of spectators was already gathered. As La Fayette approached, a bugle sounded and silence fell over the crowd. Jefferson, bestowing the highest honour upon his guest that the owner of a great country estate might offer, advanced even beyond the entrance to his house, and with the faltering steps of extreme old age, came to meet his aged visitor. He and the Marquis de La Fayette embraced, and in the impressive silence they sobbed as they enfolded one another in their arms.[2]

It was already common to make the 'pilgrimage' to 'the sage of Monticello'; but the visit of La Fayette was the most significant among many. It was a moment of especial iconographical significance in his triumphal return to the United States and tour of 1824–25 – as momentous even as his earlier memorial visit to the tomb of Washington at Mount Vernon.[3] Since the death of Washington, the

1

'patriarch' of Monticello (as Jefferson described himself to the Marquis) had assumed for La Fayette the role of mentor and confidant. In his correspondence with Jefferson, La Fayette had poured out his hopes and fears for the progress of Franco-American 'liberty' on both sides of the Atlantic. Now, at last, the writer of the Declaration of Independence and Europe's most famous recruit to the War of American Independence were united again after the separation of decades of European and world war. When they embraced and wept, the meeting signified more than personal friendship expressed in the sentimental language of the heart. It indicated too that the revolutionary principles to which they were committed in the American and French revolutions were essentially the same and remained constant even after the intervening decades of war. In Byron's words:

> Yet, Freedom! Yet thy banner, torn but flying,
> Streams like the thunder storm *against* the wind...
> (*Childe Harold*, IV, 98–9)

The visit to Monticello was involved, therefore, with the appropriate signifiers of La Fayette's revolutionary principles. At Richmond, as he had first crossed into Virginia, a great Masonic banquet had been held to welcome him as a hero (like Washington) of that radical order. At a march past, a military band had played French and American 'national airs' (so Levasseur recalled) and Masonic grandees had processed, displaying the religious symbols of their Order, signifying thus divine approval of the cause of national liberation. Later, after the domestic reception of friendship at Monticello, when the 'hero', accompanied by his host 'the sage', descended from the lofty villa (celebrated by 'a thousand daughters of the mountains' as they went), they were entertained at a great banquet in the Pantheon of Jefferson's University of Virginia: 'the future temple of literature and science, erected *beyond* the point where the flag of the invader has ever floated'. At the portico of the 'temple' the Marquis was welcomed as it were to a sacred national site 'erected on the hills of *liberty*' by 'the wisdom of our sages, and the *blood* of our heroes'. Might the '*evening* ray' of La Fayette's glory, it was proclaimed, 'shine across the gloom and oppression of other nations'. It was a sentiment echoed by Jefferson himself in the laurel-wreathed banquet which followed, although Jefferson, now too enfeebled to speak in public, gave his speech to another to read. La Fayette had 'made our cause his own, as in truth it was that of his native country also'. In time 'the rights of self-government; rights which have blessed ourselves... will bless, in their sequence, all the nations of the earth'. The toasts were numerous to 'Liberty – which has virtue for its guest and gratitude for its feast' (Madison's words).

> The hollow vault of heaven is rent with shouts,
> Wild din and hurry of tumultuous joy
> Waves the wide throng – for lo! in perfect strength, La Fayette
> comes!

Something of the romantic and quasi-religious enthusiasm of the visit must be felt before stepping back from the experience of historical celebration to examine the signification of signs. For, as Madame de Staël had written, without devotion and enthusiasm there is no true nationalism: *voilà le genre de lumières redoutable pour les vertus nationales!*[4] (this is the kind of enlightenment formidable for national virtues). It seems that the emotional moment before the portico of the domed villa of Monticello, so carefully stage-managed, and so moving to the participants, was directed towards establishing for Jefferson and his villa a meaning which united the private world of sensibility (the friendship of 'hero' and 'sage') and the public world of national self-celebration. It was a climatic moment (iconographically situated appropriately on the mountain top) between the Masonic celebration at Richmond and the secular celebration in the Pantheon of the university which Jefferson himself had founded. Between these two public events La Fayette withdrew with Jefferson (for some days) into the privacy of conversation and reminiscence in the villa on its lofty height. It was an invitation from one citizen of America to another (honorary) citizen to be 'at home'.[5]

But the private space had public signification also. Any reader of the symbolic order of architecture – and La Fayette had come from a Masonic banquet – would have known the Palladian claim that the portico of the classical villa and the form of the classical temple were directly related (*Four Books on Architecture* II, xvi). Private virtue and public magnificence were thus iconographically related by the ancients. So too Monticello was intrinsically related to the Pantheon as the 'temple' of the University of Virginia, for both buildings share a common architectural grammar of portico and (religious) dome (Plates 1 and 2). Jefferson, as it were, cloned his villa in the major public building of his university, and united both by an iconography of secular religion. The secular/sacred, private/public motif would have been apparent to Jefferson's Masonic visitor even in the penetralia of Monticello. Each of the major public rooms derives its order of architecture from the temple architecture of Rome. La Fayette, in his progress either into the villa, or from the villa to the university, was moving along a continuing spectrum of associations. 'At home' in the villa, he had been welcomed by an intimate embrace; at the Pantheon, he was greeted by the formality of public speeches on the portico and beneath the symbolic 'hollow vault of heaven' of the dome. The theme was common. It was the birth of a nation which was being sanctified, whether in the domestic or in the public sphere and, ultimately, for all nations beneath the divine heavens. Well recognising the nature of the symbolic architecture of the new nation (in Capitol or State House, as well as in villa and university), La Fayette, in his farewell address to the Continental Congress at Trenton, 11 December 1824, envisaged the whole of the United States as an architectural icon: 'May this Immense temple of freedom Ever Stand a lesson to oppressors, an Example to the oppressed, a Sanctuary for the Rights of Mankind.'[6]

The year of La Fayette's visit to Monticello is famous in the history of European romanticism as the year also of Byron's death at Missolonghi fighting in another national war of 'freedom...for the Rights of Mankind'. The appeal to the United States as a sanctuary for freedom belongs by 1824 to what one might call a romantic 'Koine' (a common language shared by speakers of different tongues) through which La Fayette might symbolically serve to unite the America of 1776 with the new wave of nationalist revolutions of Europe in the 1820s. Thus, in the Pantheon of Jefferson's university, the 'Volunteer' toast had been to 'Greece, may her cause be exposed by other Byrons, who shall live to be other La Fayettes.' The ninth toast had been to 'Greece – the Ottoman no longer tramples on the grave of Leonidas.' It followed a toast to the American Constitution and to Brutus as tyrannicide and preceded a tenth (it was a magniloquent evening) to national military power, may it continue now in 'the spirit of our Fathers'. Leonidas, Brutus, the men of '76, La Fayette and Byron were all national liberators. As it was in classic antiquity, so is it now in the United States, and from thence freedom's battle has spread to the emergent nations of post-imperial Europe.[7]

It is self-apparent that this is not a Koine expressed in words alone. The entire iconography of the visit would be familiar to La Fayette, for it was revolutionary France in particular which had instituted the (spontaneous) *Fête* as an expression of the National Will – *e pluribus unum* – and his own role had been central in the great processional of the *Fête de la Fédération* in the Champs de Mars on 14 July 1790 – the original model for a long sequence of patriotic expressions of national unity and national dedication.[8] So now in 1824 (in seeming spontaneity, carefully orchestrated) 'the Nation's Guest' saw 'a nation's gratitude' as 'thousands of freemen' sprang from wood and mountain and 'a thousand daughters of the mountains' expressed the fecundity as well as the united joy of the free people.[9] The *Volk* spontaneously rise from the *Land* (to use a more theoreticised vocabulary of romantic nationalism). But, as the examples of Leonidas, Brutus, the men of '76, La Fayette and Byron show, nations are preserved and made by *Blut und Eisen* – 'the *blood* of our heroes' – an argument which Turgot, Fichte and Herder had endorsed before Bismarck, or later the followers of Nietzsche.[10] The spontaneous national ceremony of the free yeomanry (to return to the vocabulary of La Fayette's tour) was also an expression of military power. A military band played the national airs of France and the United States; cavalry environed General La Fayette on his progress; a bugle seemed to command silence at Monticello. The banquet was held '*beyond* the point where the flag of the invader has ever floated' – and, presumably, the star-spangled banner was prominently displayed. The signifiers of militant romantic nationalism are commonplace, and were well established by 1824.

Thus, the iconographic signification of the celebration of 'the Nation's Guest' on his tour of 1824–25 was to confirm a myth of national unity and national origin – the myth of Independence Day.[11] In 1776 a nation had spontaneously sprung to arms to establish its 'liberty'. As Jefferson recorded the event in his *Autobiography*, the delegates from Virginia, on 7 June 1776, had been driven by 'the voice of the people' to join 'the general voice of America' in the resolution to be 'free and independent'. Across the sea, Europe too had heard the message, and La Fayette was one of the first to respond to the call of liberty. Now, in 1824, perhaps there was a certain irony that it was only through the person of a European visitor that the nation could embody its unity – all that was left of Washington was a tomb – but the tour of La Fayette from end to end of the nation was to enable each place to reiterate the myth through appropriate iconography and speech. It was an 'occasion which rallies us to a single subject... [and] strengthens the habit of considering our country as one and indivisible' (Jefferson to Francis W. Gilmer, 12 October 1824). Since La Fayette was a Freemason, that iconography often took architectural form, and when the architecture did not exist, it was created. La Fayette repeatedly laid cornerstones as signs of the foundation of the nation. As in revolutionary Paris, he progressed through triumphal arches – thus the arch of Septimus Severus, decorated with symbols of the republic, was recreated in La Fayette's honour in front of Independence Hall in Philadelphia. In New York he was met with a vast pyramid (a fundamental architectural and Masonic signifier) at the top of which the name 'La Fayette' blazed like the 'all-seeing eye' of Providence itself. The iconography was commodified. The English potteries flooded the American market with commemorative ware. A favoured subject was La Fayette at the tomb of Washington. The triumphal arch at Philadelphia is recorded on silk handkerchiefs. (There were also commemorative sheet music and trowels, drums and ribbons, even whiskey flasks, for patriotism and commerce were united in the States.) But before the portico and dome of the Pantheon *redivivus* at Monticello that Thursday, 4 November 1824 there had been no need to build a new national signifier. Jefferson had already created the permanent architectural form.

This was the national context of La Fayette's meeting with Jefferson at Monticello. The wider, European signification of the meeting of the two men had long been established. It is clearest in their correspondence, where La Fayette, in particular, was insistent on the Europeanisation of the American revolution. In spirit, although not in political practice, it is a myth of romantic nationalism to which Jefferson was ready to accede. It places the Declaration of Independence as the initiatory act from which the liberation of the nations of Europe (and then the entire world) would proceed. Had not Mirabeau said, 'Is there at present in Europe even one single government... which according to the declaration would not have to be ousted?'[12] It was a liberationist movement halted for a while by counter-revolution, but now exploding like a force of Nature in the post-Napoleonic world. The long correspondence between Jefferson and La Fayette is a typical history of romantic hope fighting against the forces of darkness in what Shelley had called in the preface to *The Revolt of Islam* 'an age of despair', and what Jefferson had even more darkly called one of the three worst ages the world had known.[13] La Fayette, like Shelley's Prometheus, is a figure who always hopes ''til hope creates/From its own wreck the thing it contemplates', and in this mythology America is, as it were, the land of Prometheus Unbound: 'the blessed shores of liberty' on which La Fayette's 'Heart throbbed with joy'.

In this romantic story there are few surprises, for the letters between La Fayette and Jefferson employ the standard vocabulary of Whig/liberal/nationalist idealism, and, as Lloyd Kramer has argued, it is this idealistic creation of romantic history which gave to La Fayette and his circle their pivotal role and apparent importance. The historical process is one in which the two correspondents claim to have been specifically privileged. Jefferson, by writing the Declaration of Independence, had shown the way; France, guided by La Fayette, was to follow. As Jefferson wrote to Madison (28 August 1789), the American experience was 'treated like that of the bible, open to explanation, but not to question'. But the clock of historical progress had begun to run down at a specific moment in 1789. That moment was of particular personal significance for Jefferson and La Fayette for it was one in which the romantic concept of the inevitable progress of 'liberty' was first halted by the recalcitrant nature of things. There was a time in 1789 when the author of the Declaration of Independence had collaborated with La Fayette in drawing up a Declaration of Rights for France. At a crucial moment he had given a dinner party for the leaders of the liberals to confer upon a Constitution for France (both acts of gross impropriety for a foreign Minister, but the historical possibilities seemed too important for diplomatic protocol). It was an event to which Jefferson was to give particular signification in his *Autobiography*, and again when writing to La Fayette to welcome him to Monticello in 1824.

> The discussions began at the hour of four, and were continued till ten o'clock in the evening; during which time I was a silent witness to a coolness and candor of argument unusual in the conflicts of public opinion; to a logical reasoning, and chaste eloquence, disfigured by no gaudy tinsel of rhetoric or declamation, and truly worthy of being placed in parallel with the finest dialogues of antiquity, as handed to us by Xenophon, by Plato and Cicero.[14]

But, despite the greatness of the men, and the importance of the moment, nothing came of La Fayette's Declaration or the new Constitution. Instead of achieving the effect of the American prototypes, they were swept away in the betrayal of the revolution by the Jacobins; the conspiracy of the crowned heads of Europe against France; Bonapartism; the restoration of the Bourbons.

It is, in general, a standard liberal history on which Jefferson and La Fayette were both agreed. 'You were right' in 1789, he assured La Fayette, but from the 'fatal error of the republicans',

> from their separation from yourself and the constitutionalists, in their councils, flowed all the subsequent sufferings and crimes of the French nation.... The foreigner gained time to anarchise by gold the government he could not overthrow by arms, to crush in their own councils the genuine republicans, by the fraternal embraces of exaggerated and hired pretenders, and to turn the machine of Jacobinism from the change to the destruction of order; and, in the end, the limited monarchy they have secured was exchanged for the unprincipled and bloody tyranny of Robespierre, and the equally unprincipled and maniac tyranny of Bonaparte.

La Fayette's subsequent history of liberalism after the fall of Bonaparte sustains the same historical Koine – like the Bourbons he may be said to have forgotten nothing, and to have learned nothing. The rise of liberalism and nationalism in the Iberian peninsula, in Italy, Greece, South America all testified to the inextinguishable principles of what he called 'American liberty'. Typical is a letter of 10 December 1817:

> The principle of National instead of Special Governments is working under the Bed of lies which the Sainte alliance are Holding over the European world. France, vanquished, fettered, and watched as it is, does still Hold the Intellectual and patriotic lead. Italy feels indignant to Be no more a Nation. There is in Spain But a liberal party; but Small as it is, as well as in Portugal, there is to Be found Spirit and Sympathy. You know the Germans. There are excentricities in their patriotism as well as in their philosophy. Yet much is Boiling in the Northern parts of that Country... Old despotism Has But little to live in the Civilized

world. It will be divided between the British and American doctrines. The later I Hope will prevail.

These were the views, he told Jefferson, that he had enunciated at a 4 July dinner in Europe. They were also fed back to America through La Fayette's pervasive influence on Fenimore Cooper. Jefferson, when he was free of the diplomatic exigencies of the Presidency, had encouraged La Fayette with numinous and enthusiastic discourse:

If there be god, & he is just his day will come. He will never abandon the whole race of man to be eaten up by the leviathans and mammoths of a day. (To La Fayette, 20 January 1811)

He continued, in a complacent vein from the safety of Monticello: 'I enjoy good health & am happy in contemplating the peace, prosperity, liberty & safety of my country, & especially the wide ocean, the barrier of all these.'

Yet the threat of counter-revolution had always been present even in the American republic – so Jefferson feared. Although the 'monarchical-aristocratical system' represented by Federalist 'Tories' (and traitors) had been crushed in the 1790s by Jeffersonian republicanism, yet even as late as 1815 he wrote that the eternal forces of alien sedition were seeking to destabilise the republic. 'The Marats, the Dantons, and Robespierres of Massachusetts are in the same pay, under the same orders, and making the same efforts to anarchise us, that their prototypes in France did there' (to La Fayette, 14 February 1815). To which 'treason' and 'parricide' he added, in 1817, the religious bigots of Connecticut and even the Quakers of Delaware, 'Dispersed, as the Jews, they still form, as they do, one nation, foreign to the land they live in' (to La Fayette, 14 May 1817). Fortunately, the religious and racial enemies of the true republican nation 'have very different materials to work on. The yeomanry of the United States are not the *canaille* of Paris' (to La Fayette, 14 February 1815). A Virginian gentleman farmer, like the owner of La Grange, had little in common with *sans culottism*.

Although the correspondence with La Fayette may represent only the kind of history the Marquis wanted to hear, Jefferson's own *Autobiography* underlines his identification with the 'liberals'. The unfinished work drew to its close with an impassioned declaration of the politics of revolution: it will become a seamless progression again for the 'resurrection to a new life' of the people of the world:

> As yet, we are but in the first chapter of its history. The appeal to the rights of man, which had been made in the United States, was taken up by France, first of the European nations. From her, the spirit has spread over those of the South. The tyrants of the North have allied indeed against it, but it is irresistible. Their opposition will only multiply its millions of human victims; their own satellites will catch it, and the condition of man through the civilized world will be finally and greatly ameliorated.[15]

That was the optimistic language of romantic hope, written, one presumes, for public record, but in a work never completed. It is vain to speculate why Jefferson never finished his *Autobiography*, which breaks off at the very moment when the revolution in France passed out of the hands of the liberals, and when Jefferson returned to the vicious internal controversies of American politics in the 1790s. When he looked back on those times in 1824 Jefferson was to share with the Marquis a sense of the desolation of many of the high hopes which they both had shared. Writing to invite and welcome La Fayette to Monticello, Jefferson's mind did not turn to an optimistic vision of the future but to the *Sturm und Drang* of the past:

> what recollections, dear friend, will this call up to you and me. What a history have we to run over from the evening that yourself, Mousnier, Bernau and other patriots settled, in my house in Paris, the outlines of the constitution you wished. And to trace it through all the disastrous chapters of Robespierre, Barras, Bonaparte, and the Bourbons.... (To La Fayette, 9 October 1824)

The high hopes of 1789 and their disappointment will be the theme of their time together at Monticello. The egotistical sublime of the sage of Monticello recalls with satisfaction that it was in 'my house' in Paris that the proper destiny of France was planned, as it is to his house now that the Marquis journeys once again. Then, as now, it is Jefferson's own home which is the focal point of history, political in 1789, now as part of the iconography of American romantic nationalism. 'Dear friend', he writes, in the language of sensibility, preparing for their embrace and for the tears which were seen to fall, both before the villa and again in the Pantheon, partly in joy at the friends' reunion, and partly, it would seem, in recollection of the sadness of the times through which they had passed. Or, as the poet of an earlier nationalist movement had written:

> O socii, neque enim ignari sumus ante malorum;
> O passi graviora, dabit deus his quoque finem.
> .... Revocate animos, maestumque timorem
> Mittite. Forsan et haec olim meminisse iuvabit.

(Comrades, we have been no strangers to affliction. We have survived worse things. God will put an end to this also. Revive your spirits, put aside sorrow and fear. Perhaps even this, one day, will be sweet to remember. *Aeneid* I, 199–203)

The fête of 4 November 1824 at Monticello has been interpreted here as an icon in a mythic history of the inception and spread of romantic nationalism in America and Europe. It was an attempt to fix the meaning and being of a newly 'liberated' nation by a return to a sacred ceremony of militant foundation. Perhaps, following David Miller, it should be called an 'ethical myth' to distinguish those myths of nationality of which one approves from some of the other dark places of the earth where nationalism has been engendered.[16] Or, perhaps it is a 'necessary myth' both in the sense (in general) that without myth there is no nation, or, more specifically that for Jefferson and La Fayette some story was necessary to 'keep hope alive' (the phrase, from Jesse Jackson, is used with full sense of its irony in this context). Either way, the iconography and language belong to an indeterminate, symbolic and emotional order somewhere between scientific history, with its desire to establish the truth, the whole truth, and nothing but the truth (an unobtainable object of desire), and the self-interested aims of ideological propaganda (the equivocation of the fiend who lies like truth).

What follows is a history of Jeffersonianism which is concerned with the making of a symbolic order rather than with the hard facts of political biography. It belongs to what Hayden White has called 'metahistory', and thus to the realm of the metaphorical rather than the 'literal' (where the 'letter' and 'truth' are supposedly one).[17] This is also a history of Jefferson which seemingly begins at the wrong time – the end of his life – although not at the wrong place (since it is difficult to think of Jefferson without thinking of Monticello). To begin at the end is to come to Jefferson topsy-turvy. Although, on the other hand, where might the beginning be? On 4 July 1776? Or with Jefferson's birth as a subject of the British empire in the imperial colony of Virginia? Or with the evolution of post-Elizabethan English (or British) nationalism as a template for identity of blood and language, religion and commerce in the colonies? Or with the intellectual traditions of Jefferson's thought, which reach back in an infinite regress beyond the classical world to the origin of origins: God and Nature? To begin at the end with an icon of romantic nationalism is to deracinate Jefferson – but of roots there could be no end.

It separates him also from his representative status as a figure of the cosmopolitan Enlightenment, or, more specifically what Henry May calls the millennialism of 'the revolutionary enlightenment',[18] or even from what has been called in a contradiction of terms, 'the American enlightenment' (a contradiction because the Americanisation of a cosmopolitan *Weltordnung* recruits what was a universalist philosophy for local nationalist ends). By beginning at the end it has been taken as 'self-evident' (to use a Jeffersonian word) that he belongs to the epoch of romantic nationalism, sharing a Koine of romantic discourse with La Fayette, which, thus, would have been immediately intelligible and generally acceptable, for example, to Byron and Shelley, de Staël and Sismondi, Kosciusko and Mavrocordato. The very word 'Koine' itself carries nationalist implications, for it was the demotic language of Hellenic civilisation, and thus a language which distinguished those who belonged to 'Hellas' from the 'barbarians' (those alien others) who are beyond the pale. It is preferred, therefore, to words like *mentalité* or 'discourse' which, because they are now part of the familiar language of contemporary theory, may suggest a precision of formulation and a theoretical rigour which risk foreclosing an argument before it has even begun. Rather than seeking a misleading precision, the indefinite pairing together of the indefinite words 'romantic' and 'nationalism' (the imprecision is strategic) carries with it all the subliminal implications of the historical penumbra – all that might be seen as flowing from Rousseau, Herder and Fichte through to the twentieth century.

In so doing, the phrase 'romantic nationalism' obliterates the fundamental distinction made by Hans Kohn, between the nationalist traditions of 'the west', founded on the idea of liberty, and the mystic totalitarianism of 'the east'.[19] But Kohn was writing in a world at war with National Socialism. It was important for his purposes that Jefferson, as a founding father of the American nation, should belong to 'the free world' of the west. It was a view reiterated by Yehoshua Arieli during the period of the Cold War and by Liah Greenfield on a wave of subsequent triumphalism.[20] For Arieli, constitutional (Whig) liberty is the distinguishing ideology of the United States which, for wave after wave of immigrants, obliterated ancient national identities in a freely-chosen commitment to democratic constitutional principles. For Lloyd Kramer, writing on the signification of La Fayette for the romantic era, the idea is, thus, self-evident (in 1996) that the metahistory of American and French constitutional liberalism (the La Fayette/Jefferson symbiosis) had nothing to do with the later development of the totalitarian nation-state or what he describes (in an interesting rearrangement of words) as 'socialist nationalism'.[21] In this view of history, therefore, there is a fundamental divide between the emergent 'western' democratic nationalism of the United States (represented *ab origine* by works such as Paine's *Common Sense*) and the kind of 'mystic' totalitarianism of the 'east' (for which Rousseau's *Considerations on the Government of Poland* may stand as a typical example). For Paine, all government is 'the badge of lost innocence' and the purpose of the American revolution was to secure 'freedom and property to all men'. Thus, in Paine's ideal 'America' the nation would exist only to liberate the individual from any form of control not self-approved. But in Rousseau's equally ideal 'Poland' the nation would be everything: 'A child on opening its eyes for the first time should see the nation, and until death he should see nothing but her. Every true national imbibes with his mother's milk the love of *la patrie*.... This love encompasses his entire existence; he sees only the nation, he loves only the nation; alone, he is nothing; the moment he is without the nation he ceases to exist....'[22]

Rather than holding fast to the ideology of 'western freedom', to plunge instead wilfully *in medias res* into the epic turmoil of a mythic history of an undifferentiated romantic nationalism is to obliterate distinctions seemingly firmly established. In deracinating Jefferson from his origins in the (self-declared) Enlightenment, the purpose, therefore, is not to reroot him in the comfort of some teleological history which has the confirmation of an ideal 'western' or 'free' American nationhood as its end (even though that is the end which the fête of 4 November seems to be celebrating). For that teleology is itself a romantic strategy by which an ideal and imaginary order – 'the free west' – is enabled to precipitate on to an 'eastern' other everything in the self one might wish to disown: millennial mysticism, racial imperatives, or any excess of force one might designate (imprecisely) as 'fascist'. Instead, the hypothesis here is that the spectrum of romantic nationalism was open (as it were, from Paine to Rousseau) and one might be, at any time, anywhere upon it. The aim is not to define Jefferson, but to submerge the historical individual as a sentient being in the *Sturm und Drang* of romantic experience. (But then, the very concept of *Sturm und Drang* originates in the Germanic interpretation of the American revolution.) When Jefferson described to La Fayette contemporary experience as like living on a 'volcano', that image suggests Shelley or Blake more than the world of the Enlightenment. The volcanic eruption was that of fifty years of ideological, imperial and national war; war between nations and emergent nations; war within nations. The existence of a Koine of romantic nationalism does not mean that the language was either fixed or unproblematical. On the contrary, everything was contested and everything in process of change. All that is asked here, therefore, is that no originary nor teleological determinates should remove Jefferson from that process to pre-empt his position either as some rock of the Enlightenment then, or some bastion of anti-totalitarianism now for our own age. Something ('the nation') indeterminate, imaginary, ideal was in process of birth.

Of course, any modern history of nationalism in the United States is likely to accept as uncontentious the premise that the nation was not 'given' as an historical entity but 'invented'. As Gordon Wood has written, 'The revolutionary leaders never intended to make a national revolution in any modern sense' and the collapse of the United States through internal dissension was as probable an outcome of the revolution as the emergence of a strong nation-state.[23] There is no reason to suppose that there was universal consent for the claim of David Humphreys that 'This is the time for fixing our national character and national manners'[24] as the (disunited) United States emerged out of what David Ramsay described in *The History of the American Revolution* (1789) as a British civil war. Although the eventual 'cause' enunciated by the Declaration of 1776 was 'independence' for the colonial States, it could not be the predetermined establishment of the 'romantic nation' since neither the thing nor the idea existed. Thus, John Adams passed up the task of drafting a certain declaratory act in the summer of 1776 (an oversight he came to regret) because there were more important concerns: a war to be fought (which without French men and *matériel* might be lost); State constitutions to be made (to protect the property and power of the white colonialists). It was Jefferson in Paris who, ten years later, suggested to Trumbull that the Declaration of Independence *now* might form the subject of an iconographic painting fixing the foundational moment of the United States; it was not until 1817 that the painting (which is now framed by the *fasces* as an American revolutionary sign) was incorporated into the mythic history of the Capitol rotunda (a building whose iconic function owes much to Jefferson). It was Jefferson also who misremembered (conveniently) that the Declaration was signed on 4 July – and to confirm this fiction the 4 July oration had already developed. It is uncertain by what date Jefferson's writing desk itself had become a national icon, but when recently exhibited at Monticello the desk on which the Declaration was drafted required a 24-hour guard – a sign of its fetish-character (and of the gap between Jefferson's idealisation of the *Volk* and the real behaviour of people). In these kinds of ways the 'rebellion' in the colonies gradually and *ad hoc* acquired a mythology of national signs. But in the beginning there had been merely a vacuum to be filled.

Yet, by the end of the second British war of 1812–15, there existed a clearly emergent articulated nationalism. This, at least, is a reasonable working hypothesis. It was this war especially, so Monroe told Madison, which 'raised up and consolidated a national character, dear to the hearts of the people'. Albert Gallatin claimed that 'The people are now more American: they feel and act more as a Nation', a view given a 'brave new world' gloss by the later authority of Henry Adams, for the war confirmed, he claimed, that 'the national character had already diverged from any foreign type.... The American in his political character was a new variety of man.'[25] If fighting wars does indeed establish 'the national character' in the hard school of *Blut und Eisen*, then the 'new variety of man' Adams described is familiar to any historian of romantic nationalism from the Jacobins (*Allons enfants de la patrie . . .*) to Bismarck, Nietzsche and Padraic Pearse. Adams's designation merely reveals that his conception of 'the national character' in the United States after 1812 is in symbiotic relationship with the heroic school of European romanticism. George Bancroft (who was not without influence on the nationalist interpretation of American history), Joseph Cogwell,

Edward Everett, George Ticknor (among others) absorbed Germanic national culture; nationalism and transcendentalism were to merge in Emerson's invocation of the Carlylean hero – those great and perfect persons on whom the future of mankind depends. The idea of 'manifest destiny', although post-Jefferson, depended in large measure on Jefferson's acquisition of the western frontier by 'the Louisiana purchase', and it might be argued that the unfettered individualism enunciated by the Declaration of Independence leads directly to the proto-Darwinism iconised by Leutze's 'Westward the Course of Empire'. The armed white races, as Leutze depicts them, roll their wagons towards the setting sun in a perpetual quest for *Lebensraum*. In the eternal *Kampf* which determines the fittest to survive, 'Let them compete, and success to the strongest, the wisest, and the best.'[26] This, it was to be claimed, was 'a truly national ideology'. Thus the laws of God and Nature determined that lesser breeds would fail before Adams's 'new variety of man'.

This historical process is not a development towards some termination susceptible of definition. What is outlined here is only *one* metahistory among many, and is offered only as unsettling the more complacent histories of 'western freedom'. One may pick out significant moments in the flux of events, but one must not mistake the moment for closure. Witness Edward Everett's Phi Beta Kappa oration before La Fayette in 1824 at Cambridge, Massachusetts, which is without doubt an expression of one form of romantic nationalism, but which forecloses nothing. Everett, by 1824, could take as self-evident the existence of a fully developed theory of nationalism, although it is only *one* theory among many. For Everett all history is understood in terms of the rise and fall of nation states (of which Greece and Rome are originary examples). The process is inevitable, for the 'destiny' of nation-states, each with its national character and language, is divinely ordained 'wheresoever Providence gathers into a nation the tribes of men'. But an especial Providence moves 'the masses' of 'our country... the mightiest kindred people known in history... uniting into one great national feeling the hearts of so many freemen; all to be guided, persuaded, moved, and swayed, by the master spirits of the time!' The American nation is thus the greatest nation to emerge providentially in the course of history, and the great men of America accordingly are the master-spirits of all ages. *Mutatis mutandis* Everett's view of history is one which Fichte or Carlyle would readily recognise. Others, elsewhere, might argue much the same for Britannia or Germania: 'An historical revision on a unique scale has been imposed upon us by the Creator' as a later and more persuasive orator than Everett was to compellingly argue.[27]

But this was only one way of putting it. Emerson's more famous nationalist address (of 1837) was, in fact, provoked by disagreement with Everett. Or one might, more traditionally, prefer some other definition of what it was to be an American and move further forward yet in time to Lincoln at Gettysburg. The Gettysburg speech rededicates a nation in terms of the moral purity of its origins. The morally fittest to survive had been determined by war. Or, perhaps, one should look further forward yet to Frederick Jackson Turner's claim that while the frontier remained open, America was always in process of making itself anew. What was manifest in destiny was always to have a new destiny until the process was ended geographically and historically at the Pacific Ocean. The selection of any such points of closure would predetermine whatever it was precedes them in the making of the nation, and the later one comes in history the more diverse and complex the materials to be harmonised into the indefinable concept of the romantic nation. Therefore, no such closure is offered here.

All that is asked is the recognition that between the declaratory act of independence of 1776, and the return of La Fayette to America in 1824, somehow a way of signifying the revolution was developing which may be appropriately described as one manifestation of romantic nationalism. It is a process for which neither origin nor termination may be given. This indeterminacy is essential. 'The nation' is always suspended between what Machiavelli would call a *ritorno* to the purity of some mythical moment of foundation (Jefferson's Declaration – or, for some, the landing on Plymouth Rock) and always receding beyond some 'new frontier' of futurity. In 1824, paradoxically, national identity symbolically centred upon a European hero (free, thus, from any claims of class or party), who was an almost expired representative of a revolution fast dissolving into the myths of history. Jefferson, on the steps of Monticello, was himself a kind of antediluvian patriarch from the same period. What the nation might be, in quotidian fact now, might lie outside the imagined symbolic order altogether. If that uncertainty about what constitutes the here and now was avoided in 1824 by looking into a mythologised past, the discomfort of the present is as frequently avoided in the revolutionary period by the invocation of the indefinite future. Throughout the early history of the nation there is a continuing exploitation of a millennial language of some kind of unprecedented leap into what Paine called 'the birth-day of a new world' and Everett the 'impending future'. It was a future often said to carry with it all the best hopes of mankind – as the correspondence of Jefferson and La Fayette demonstrates, or the visionary prophecies, for instance, of Connecticut Georgic or the foundational epics of Joel Barlow.[28] But on sceptical examination, the romantic nation as it now is – somewhere between the purity of a *ritorno* and the 'new frontier' yet to be conquered – slips and slides from definition, may even be centrifugal rather than one *Volk* ('yeomanry' as Everett calls them) united *e pluribus*. Indeed, one contrary interpretation of the symbolic order of things would be to see, only partially masked by a revolutionary iconography of universal unity, the nation headed not towards the greatest destiny ever known in history, but towards civil war – a war latent even in the very originary compromises of the sacramental text of the Constitution. But that would be merely to impose another teleological reading upon history, as if certain causes have necessary consequences.

The entry here *in medias res* without origin or telos is, thus, an attempt to see things as it were through the experience of those agents and subjects involved in seeking to make a symbolic order from the chaos of events. If there is a theoretical position, it is closest to that Schlegelian concept of irony which sees the romantic protagonist as inextricably caught up in a process of becoming in which contraries are contained only within the process of unending change. Or, to quote a later, and equally romantic theorist, Jefferson is like the 'angel of history' in Benjamin's *Illuminations*, blown by a storm from paradise: 'this storm irresistibly propels him into the future'; history 'keeps piling wreckage and hurls it at his feet' but that wreckage, subsequently, we call 'progress'.

If this is too romantically vague, one might turn to what Goethe called the *Urphänomenon* which coalesces word and thing, idea and experience in representative signification (*Bedeutung*). A classic text, Washington's 'Farewell Address', seen as such an *Urphänomenon*, may illustrate both the indefiniteness of things and of the need to create an imaginary order on the hoof, as it were, through a changing historical landscape. This definitive and originary (Ur)text is a kind of last will and testament of *the* Founding Father to his people – a secular Moses to the Israelites – charting the future course of the nation. But (as is now well known) it was, of course, not what Washington originally wrote. It is a Hamiltonian (and anti-Jeffersonian) recension of another (suppressed) text, the partially lost words of what Washington wanted to declare (in some bitterness of spirit) about trying to ride the storm of contesting forces in the republic. But it was inexpedient to broadcast that interpretation of things. The 'Address' as published, however, still contains within it elements of division, for the very necessity for the discourse to come into being at all arises from the fear that things are going to fall apart. Hence his need to move 'the will of the Nation' (a phrase Rousseau, Bonaparte and Goebbels would all have understood, albeit with different and contested significations). That 'will' must be to 'remain one People'. That commitment to national unity (the 'fascist' imperative) is the only preservative against the factious divisions inspired by 'the Alien' outside, and sedition within. Somehow party political and geographical divisions must be reconciled. 'The name of AMERICAN, which belongs to you in your national capacity, must always exalt the just pride of Patriotism ... more than any appelation derived from local discriminations.' The statement that national unity *must* 'exalt' the 'AMERICAN' is as much an appeal as a statement of fact, and, as the history of the 1790s was to show, party division was far from an exalting experience. If Washington had not perceived, and bitterly experienced, the divisive tendencies of party and place, there would have been no need to chauvinistically invoke those visions of continental conquest implied by 'the name AMERICAN'.

This sense that the symbolic order is always threatened by dissolution might be illustrated too in other Urtexts of the romantic nation. De Crèvecoeur's *Letters from an American Farmer*, dedicated in one manifestation to La Fayette, possesses (in French or English) much the same classic authority as Washington's 'Farewell Address'. Letter III, 'What is an American?' is still anthologised in the (changing) canon represented by the Norton Anthology of American Literature. The Letters are also a defining text for the American image in Europe. They idealise a 'new race of men' sowing the 'seed of future nations' west of the Atlantic. It is the 'American farmer' (Everett's 'yeoman') who embodies the national type – a race sprung from the land and of the land. But to rest with that image of the happy husbandman is to subscribe to what Renan described as the selective amnesia of nationalism. It is to ignore those aspects of the published letters which do not fit the racial stereotype (the violence of the frontiersmen, the iniquities of slavery, which de Crèvecoeur graphically depicts). It is to forget also those letters for which de Crèvecoeur could find no publisher either in the United States or in Europe. Like Washington's suppressed text of the Farewell Address, they stated what no one wanted to hear. Not until the twentieth century was it possible to read de Crèvecoeur's account of the bigotry and violence of the civil war of 1776. The suppressed letters express the reason why he, and tens of thousands of other 'aliens' (to use Washington's word) quit the so-called 'united' States of America. There were proportionally more *émigrés* from American terrorism than from the Terror in France, and these *émigrés* did not return. But the fate of these American 'Tories' ('traitors', as Jefferson called them) was to be written out of the *Urphänomenon*. The victors write history.

The establishment of who it was constituted 'we, the people' was the most contested element in the creation of the *Volk*. But even the constitution of the *Land* itself was uncertain. The 'frontier', from the beginning, had tended to be an indefinite line extended westward over unknown country to the Pacific – territory to be contested with other imperial powers and with the aboriginal inhabitants. 'The Louisiana Purchase' was to make 'the west' an early and crucial element in definition of the *Heimat* – what it is that constitutes the 'home' land. Consider, for instance, the initial intention of Jedidiah Morse's *American Geography* (the first national rather than State-based account of the United States. The nationalist intention is 'to impress the minds of American Youth with an idea of the superior importance of their own country, as well as to attach them to its interests'. Yet, as the 'geography' evolved, Morse had to confess subsequently to Young America that, even as he wrote, the subject changed before him: 'so fast do alterations and revolutions succeed each other, that it is not an easy matter... to keep pace with them. What is this year geographical truth, may the next year be geographical error.' So fast does the idea of the 'native land' change that no text can keep abreast of the Heraclitean flux of things and the endless process of conquest and discovery.[29]

Or consider an issue more problematical and fundamental yet in romantic nationalism: the question of 'the national language', which Webster saw as intrinsic in the founding of the 'national character' of the American 'family'. If language, as Herder and Walter Channing claimed, is 'essentially peculiar to every nation' then, for the

American, it might seem that the colonies could never achieve independent self-definition but must remain culturally always symbiotically dependent upon English origins, although those origins are repeatedly disowned. What is it, then, that is 'original' in the American language, both in the sense of *ab origine* – from the beginning, and in the romantic sense of 'originality' – made new? How might either view of the language relate to those other 'aboriginal' tongues which might claim priority in the American continent? How might an 'independent' and nationally authentic American 'literature' develop? This is an issue which need only be stated to be recognised, for it has been often explored, and not yet resolved.[30]

This is merely to flash a series of snapshots into the darkness of the indefiniteness of romantic nationalism – to establish some *Urphänomena* (evidential referents) for the destabilisation of Jefferson from stable origin or defining telos. The emphasis here is not upon the orderliness of symbols in the metahistory of the nation, but rather upon the momentariness of their emergence. This indefinite momentariness of the nation was well understood by Renan, whose essay on nineteenth-century nationalism is still, in many ways, the best point of entry into the subject. In an often reiterated phrase, Renan described the nation as constituted only by a 'daily plebiscite'. The phrase is merely metaphorical, but the sense that the national idea is ever made up anew is captured by the word 'daily'. The metaphor reveals also Renan's nineteenth-century democratical ambience, for the word 'plebiscite' implies the existence of some agency of consultation through which 'we, the people' may express ourselves. It also raises the question of who 'we' might be. But what constitutes the franchise, and what role exists in the nation for those unfranchised, or who deny the majority voice? Any plebiscite in Jefferson's Virginia would, of course, have excluded the overwhelming majority of 'the people'.

Perhaps one might suggest instead of an unrealisable 'plebiscite' that the nation is rather constituted by an act of daily 'will' (to adopt Washington's word). It is by the reiterated triumph of the will (to substitute Leni Riefenstahl for Washington) that the people are made and sustained. One might quote, from the originary time of war, Paine's 'These are the times that try men's souls', or 'The summer soldier and the sunshine patriot will, in this crisis, shrink from the service of their country.' If Renan's icon of the state might be Trumbull's image of Washington laying down his sword to seek the suffrage of the people, then, for those who see rather the nation as sustained by the triumph of the will, the image might be some group of patriot soldiers raising the battle-flag of the republic upon some contested hill. Both images are familiar to any reader of the national icons of Washington, DC.

So indefinite and complex is the nature of the daily redefinition of the romantic nation that, perhaps, one might call Plato to philosophise Renan or Riefenstahl. In Platonic epistemology all meaning is always deferred, for it is always caught up in the differential processes of dialectical exploration. 'Reality' (here 'the nation') always lies somewhere beyond the compass of human signs, as an ideal 'form' which can never be present. It is best suggested by poetic metaphor, for poetic symbolism is always tangentially related to (unrealisable) truth. If this vocabulary of deferral suggests a more 'modern' critical idiom, Derrida is only a late commentator on Plato. If there is no origin nor telos which can be given definitive form, there is only a process of exploration. The new world is always somewhere over the horizon; the promised land remains always a promise of futurity. There is only an unfulfillable striving for an unrealisable goal.

> Who shall tempt with wand'ring feet
> The dark unbottom'd infinite abyss
> And through the palpable obscure find out
> His uncouth way...?
>
> (*Paradise Lost* II, 404–7)

To approach Jefferson by way of allusion to Milton's Satan is, perhaps, to go too far in mythologising the statesman from the perspective of a Federalist metahistory. But Jefferson's defeat of his Federalist opponents should not expunge from the experience of history their image of the 'Satanic' Jefferson: fanatical Jacobinical aetheist, 'whirligig' Machiavellian hypocrite, the 'raw head and bloody bones' which he protested that his enemies made him. But, for Jefferson, the Satanic pose was not without its attractions. His Commonplace Book shows that Satan's great speeches of rebellion were among his favourite passages from Milton in his early years, and at the end of his life, writing to George W. Lewis (25 October 1825) he invoked, as a 'Saxon' principle, Satan's 'courage never to submit or yield'. In Blakean eschatology, Satan's resistance to a monarchical God made him the true hero of the poem, and the leading statement of the Jefferson Memorial in Washington is a quasi-Blakean oath declaring eternal 'resistance to tyranny'. Indeed, it might be argued plausibly that the invention of a series of 'tyrants' to be resisted is the *leitmotiv* of Jefferson's political career: George III and Great Britain, American Tories and monarchical-aristocratical Federalists, Napoleon Bonaparte and the British navy.... It is not a material history that we are seeking scientifically to define, but rather a symbolic perspective upon history which needs to be imaginatively revitalised. Things are as they are perceived by the agents in history. What is it that is perceived, and what form is taken by the symbolic order?

In this context, Miltonic eschatology is enabling historically, for it provides a specific, textual focus illustrative of something widely diffused in the culture of the new 'American' nation and the Jeffersonian *Weltordnung*. (Since the Miltonic epic is also self-evidently a fiction, it is useful also in this study of metahistory because its fictitious nature cannot be mistaken for fact.) Initially the Miltonic story of paradise lost – and paradise to be found again in the fullness of time – belongs to the originary culture of the 'pilgrim fathers'. This is, for their Protestant world, the definitive epic which, reordering the culture of classical antiquity, 'justifies' modern history *sub specie aeternitatis*. It is also a story, its polarities strangely reversed by the passage of time, which is central to the romantic consciousness of the English-speaking cultures both sides of the Atlantic. It shapes the millennial mythologies of writers as diverse as Blake and Barlow, Shelley and Humphreys, and is a deep underpresence in Wordsworthian pastoral and Connecticut Georgic. Resisting tyranny, newly perfected Man in Blake breaks all bounds; Prometheus is unbound in Shelley; in a return to Nature paradise is regained, and that paradisical Nature, as if newly minted by the hand of God, awaits the new race of man in America. The myth was equally powerful in France. The French revolution, initially shaped in some measure by the American dream, manifested a similar (secularised) eschatological view of history – hence the urge towards the establishment of the perfected State in Jacobinism (and, by long sorites, the millennialism of Utopian socialism).

This sketch of metahistory is, of course, imprecisely general. But all these diverse manifestations of Miltonic, millennial epic are founded on a teleological premise: that human (or divine) history is perpetually polarised (however the polarities flow) between the principles of light and darkness, between (in the discourse of romanticism) that tyranny which produces slavery, and liberty freely chosen. The consequences of the individual's choice between that darkness and that light affect all mankind. This is the kind of metahistory to which Jefferson belonged. Which is not to claim (absurdly) that his statecraft was shaped by reading Milton. But as a figure caught up, willy-nilly, in what one calls the 'romantic' era, his symbolic history is part of what once was called the romantic *Zeitgeist* and what might now be called the cultural *episteme*. Jeffersonian polarities, indeed, have been claimed (by his biographers) to be intrinsic in his 'passionate imagination' which impulsively divided the nature of things by a binary rhetoric of tyranny and liberty, wolves and sheep, hammer and anvil and (as far as his own personality was concerned) head and heart.[31] Seeking, towards the end of his life, to philosophise his statecraft, he told John Adams (letter of 27 June 1813) that the history of mankind 'thro' all time' can be written as a binary struggle between 'Tory' and 'Whig', that is, between authority which always seeks to accrue more power to itself, and those free individuals who exercise their sacred right to resist that power. These were issues 'which kept the states of Greece and Rome in eternal convulsions, as they now schismatize every people whose minds and mouths are not shut up by the gag of a despot. And in fact the terms of whig and tory belong to natural, as well as civil history.' They are intrinsic, thus, in the very polarities of the mind of Man. Since Jefferson was seeking to make his peace with the Federalist Adams, he put the issue as one of general philosophy. But, in the vocabulary of the War of Independence, the word 'Tory' is the equivalent of 'traitor'. The Tory was the enemy within the nation, the agent and exponent of what Jefferson saw as the evils of European despotism, and there is little doubt that Jefferson saw the struggle (which is eternal) between freedom and tyranny as running through the 1790s in the new nation. This was the cause of the 'violent contests...conducted by the parties with an animosity, a bitterness, and an indecency, which has never been exceeded' he told Adams. Among his own circle he made it clear (in private) that his aim was to extirpate the enemy within. He told Madison (1 October 1792) that Hamilton was guilty of 'high treason' and should 'suffer death accordingly'. After his election to the presidency he told Levi Lincoln (25 October 1802) that his aim was sink his enemies 'into an abyss from which there shall be no resurrection'. The eschatological imagery closes the mouth of hell on the Federalist traitor forever.

This is, of course, a simplistic symbolic history through which to approach a phenomenon as complex, various, and ultimately indefinable as Jefferson's relation to the romantic nation. The simplicity is wilful, as is the avoidance of the complexities of 'theory'. As it were, a picture, yet to be drawn, is being defined only by its frame, or, to change the image, the inception of romantic nationalism in the American revolution is a kind of magnetic field between positive and negative polarities. In Jefferson's simple picture of things tyranny and freedom are clearly visible opposites (George III and himself). On closer examination, however, the entire magnetic field is permeated by contrary tendencies. Consider, for example, the first two paragraphs (in Jefferson's draft) of the Declaration of Independence (the foundational document of romantic nationalism):

> When, in the course of human events, it becomes necessary for one people to dissolve the political bands which have connected them with another, and to assume among the powers of the earth the separate and equal station which the laws of nature and of nature's God entitle them....
>
> We hold these truths to be self-evident: that all men are created equal; that they are endowed by their Creator with inherent and inalienable rights; that among these are life, liberty, and the pursuit of happiness....

The words are so familiar that only the beginning of the first two paragraphs need citation as a mere *aide-mémoire*. It is difficult now to recover the emotional power of their disruptive and incalculable potential then. It is more difficult yet to perceive that, like the polarity of the Miltonic myth, they contain the elements of a dialectical opposition between freedom and power, whig and tory which is *within* the new nation itself. The initiatory rhetoric is uncertain, even contradictory at the very point at which it sounds most self-assured. What is it, in the first place, which constitutes 'one people'? The first paragraph invokes a collective identity whom necessity compels to separate from another (or should one, more theoretically, write 'an Other'?). As the Declaration goes on to argue, it is the 'absolute despotism' of that other which compels resistance, for it is 'the right of the people' to dissolve the 'bands' in which they are enchained and to assume their proper station 'among the powers of the earth'. Here we have what is to become the standard discourse of romantic national liberation movements (growing from Whig discourse and developing towards what we now call 'postcolonialism'). Emergent nations have the right to free themselves from an imperial oppressor. It is taken as self-evident that this collective identity exists, and is, thus, separable from the alien other – Jefferson assumes it needs no definition – *Vox populi, vox Dei* as an earlier formulation has it; *ein Volk, ein Vaterland* in the words of a later romantic nationalism. Acting together 'the people' will now assume a role among the 'powers' of the earth. The implication is that the individual will is subjected, thus, to the collective, and the collective will is empowered. Nations are expressions of force.

The beginning of the second paragraph, on the other hand, is anarchical. Whatever the philosophical tradition in which it originates, the statement of 'inherent rights' projected into 'the course of human events', now makes the individual the autonomous source of those rights (Congress struck out the word, 'inherent' but could not remove the tendency). I define my rights, I define what is liberty, and I define what I mean by 'happiness' which, by God, I have the right to pursue. It is a declaration inviting each individual to perpetual rebellion against any external authority over the will, for it is the individual alone who is rightfully empowered. It was Jefferson himself, taking his words from Franklin, who adopted as his own the motto 'Rebellion to tyrants is obedience to God.' It is a typically romantic reshaping of Miltonic eschatology, but so central to his view of his historic role that he chose it as the personal seal with which he marked his letters (and he added it to du Simitière's iconography for the arms of Virginia). The phrase, of course, seeks to recruit God himself for the cause of rebellion – what fundamentalist postcolonialist would disown the strategy? – and thus seeks to sustain some source of divine authority to which one should be 'obedient'. But ultimately it remains the individual who defines what he (or she) declares to be 'right'. Who else, in a State not theocratic, is to define the divine will? – and, for Jefferson, theocracy has no part in the state.

The relationship between individual rights (on the one hand) and the State as the collective expression of 'the people' (on the other) is a nice speculation of political philosophy. It was debated at length by Jefferson and Madison, and it is an issue which the addition of the 'Bill of Rights' to the American Constitution sought to resolve legally for the nation. But, 'in the course of human events' the Declaration of Independence was not a nice speculation of philosophy but marked the initiation of fifty years of global war and disruptive ideological, nationalist and imperialist violence. The vicious political divisions within the (dis)United States originated, in part, in ongoing attempts to resolve the contradiction of the Declaration between the State as a 'power' and resistant claims of other kinds of 'right'. In this context one need not only recall but restore to contestation certain familiar passages of the 1790s; that is, to read Jefferson without the benefit of hindsight, but at a time when the whole order of things among the European peoples had been fundamentally torn apart. Consider his letter to William Short, of 3 January 1793, for instance, which takes up again the word 'necessary' from the Declaration of Independence. Now it is an 'absolute necessity' (a pleonastic emphasis in time of crisis) for the Jacobins in France to act as they do – 'and the Nation was with them in the opinion':

> In the struggle which was necessary, many guilty persons fell without the forms of trial, and with them some of the innocent. These I deplore as much as any body, and shall deplore some of them to the day of my death. But I deplore them as I should have done had they fallen in a battle. It was necessary to use the arm of the people, a machine not quite so blind as balls and bombs, but blind to a certain degree. A few of their cordial friends met at their hands the fate of enemies. But time and truth will rescue and embalm their memories, while their posterity will be enjoying that very liberty for which they would never have hesitated to offer up their lives. The liberty of the whole earth was depending on the issue of the contest, and was ever such a prize won with so little innocent blood? My own affections have been deeply wounded by some of the martyrs of this cause, but rather than it should have failed, I would have seen half the earth desolated. Were there but an Adam and Eve left in every country, and left free, it would be better than it is now. I have expressed to you my sentiments, because they are those of ninety nine in a hundred of our citizens.

'Necessity' leaves no room for argument. War was unavoidable in 1776 – so too is the Terror now. Significantly 'the people' of 1776 have changed to 'the Nation' (capitalised) – Whig philosophy tending now towards the Abbé Sieyès: 'the nation is prior to everything. It is the source of everything. Its will is always legal; indeed it is the law itself.' (*What is the Third Estate?*) It is deplorable that among the 'guilty' who have been executed, innocents may have fallen also, including some of those of La Fayette's circle who had gathered (like Plato or Cicero of old, one recollects) in Jefferson's house and at his table to establish the spirit of the laws for the new nation. Others were imprisoned or in exile. But rather than the revolutionary cause should fail 'I would have seen half the earth desolated.' So absolute is his demand that he would return, if need be, to an originary Adam and Eve in each nation. The Miltonic eschatology is overt (as a sort of parody of Robespierre guillotining the whole French nation as unworthy of the revolution). Fortunately for the Adams and Eves of the United States, this is not a view personal to Jefferson. On the contrary, it is the view of 'our citizens' (with the exception of an infinitesimal rump). The insignificant opposition were the enemy within whom he was to define in the notorious Mazzei letter of 24 April 1796 as the 'Anglican monarchical aristocratical party', who had, unfortunately, corrupted even George Washington himself. Since, in France, the absolute necessity of the Terror was truncating the monarchical-aristocratical opposition, it is not surprising that Jefferson's enemies saw him as a Jacobin.

Seen in retrospect, the 'lava of the imagination' (a Byronic phrase) of Jefferson's proto-Jacobinical utterances solidifies in the wider tracts of political history. (Jefferson on whale-oil is a different kettle of fish!) Since potentially revolutionary events in the United States such as Shays's rebellion, or the 'whiskey' revolt came to little, and Citizen Genet's attempts at direct action democracy were swiftly snuffed out, the United States produced no social revolution on a European model. The American Democratic Societies, which Washington feared, appear, on close examination, as associations of solid citizenry, the 'Alien and Sedition' laws were mild in their operation, a vituperative press, in the main, escaped from the 'gagging' powers which Toryism obtained by savage prosecutions in Britain. No Jacquerie (white or black) cut the throats of the slaveowners of Mount Vernon or Monticello. Or, put another way, in the United States, as in Britain, 'the ancient social order' (Castlereagh's phrase) survived intact. The men of property of '76 retained that property.[32]

But, in relating the experience of the English-speaking peoples both sides of the Atlantic, one must reactivate the sense of danger and the passions with which events were dramatically invested. For, to be wise after the event is not to know the event. There is, on both sides of the Atlantic, the same conflict in both societies between the 'Tory' 'alarmism' and 'Whig' 'anarchy' – both 'factions' representing the other as dangerously extremist. No one can doubt the deep sense of fundamental destabilisation in the entire European world in the 1790s, and the United States was another, albeit newly constituted, European nation (with an untried form of republican government) in potential conflict with the great transcontinental powers of Britain, France and Spain. The experience of the 1790s was, therefore, something which the participants did not easily forget. Looking back on the epoch, Jefferson wrote to John Adams (15 June 1813):

> Whether the character of the times is justly portrayed or not, posterity will decide. But on one feature of them they can never decide, the *sensations* [my italics] excited in free yet firm minds, by the terrorism of the day. None can conceive who did not witness them....

The word 'terrorism' imports into American experience 'sensations' directly derived from the experience of 'the Terror' in France (and Jefferson adds 'England and it's [*sic*] alarmists were equally under consideration'). The Tories in the United States, so he claims even now in old age, combined the tendencies of Pittite extremism in Britain with the potential ruthlessness of class-war in France. Hence the Alien and Sedition laws which struck directly even at members of his own circle. It is an extreme claim which drew the strongest response from Adams in reply who, as President, claimed to have had to directly address 'terrorism' in action:

> You never felt the Terrorism of Chaises Rebellion in Massachusetts. I believe You never felt the Terrorism of Gallatins Insurrection in Pensilvania: You certainly never reallized the Terrorism of Frie's, most outrageous Riot and Rescue, as I call it, Treason, Rebellion as the World and great Judges and two Juries pronounced it. You certainly never felt the Terrorism, excited by Genet in 1793, when ten thousand People in the Streets of Philadelphia, day after day, threatened to drag Washington out of his House, and effect a Revolution in Government, or compel it to declare War in favour of the French Revolution...nothing but the Yellow Fever [which paralysed Philadelphia]...could have saved the United States from a total Revolution of Government...when

I myself judged it prudent and *necessary* [my italics] to order Chests of Arms from the War Office to be brought through bye Lanes and back Doors: determined to defend my House at the Expence of my Life, and the Lives of the few, very few Domesticks and Friends within it. What think you of Terrorism, Mr. Jefferson? Shall I investigate the Causes, the Motives, the Incentives to these Terrorisms?

Not least of these incentives were the activities of Jefferson himself, and his patronage of men like Philip Freneau (the gutter journalist) and Citizen Tom Paine. The 'ten thousand people' on the streets of Philadelphia calling for war in support of the French Revolution are not the united nation for which Jefferson claimed to speak but represent for Adams a dangerous and violent mob. Perhaps this is paranoia. Perhaps, too, Jefferson showed paranoia in his fear, clear from the Anas as well as the Mazzei letter, that even Washington had (when he was aged and feeble) betrayed the people into the hands of Toryism – the international conspiracy of kings. But it was not a judgement written out of the heat of the moment when Jefferson claimed in his *Autobiography* that the 'crimes and cruelties' of Europe had passed to America, and that he had lived through an epoch of 'the total extinction of national morality'. The passage of 25 years had not softened the bitterness of memory.

It is commonplace to see Jefferson's inauguration as President as marking the end of this turmoil of the 1790s and the renewed definition of the American nation. At least, that is the Jeffersonian view. 'The revolution of 1800' was intended to rededicate the nation to the fundamental first principles of republican simplicity. Hence, iconographically, Jefferson's rejection of the Augustan triumph of Washington's Inaugural procession (and his notorious 'pell mell' dinners and slovenliness of dress). The First Inaugural was to serve as an historical marker of a crucial moment of history. It is both a classic statement of Whig constitutional theory and a call for national unity to 'the honest patriot' of the 'rising nation' which was founded by 'the wisdom of our sages and the blood of our heroes'. It has been a misfortune that the rising nation with its 'destinies beyond the reach of mortal eye' should have felt

the throes and convulsions of the ancient world, during the agonizing spasms of infuriated man, seeking through blood and slaughter his long lost liberty...

But the worst of the storm has avoided the nation:

> Kindly separated by nature and a wide ocean from the exterm-
> inating havoc of one quarter of the globe; too high minded to
> endure the degradation of others; possessing a chosen country,
> with room enough for our descendants to the thousandth and
> thousandth generation....

The internal divisions of party have now subsided. In our chosen
country now 'We are all republicans – we are all federalists.'

As with the Declaration of Independence, one needs only to be
reminded of the justly famous phrases. The First Inaugural is a work
of symbolic national history – a piece of romantic 'poetry' in
Shelley's sense of the word – a work of imagination, by a would-
be legislator of mankind, inaugurating, he told Priestley, a new
'chapter in the history of man' (21 March 1801). But, like Washington
in his Farewell, Jefferson speaks as the leader of a nation needing
unification. The more Jefferson lays emphasis upon the unitary
nation, the greater the implication of the existence of some centrifugal force. In the famous assertion 'We are all republicans – we are all
federalists', he seems to be returning to Paine's call for national unity
in *Common Sense*: 'Let the names of Whig and Tory be extinct.'[33] But,
as is well-recognised now, the lower case setting of 'republicans' and
'federalists' indicates that Jefferson is not referring to contemporary
political parties (that would require capitalisation). He would seem,
rather, to be alluding to those Whig and Tory principles which he
was to claim existed 'thro' all time'. By so doing he collapses the
former polarities of history by uniting the Federal (Tory) concern
with power with his own popular base in Republican (Whig) resistance to power. Thus, the contradiction of the first paragraphs of the
Declaration of Independence is resolved by justifying power in the
nation as the expression of unified individual wills centred in himself as the collective voice of 'We' the people. The rhetoric excludes
all possibility of reasonable dissent from those 'united for the common good'. It is the presidential function 'to give activity to a mass
mind'[34] for, as he stated to J. Garland Jefferson (25 January 1810),

> In a government like ours, it is the duty of the Chief Magistrate, in
> order... to do all the good which his station requires... to unite in
> himself the confidence of the whole people. This alone, in any
> case where the energy of the nation is required, can produce

a union of the powers of the whole, and point them in a single direction, as if all constituted but one body and one mind....

One body, one mind, one leader.

The First Inaugural Address to the American people is a unique moment for Jefferson. There is (in the rhetoric) a symbiosis between self and the nation. In terms of the polarities of mythic history between the forces of Truth and Error, freedom and tyranny, Whig and Tory, there is a healing of the eternal *Zerissenheit* by the ceremony of national unity: *e pluribus unum*. In the feeling of nationhood there is no distinction within the people between Self and Other. The romantic nation heals that psychological alienation which is the other face of romanticism for those who have no 'deep, abiding home' (Wordsworth's phrase). In the larger context of European romanticism, one may place the First Inaugural over against the the fragmented 'mirror' of the homeless 'pilgrimage' of *Childe Harold*, or, more profoundly inward, the eternal divide between Shelley's Prometheus and Jupiter where the conflicts of history emerge from the perennial divisions within the universal mind of Man. The alienation of history ends in Jefferson's America, for to belong to the nation is to belong, in Jefferson's imagery, to a great family secure in its 'chosen country' for its children's children 'to the thousandth and thousandth generation'. It is secure too in its chosen leader, 'the Great Father', as Jefferson was to call himself to the aboriginal tribes not yet incorporated into the Fatherland.

Such a moment of visionary stasis was unrepeatable for Jefferson. (One might compare, from about the same date, Fichte's call to the Germanic peoples to unite to rediscover their historic homeland and culture, or, later, Lincoln rededicating the American nation at Gettysburg.) The mythic moment of the First Inaugural can only exist at the still point of the turning world at which 25 years of 'resistance' to 'alien' power without and 'sedition' within changes by empowerment. But, by the very logic of the myth, the Great Father empowered becomes himself the authority which *must* be resisted. Hence, in the Second Inaugural, the catalogue of that 'minority' in the nation whose 'Error' is still not enlightened by the 'Truth' of a zealous and pure administration: recalcitrant aboriginals misled in seeking to follow their ancient customs; 'doubting brethren' not yet drawn into the 'mass'; a viciously hostile press against whom the suspended law might yet serve as a salutary check.... Although the Second Inaugural is sometimes cited as an important enunciation of the freedom of the press in America, the polarities of Truth and Error on which it is based are very different from the classic position of Milton's *Areopagitica*. For Milton the wheat and tares grow up together so closely in this fallen world that they are inseparable (hence the ease with which the polarities of *Paradise Lost* may be reversed). For Jefferson, Truth appears to be symbiotically related to his Republican party, authorised by 'the will of the majority', with the implication that once Error has ended its unAmerican career, the United States will be a one-party nation. Jefferson's peroration ends with an enunciation of national unity in which the President, in traditional imagery, is a Mosaic figure, seeking in his office the aid of 'that Being...who led our forefathers, as Israel of old'. In short, resistance to Jefferson is disobedience to God.

It is difficult to construct and permanently sustain the symbolic order in the hurly-burly of contentious office. Jefferson's second term as President was unfortunate, divisive and personally hurtful. He left the nation on the brink of involvement in the Napoleonic Wars. That, however, is the matter of political biography. The concern here is with the mythic history of the romantic nation. Beyond 'the fury and the mire of human veins' there is a search by Jefferson for some permanent memorial which would express the national being. Words slip and slide, and after the First Inaugural there is no written Jefferson legacy of symbolic weight, only the uncompleted *Autobiography*, the controversial annotations of the 'Anas' and the daily mass of an overwhelming correspondence not yet fully edited. The dialectic of the late exchange of letters with John Adams is, perhaps, the nearest Jefferson came to trying to set the written record straight.

Thus, in contradistinction to the contentions of dialectical debate, the iconographic order of architecture, sanctioned by the long experience of the European peoples, might seem to offer something more permanent and less contentious than dialectic debate. As William H. Pierson has written:

As one of the pivotal idealists of the revolution and as one of the creative figures in the formation of the new republic, Jefferson spoke for an aspiring America. His architecture, therefore, takes on its full meaning...when viewed as both instrument and symbol of his social and political purpose, Jefferson became the first American leader to think in terms of cultural as well as political independence and to him this independence could nowhere be better expressed than in architecture.[35]

In this expressive purpose, the most obvious icon was the creation, out of the very wilderness, of a national capital and Capitol. It was Jefferson who was the prime mover in the attempt to create the symbolic city of Washington – 'the only monument of human rights'. This was a scheme of a *quasi*-Napoleonic imagination, or like an embodiment of one of the visionary projects of Ledoux or Boullée. (More specifically, the design of the Mall derives, via L'Enfant, from Louis XIV's Versailles and the White House stands in place of the Trianon palace.) But the complexity of the magnilo-quent project was beyond Jefferson's personal control, and evolved through many years, through many hands, acquiring new significa-tions in the process. During Jefferson's presidency, the great design of a national capital, like Napoleon's alternative symbolic order for Europe, floundered in the real morass of recalcitrant nature. In blunt, simple terms, Jefferson's Washington was a pretentious mess – a swampy, mosquito-infested building-site of 'magnificent intention' (Dickens's phrase) rather than a city, and a visionary city without any natural reason for existence except the desire of the imagination to construct (close to the Virginian heartland) a national icon. It is an irony of history that the British army did the new nation an unwitting favour in torching the original Capitol and consequently it is through the work of a British architect (Benjamin Latrobe) that professional skill at last was brought to bear on the design and function of the (second) Capitol. Even now the Mall remains a civic centre without any practical function, the world's largest traffic island, and a vacuum to which have been added over the centuries an ongoing assortment of national monuments and national museums. In that respect it is an embodiment of Renan's argument that the nation makes itself up as it goes along, remem-bering and forgetting at will, and the story of Washington, DC, is an ultra-Jeffersonian history.[36]

Jefferson's own great and continuing self-controlled projects were Monticello, and, deriving directly from Monticello, his final icono-graphical scheme, the campus of the University of Virginia. In the university the 'vestal flame' of true republicanism, embodied by 'the sage' of Monticello while he still survived, might be handed on to the rising generation of Virginia. To complete Monticello as an expression of his own cultural ideals, and return to Monticello became an imperative for Jefferson (as it is the imperative of these essays). He was tired by the strains of office, and, perhaps like Washington, disenchanted by the conflicts within a self-divided and recalcitrant people. 'By God,' Washington had said, 'he had rather be in his grave than in his present situation; that he had rather be on his farm than to be made Emperor of the world.'[37]

If a similar disenchantment came to Jefferson also, and there is ample biographical evidence, perhaps this may explain Jefferson's final monumental icon of his national role, the obelisk which marks his grave at Monticello. Like the First Inaugural, this too records a moment of stasis, now in the permanence of death. But, rather than listing Jefferson's achievements as the embodiment of the united nation, instead, in an extraordinary paradoxical silence, all mention of his presidency is omitted. This is not the diffidence of modesty, for that kind of modesty would record merely the name of the man which might speak (or not) for itself. Other acts are recorded – the Declaration of Independence, the statute of religious freedom for Virginia, the founding of the University of Virginia – but nothing which would link Jefferson's name with the visionary city named after Washington.

Ultimately that monumental silence cannot be explained. It indicates how uncertain may be the traces left by history. But there is an immense gap between the great rededication of the First Inaugural, and the enigmatic silence of the obelisk at Monticello. That silence warns of the dangers in the leap from iconography to iconology – from the attempt to find specific meanings for signs within a culture to the interpretation of that culture from the traces left by signs. One may, at best, fill the silence of the obelisk with guesses about the recalcitrance of things and the 'necessity' of history which may not, after all, tend to the creation of that promised land which has been chosen to the thousandth generation. His presidency, we know, left a bitter after-taste. During the embargo crisis, the *Volk* had not shown that 'disinterested' virtue attributed to the heroic generation which founded the republic, and of which La Fayette was the archetype. The self-interest of a nascent capitalist (Hamiltonian) economy was far removed also from the Jeffersonian ideal of a perpetual agrarian republic. Perhaps too the new *Lebensraum* purchased by the President in the west ('the Louisiana purchase') might not after all provide a continuing safeguard of agrarian virtue. As Lawson Peebles has argued, the reports brought back by the Lewis and Clark expedition revealed not the fair land of Virginia inexhaustibly cloned, but a violent, unspeakable wilderness – the region Thoreau was to call that 'of Chaos and Old Night' where to be heroic was to suck the milk of the wolf.[38]

This is mere speculation. It is certain, however, that Jefferson's presidency had found no solution to the insoluble problem of race within the growing nation (an issue on which he abrogated all leadership). It was a problem which came to weigh increasingly heavily upon him. 'The fire-bell in the night' of the Missouri compromise disunited the States over the issue of slavery. In a notorious phrase 'we' (that collective word again) 'hold the wolf by the ears' and cannot safely either hold him or let him go. In a vein of pessimistic prophecy, quite different from the First Inaugural, he seems to have foreseen something of the gathering storm ahead:

> I regret that I am now to die in the belief, that the useless sacrifice of themselves by the generation of 1776, to acquire self-government and happiness to their country, is to be thrown away by the unwise and unworthy passions of their sons, and that my only consolation is to be, that I live not to weep over it. (Letter to John Holmes, 22 April 1822)

As a later romantic nationalist expressed it, in a nascent nation dividing in civil war:

> Things fall apart, the centre cannot hold.
> Mere anarchy is loosed upon the world.

In this mythic history of the Jeffersonian nation as an evolving symbolic form, the words 'romantic nationalism' have been left deliberately vague and, thus, provocative. One might, less provocatively, write in Herderian vein of those nationalisms which evolved between the Declaration of Independence and Jefferson's death, for each nation, Herder argued, is unique, and, thus, exceptional.[39] The evolving nation is called 'romantic' here because 'the nation' exists as it is felt by the emotions, and it is more readily expressed in symbolism than by definitive logic. It is an 'imaginary community' (to use Benedict Anderson's often-repeated phrase), and alternative attempts to establish the basis of nationality by rational and scientific means have been fraught with difficulty. Yet the community, though imaginary, undoubtedly exists. As the first romantic nation, the United States forced its way into being without the template of a theory of what it was to be a nation, but it was a model for those movements which followed, especially those nations created by the dynamic and rhetoric of anti-imperialism. The act of 'resistance' to imperialistic 'tyranny' was to be accompanied by progressively knowing acts of self-definition – so Germany, Greece, Italy....[40] Thus, by the time one comes to a late romantic act of nation-building, for instance in Ireland, a theory of national being may be taken as matter of fact. Young Ireland and then Padraic Pearse could draw on an Identikit model for the invention of the entity 'Ireland'. Their movement depended upon the creation (by intellectual leaders like the schoolmaster Pearse) of an image of a demonised imperial oppressor, and a model of history in which an originary and emergent Irish people possess natural rights to their historic homeland within its natural frontiers. What defines the people is the national culture of Ireland (including an 'Irish' language) which becomes the basis for the national education of the people. Symbols, such as the Irish flag or Cathleen ni Houlihan, become essential icons in simplifying historical complexity into unificatory signs. Pearse knew too the importance of the creation of a pantheon of heroes for the people, and the sanctification of heroic struggle by blood sacrifice (his own included). For Pearse, as for Jefferson, the tree of liberty needs watering by blood.

Between the Declaration of Independence (1776) and Padraic Pearse's proclamation of the Irish republic (1916), there is an immense historic distance, and, thus, the term 'romantic nationalism' becomes more indefinite yet. There is a continuing process which extends well into the twentieth century, and in the continuing evolution of post-colonialism may not be finished yet. In that respect, Jefferson is our contemporary, since 'we' are involved in a process which he initiated. The mutability of that process is the prime reason why this preliminary frame for the Jeffersonian national landscape has resisted preferring one categorisation of romantic nationalism to another and has chosen as an originary moment merely one spot of time from an infinitude of others – La Fayette's visit to Monticello. It was chosen because there the link between America and Europe is manifest. Among the plentitude of theories of nationalism, however, there is one American and European text which has been accorded such definitive status in the shaping of national self-consciousness in the United States that it would be perverse to deny its significance or to pass it by without at least summary comment. That text, of course, is de Tocqueville's *Democracy in America*.

It seemed self-evident to de Tocqueville that any account of 'democracy' in America was intrinsically involved with the idea of nationality. Indeed, he observed that patriotic pride in the 'Anglo-Americans' (as he racially designated the people) was an extreme and excessive quality (as another Frenchman, Volney, had discovered when his unAmerican activities made him a prime target for expulsion in 1798 as a seditious alien critic of the the nation).[41] To understand a nation, de Tocqueville claimed, one must turn to its origins, for in the birth of a nation, as of a child, one may trace the essential characteristics of its future being – 'the national character'. If we know how the people first came to possess the land, if we are aware of their common racial origins, their essential tongue and culture, then much which now seems complex may be reduced to its originary simplicity. His idea of the birth of the nation is luminously free from the collective mysticism with which German theory was to involve people and land, language and culture and the whole mystery of race, but de Tocqueville's very matter-of-factness, his role as an empirical and detached European observer, merely lends the weight of apparent science to his presuppositions about the existence of 'national character' in the race. (It was left to Emerson in 1837 to meld German mysticism with patriotic fervour in his invocation in 'The American Scholar' of 'a nation of men . . . inspired by the Divine Soul'.)

On de Tocqueville's assumptions, the common language of the Anglo-Americans is the Plymouth Rock of nationality, the essential element which unites the common 'family' in North and South. 'The tie of language is, perhaps, the strongest and the most durable that can unite mankind.' It is so fundamental an assumption that it commonly disappears, invisible like the air, yet all-pervasive and vital. Yet the implications of the choice of English as the hegemonic language of the Federal State are immense. That hegemonic tendency is manifest, for instance, in 'the Louisiana purchase' when Jefferson imposed what was a foreign tongue (along with a governor) on the new peoples in the territory. To be American requires that you speak the language of the Anglo-Americans.

Equally important for de Tocqueville in the foundation of national character is the religion of the originary people. In this respect, de Tocqueville privileged the 'republican' and 'democratic' Pilgrim Fathers of the North over the slave-owning aristocracy of the South. 'Their union on the soil of America at once presented the singular phenomenon of a society containing neither lords nor common people, and we may also say neither rich nor poor.' Ideologically, therefore, the future civil war has already been decided in terms of Northern values, for these represent what are the essential values of the nation. Religion, 'the soil of America' and the tie of language are so strong that for large sections of his discussion of nationality de Tocqueville abandoned himself to the words of the originary people, the new 'seed of Abraham and the children of Jacob'. 'God brought a vine into this wilderness... he cast out the heathen and planted it... he made room for it and caused it to take deep root; and it filled the land.' Nor does he suppress the tendency of that religious fundamentalism: 'Whosoever shall worship any other God than the Lord shall surely be put to death.'

The birth of the nation, therefore, is closely linked to a missionary fundamentalism, unable to exist under imperial oppression, and committed to establishing itself in its own land and filling that land with those who see themselves as God's chosen people. The *Urtext*, the foundational epic, is the Mosaic account of 'The Conquest of Canaan' (to gloss de Tocqueville by using the title of Timothy Dwight's American epic), and the cleansing of the soil from any alien Other. That racial and ideological effectiveness carries with it in de Tocqueville a strong element of proto-Darwinism as he describes the irresistible rise of the Anglo-American nation. The stock were well-fitted to survive the rigours of the 'wilderness' – a view which had been developed already in the 1790s by Volney. 'As they go forward, the barriers which imprisoned society... which for centuries had been controlling the world, vanish; a course almost without limits; a field without horizon, is revealed: the human spirit rushes forward and traverses them in every direction.' This limitless forward vision is 'romantic', recognisably part of 'the American dream' of an ever-expanding frontier, and Jeffersonian.

It is also racial. De Tocqueville was well aware that the Anglo-Americans were only one of several peoples competing for the 'field without horizon' of the continent, and that the territory occupied by the new nation was deeply divided. Chapter XVIII on 'The Three Races' is an utterly bleak, viciously ironic, and perceptively proleptic account of the racial policies of the new nation both in regard to the Indians and the African slaves. De Tocqueville's conclusion that the Indians are doomed to extinction was not uncommon; but his refusal to accept the peaceful coexistence policies of the administration as anything but a hypocritical cant must deeply disturb any student of Jefferson. Nor does he perceive, for the South, any solution for the problem of slavery except in war or racial anarchy, terminations which Jefferson also feared.

It is difficult to reconcile the progressive enthusiasm of de Tocqueville's account of the development of democracy in the Anglo-American nation with his portrayal of the future relation of the three races in the States. It is as if, imaginatively, he breaks the nation into three, with the North committed to its course 'almost without limits, a field without a horizon' while the South and the West become other Americas – what Conrad might call the dark places of the earth. The 'real' nation had already been ethnically and ideologically cleansed, and thus is racially, linguistically and culturally one. Elsewhere the process of festering genocidal and racial conflict may run another course.

Few of the fundamental conceptions underlying de Tocqueville's analysis now command assent as viable categories for defining a nation: an originary people, an originary land, a unified culture and a common language. But the unsolvable problematisation of 'what is a nation?' is irrelevant. If nationality is an imaginary and symbolic order, it is the individual's perception that matters, felt in the blood and attached to defining signs. Since it is not a matter of science, but of emotion, these essays on Jefferson have begun in the intense emotion of the fête of 4 November 1824 and in the symbolic and imaginative pageantry of the history of the people. Hence, also, the emphasis upon the importance of the individual agent in history. For the paradox of romantic nationalism is that 'we', the nation, are 'one people' and yet the people needs and demands the example of heroic individuals. These heroic individuals are the ideal, archetypal, expression of the race, the model of the best 'we' might be. Witness, thus, those named great men in Trumbull's iconic painting of the Declaration of Independence, acting collectively, as they mutually pledge to each other their lives, fortunes, 'sacred honour', and yet led by an outstanding group of greater men yet, over whom Jefferson rises higher by a head.

The essays on Jefferson which follow merely take up *seriatim* three elements from de Tocqueville's characterisation of the Anglo-Americans: the people, the land and the cultural history of the people in that land. They are the elements already seen unified in the fête of 4 November 1824 on the lawn at Monticello before the assembled 'people' of Virginia in the great circumference of the American landscape. As Mrs Jane Cary observed, instinctively understanding the iconography of romantic nationalism, 'The whole was a scene for an artist – a grand historic picture should have commemorated this meeting.'[42] Mrs Jane Cary writes, of course, in English. Thus, a fourth, crucial, element of de Tocqueville's analysis is implied throughout these essays on people, land and cultural history. That element is the language. By this the 'Anglo-American' (to use de Tocqueville's term) is inevitably caught in the web of English (and, thus, ultimately, European) origins.

Since romantic nationalism has been claimed here to be a mythic and symbolic order, people, land and cultural history are each approached in the essays which follow as the product of creative imagination. This is the province of literature and art, and Jefferson is read and seen as if he were a verbal and visual artist, a man of imagination who orders the world in which he finds himself as much by processes of symbolism as by reason. If there is a theory behind this approach to Jefferson, it is itself romantic. It originates in a sense of the unique value of each individual. This theory, thus, is paradoxically antitheory, if by 'theory' is meant an ideological and *a priori* totalisation which obliterates the uniqueness of the individual in presuppositions about class, gender, race or power. On these ideological matters no apologetics are offered, nor any special privilege asserted. I admit only to a deep (and growing) scepticism at any attempt at holistic explanation of history.

The people, the land and cultural history are, in some measure, separated in the essays that follow. That separation is the mere product of narrative and analytical necessity, which divides ideas which are intrinsically 'organically' related. The *terminus ad quem* which iconographically embodies the whole is the villa at Monticello where La Fayette and Jefferson, Europe and Anglo-America, embraced on the lawn. The significant signs and texts chosen all lie in large measure outside Jefferson's career as a politician, for his career as statesman belongs to the realm of empirical, day-by-day practicality. The administration of a State and the idea of the nation are separable entities. In the first essay which follows, the people are seen in the icon of the Seal which Jefferson designed for the republic at the very beginning of the nation, but which was never struck in the form that he desired. Next, the land, being itself a visual sign, is textualised as icon in the *Notes on the State of Virginia* – 'notes' written early in Jefferson's career (1781), imperfect, in their composition, because it was a period of bloody wounds he was unwilling to reopen (so he claimed); never formally revised, although he thought of this in old age, and abandoned because the world had now moved on too far since 1781.

The Seal and the *Notes* serve as prologue to the essays on the significations of the villa at Monticello – the *terminus ad quem*. The villa is seen as an icon of that national culture which gives historical roots and formal models to people and land. The argument, therefore, returns to the place at which it began. As idea embodied, Monticello originates in 'the villa culture' of the ancient world. It has often been interpreted also as the expression of Jefferson's personality and humanistic ideals. This has been well explored.[43] But here it is read, both intrinsically (and subsequently in the words of its many visitors) as an ideal sign for the romantic nation. The villa is an attempt to fix in material form the true spirit of an imaginary unity, and at a time when the tumult and flux of change and war risked involving and even dissolving the nation in the European 'age of despair'.[44] Things changed even as the icon laboriously took shape through the decades of its building. Since the forms of architecture are non-verbal, Monticello was a potential means of liberation from the web of language (the English tongue) which inevitably linked the Anglo-American to the rejected culture of British imperialism. But it was a vain aspiration, for architectural forms are iconographical (carriers of meaning), and conflicting interpretation of the sign re-emerged in language through the ceaseless progress of visitors. Inevitably, therefore, Monticello involved Jefferson in a struggle between rejected origins in the past and the unknowable teleology of future interpretation. The struggle to establish meaning for the icon was, and is, indeterminable.

But why Jefferson as the particular human agent in history for this iconographic study? He has been chosen because of his typological signification. Like La Fayette, he too is a romantic hero for the nation. He belongs to a pantheon of national 'fathers' – like Alfred in England, Arminius in Germany, or Pearse in Ireland. But he is also, as a cultural icon, a great national figure which each generation in the United States has used to construct the symbolic order of the present in relation to the past. He is a kind of vast quarry from which each hews what they will for their needs. With George Washington, he is the only member of the 'founding fathers' of 1776 to be given his own monument among that peculiar historical detritus which constitutes the Mall in the national capital. In that context George Washington and Jefferson possess the status of iconological (rather than iconographical) signs for they define (or were intended to define) what is the essence of the originary nation. But Washington's obelisk is not inscribed, whereas the Jefferson Memorial is a textualised icon recording on tablets of stone the 'essential' words of the Father. Nor does Washington's obelisk represent an image of the man (perhaps, like God, he should have no human image) while Jefferson, on the other hand, like Gulliver in Lilliput, towers over 'we, the people' within the Pantheon dedicated here not to all the Gods, but to Jefferson alone. The living man has been reified and deified as a sign of the romantic nation.

But the tablets of stone have not fixed the law. (There is iconography, but no permanent iconology.) Jefferson was, in his lifetime, and throughout the nineteenth century, a figure surrounded by intense controversy, as Merrill Peterson has shown in one of the great studies of a great subject: *The Jefferson Image in the American Mind* (1960). That controversy has not ended. At the brighter end of the spectrum of interpretation one might place the hagiography of the Memorial and the Memorial Association edition of the writings, an ideal image of Jefferson admirably supported by the scholarly apologetic of Dumas Malone's biography. Less secure is the Protean image created by the subtle dialectics of Peterson's *Thomas Jefferson and the New Nation* (1970) (whose Jefferson oscillates, skilfully, between idealisms of excellence and the necessities of *Realpolitik*). These dialectics have subsequently dissolved into the mere contradictions of the self-deluding postmodern Jefferson whom Joseph J. Ellis has characterised as an *American Sphinx* (1997). But the darker end of the spectrum reaches ultimately to a black (correction: 'white') extremity of Machiavellian duplicity where Jefferson emerges as an indefensible hypocrite in relation to his slaves, objectionable in his attitudes to women, a sexual libertine, and a corrupter of the very civil liberties he claimed to defend. He is, thus,

> A man so various that he seem'd to be
> Not one, but all mankind's epitome.[45]

At one extreme, therefore, Jefferson is used for purposes of patriotic self-glorification and revered as a founder of a nation dedicated to the universal principles of human rights and individual liberty; at the other extreme there are those who would utilise him as an example of that 'white mythology' which conceals an oppressive racial imperialism in a language of universal philanthropy and whose culture conceals that 'barbarism' (Benjamin's word) designated by abusive rhetoric as 'Fascism'. In coming to the perplexed subject, perhaps all a European writer may claim in his favour is that like Tacitus he writes of things American *sine ira et studio, quorum causas procul habeo* (which one might freely translate 'without fear or favour, for I have no axe to grind'). Or if that objectivity is unobtainable (could even Tacitus achieve it?) perhaps, although lacking Tacitean style or insight, one may achieve at least a paradoxical unity between the critical irony of distance, and the empathy of understanding that even now our common predicament is involved, like Jefferson, with the ineluctable processes of romantic nationalism.

2

Jefferson Seals the Revolution

Has the pyramid lost any of its strength? The pyramid put on the reverse side of the great seal of the United States by the fathers as signifying strength and duration, has it lost any of its strength? [Voices, 'No!'] Has the republic lost any of its virility? Has the self-governing principle been weakened? Is there any present menace to our stability and duration? [Voices, 'No!'] These questions bring but one answer. The republic is sturdier and stronger than ever before. [Great applause.] Government by the people has not been retarded, but advanced. [Applause.] Freedom under the flag is more universal than when the Union was formed. Our steps have been forward, not backward. We have not stood still. 'From Plymouth Rock to the Philippines [great applause] the grand triumphant march of human liberty has never paused.' [Great applause.]

President McKinley, 1899[1]

Late in the afternoon of 4 July 1776 the Continental Congress resolved that a committee should prepare 'a device for a seal of the United States of America'.[2] The members of the committee were John Adams, Benjamin Franklin and Thomas Jefferson, drawn from the committee which had earlier drafted the Declaration of Independence. They were supplemented by an emigrant Swiss painter, Pierre-Eugène du Simitière. The Declaration and the Seal are concomitant, therefore, and the 'device' of the Seal is an originary act supplementing the textuality of the revolution with an iconography. By what image should the newly emergent 'one people' be emblazoned among 'the powers of the earth'?

The Seal is both originary, as a signifier of the birth of a nation, and teleological, seeking to define what the nation shall be. Its iconography is transitional, therefore, between a past which is in process of rejection and an 'impending future' not yet in being. Seen in terms of origins, the idea that the revolution required a seal is part of

45

inherited Whig tradition. Just as in 1688–89 in England, the revolutionaries needed to justify acts of treason as acts of legality. The signs of law and order must be maintained because, in the simplest material terms, security of property, including man's property in himself, depended on the rule of law, which in Whig tradition meant the rule of those men of property who make the law – 'we, the people' (as distinguished from 'the mob'). The alternative was what was called 'anarchy' – of which the revolution in France was to become the major example. This was not merely an internal concern. War in the former British colonies meant international war in North America. It was necessary to possess recognisable signs of government, for only what was recognisably a government could negotiate on behalf of the States with the other competing powers in the Americas and West Indies. In particular it was important to strike a deal with France, for Britain's difficulty was France's opportunity.

Merely to summarise the originary Whig context of the Seal as 'device' indicates the remoteness of the *ancien régime* of Whig history.[3] A major wrench of historical imagination is needed to read reference to 'we, the people' as meaning Whig gentlemen of property, or to respond sympathetically to Jefferson's outrage in the (suppressed) passages of the Declaration of Independence, that it was a gross act of Georgian tyranny for the British army to expropriate property by freeing negro slaves. But another difficulty of entering into that kind of Whig history is that it is in process of future transformation even as one looks at it. 'All eyes are opened, or opening, to the rights of man', Jefferson was to write to Roger Weightman in the famous (valedictory) letter of 24 June 1826. Jefferson placed the Declaration of Independence and the emergence of the Americans 'among the powers of the earth' at the centre of a great process of historical change based on the new idea of universal rights. The revolutionary concept of 'the rights of man' (and eventually of woman too) was to dissolve the old Whig identification of citizenship with property. But it was an idea only nominally universal in the old, Enlightenment, sense of 'cosmopolitan'. If 'all eyes' perceived it, in practice that perception was repeatedly associated with the claim of the right to national 'self-determination'. Thus 'universal' rights were likely to find their expression in the revolutionary epoch post–1776 only within the boundaries of the newly defined or newly emergent nation-state. 'Man' has 'rights', but it is the 'one people' of the national entity who give expression to those rights. What, then, was imagined by writing of the States as constituting 'one people'? In relation to the making of nations post-1776, how does one envisage the relationship of such a phrase to the subsequent development of the idea of 'the people', for instance by the United Irishmen (the immediate heirs of the American revolution), or in the plebiscites of Jacobin or Napoleonic France (which radically revised the American example), or in later formulations such as *Deutschevolk*, or the Churchillian 'the English-speaking peoples'? It is both a question of definition, and of future historical reverberation.

In uniting 'one people' an icon (or 'totem', to use a North American word, *nintotem*: the mark of my family) has the great virtue of simplicity.[4] It does not raise complex issues of definition (what is the nation?) but is a matter of recognition. The device of a national flag is an obvious example, witness the nationalist iconography of Leutze's *Washington Crossing the Delaware* (1851) where the star-spangled banner (anachronistically) waves in the wind of freedom above the head of the militant hero. When the flag becomes the battle-flag, the issue of definition of what constitutes 'one people' is easy. 'We' are those people who are fighting against the 'alien' – a collective self against a collective other – in this case, the evil empire of Great Britain. (Other evil empires were to follow.) With the flag often comes the national anthem. 'The Star-Spangled Banner' dates from the second war (1812–15) against the alien British invader (although only officially adopted in 1931). To which one may add those commemorative fêtes on which it is an act of national identity to show the flag: 4 July, or Washington's birthday, or the date of the confirmation of the Constitution. This is elementary matter of romantic nationalism and needs no elaboration.

It was the strength of Whig tradition that led Congress to think immediately of a Seal (a sign of legality) as a 'device' for the United States rather than the more emotive nationalist symbol of a battle-flag.[5] But as matter of fact, even of symbolic necessity, it was to be the battle-flag which preceded the Seal as the emergent national icon by five years (1777 as against 1782). The problem was that the Seal Committee, faced with the difficult task of inventing an originary 'device' which would signify the collective will of 'one people', produced diverse and complex proposals. Even when the Committee's proposal was simplified by du Simitière's professional advice, the agreement of Congress could not be obtained. Most of the recommendations were rejected; during the next six years the embattled republic neglected the matter; even after the adoption of a new design for the Seal in 1782 only the obverse was cut. Half the device now daily familiar on the Federal dollar was unused by the Founding Fathers.

But this evanescent imagery of the new republic is important because its very evanescence reveals the processes by which the symbolic order of the new nation was being invented before the idea of 'America' hardened into received icons and their accumulated textuality. In historical practice, it is well known that in making the romantic nation, the symbolic order often has to be invented before a political structure evolves and is finally accepted. It is at this time that those things which are to be included and excluded in the nation are distinguished and the choice is made of what to remember and what to expunge.

It is crucial, therefore, which people among 'the people' first constitute what comes to be accepted as the collective memory. Whom, or what, did the members of the Seal Committee represent? The major figure was Franklin. His authority on the committee rested on his substantial seniority of years and his European reputation. He was the only American of European 'fame' – to use the word as Douglass Adair has applied it to the Founding Fathers.[6] He could already be seen in the great glass of history to which new men, like Adams and Jefferson, might only now begin to aspire. This is not the Franklin of the incompleted and as yet unpublished *Autobiography*, who was later admired as an example of the American dream of rising from rags to riches by what Samuel Smiles called 'self-help'. This was rather Franklin who had put trade behind him to emerge as an American type of the universal man (to which universality Jefferson also aspired). He was a philosopher in the widest, Baconian sense of the word; the man, who as a scientist had brought down lightning from heaven, was now to add to his fame as a statesman who tore the sceptre from tyranny. His very bodily self was to become an American icon by the cultivation of his image as a homespun man of the people during his subsequent years in France. Or, put another way, if Franklin had not existed, it would have been necessary to invent him. Emergent nations need national heroes (Washington's military career, to date, was scarcely one of glory).

The symbolic signification of Adams and Jefferson on the committee, on the other hand, can only be constructed by retrospectively reading their history. It is mere coincidence that here were Washington's immediate heirs to an as-yet non-existent Presidency. Yet, between the future second President of the United States (Adams) and the third (Jefferson), there is already latent the great division between Federalism and Republicanism of the 1790s. The Tory (Adams) is set against the Whig (Jefferson) – to adopt Jefferson's historical eschatology. But both, of course, were men of property and gentlemen.

Du Simitière, a native of Geneva, on the other hand, was not a 'gentleman' (in the Adams/Jefferson sense of the word) and had been naturalised only recently as a citizen of New York (1769). He made his living as an itinerant artist, and was on the committee as the only member with experience in the design of seals (a 'professional' among 'gentlemen'). If language is an essential element in national self-definition, then du Simitière had to abandon his native tongue for the language of Adams, Franklin and Jefferson. In losing, thus, his originary culture, he represents a common phenomenon in the history of romantic nationalism: the deracinated immigrant who becomes the ultra-patriot. What Richard Patterson has called 'his great personal vision'[7] of America led him to found what is the first museum of American history in Philadelphia (1782). He sought to compile a history of the colonies, and as a painter, he was assiduous in recording the images of notable Americans who passed his way. Since the making and interpretation of national history in order to create a sense of identity is, like language, a vital element of romantic nationalism, du Simitière's place on the committee has far more weight than that of a mere draughtsman. For him the question of national identity was also a question of selfhood. He made himself an American.

More generally, the very names themselves of the Anglophone members of the committee construct a cultural matrix. Although this is a mere coincidence, it is an instructive one. The fundamental ideology of Christendom is implicit in the connotations of the word 'Adam' which recalls the Hebraic account of the origin of Man; 'Benjamin' refers collective memory to the tribes of Israel specially chosen by that God who made Adam; John was the disciple beloved by Christ, and Thomas the disciple who doubted the power of divinity. This Christian society politically is patriarchal and patrilinear as is clear from the name Jefferson (Jeffersdaughter is a linguistic absurdity in such a culture). It is also a society where freehold in land is an important element in social identity and power, hence Franklin (a freeholder but not an hereditary nobleman). This is so 'self-evident' that it is, perhaps, redundant to state the obvious. But that is the point. It is so deeply buried in the culture that it is almost invisible. But the very names of the members of the committee carry immense implications.

The history of the committee's work is fully documented in the official record of the genesis of the Seal. It is complex, but may be simply summarised. Each of the four members put forward separate proposals, those from Franklin and du Simitière eventually carrying the day. The least influential was Adams, who wrote:

> I proposed the Choice of Hercules, as engraved by Gribeline in some Editions of Lord Shaftesburys Works. The Hero resting on his Clubb. Virtue pointing to her rugged Mountain, on one Hand, and perswading him to ascend. Sloth, glancing at her flowery Paths of Pleasure, wantonly reclining on the Ground, displaying the Charms both of her Eloquence and Person, to seduce him into Vice. But this is too complicated a Group for a Seal or Medal, and it is not original.

Jefferson also chose subjects more appropriate, perhaps, to an allegorical painting than a Seal:[8]

> The Children of Israel in the Wilderness, led by a Cloud by day, and a Pillar of Fire by night, and on the other Side Hengist and Horsa, the Saxon Chiefs, from whom We claim the Honour of being descended and whose Political Principles and Form of Government We have assumed.

Another suggestion in his mind, although of uncertain date, is recorded in his account book for 1774:

> A proper device (instead of arms) for the American states united would be the Father presenting the bundle of rods to his sons. [from Aesop's *Fables*]
>   The motto 'Insuperabiles si inseparabiles' an answer given in parl[iament] to the H[ouse] of L[or]ds & Comm[ons].

The source of the motto is impeccably Whig – Sir Edward Coke, *The Fourth Part of the Institutes of the Laws of England*. The iconography of the 'bundle of rods' introduced here by Jefferson for the first time as a national sign is closely related to the *fasces* – the bundle of rods with an axe protruding, which was the representation of magisterial authority in Rome.[9] The *fasces* were to become a sign rapidly established in the early national imagery in the United States: witness Independence Hall; Houdon's statue of Washington in the State Capitol of Virginia (where his left hand rests on the *fasces*) and Godefroy's Monument to the Battle of Baltimore. They became so firmly established as a national icon that the *fasces* became a universal decorative motif in the State Capitol of Wisconsin (1907–17). For obvious reasons, one would not wish to enter upon the subsequent history of the icon from the 1920s onward.

None of the proposals from Adams or Jefferson survived. The committee submitted instead a proposal in which the reverse of the Seal should depict:

> Pharaoh sitting in an open Chariot a Crown on his head & a Sword in his hand passing through the divided Waters of the Red Sea in Pursuit of the Israelites: Rays from a Pillow [Pillar] of Fire in the Cloud, expressive of the divine Presence & Command, beaming on Moses who stands on the shore and extending his hand over the Sea causes it to overwhelm Pharaoh.
>   Motto Rebellion to Tyrants is Obedience to God.

This was from Franklin, by alternative drafts. The obverse was an heraldic scheme (sketched by du Simitière) expressed in heraldic language. The 'Arms of the United States' were displayed in 'six Quarters', comprising the heraldic signs for England, Scotland, Ireland, France, Germany and Holland, 'pointing out the Countries from which these States have been peopled'. The shield was bordered by 'thirteen Scutcheons Argent' linked by a golden chain representing each of the States, and the supporters were an armed Goddess of Liberty holding a spear and liberty cap, and the Goddess Justice with the usual sword and balance. (The latter was a substitute for du Simitière's original proposal for an American soldier with powder horn and tomahawk.) The crest was 'The Eye of Providence in a radiant Triangle whose Glory extends over the Shield and beyond the Figures.' The motto was E PLURIBUS UNUM. The date MDCCLXXVI.

As a glance at a dollar bill will show, '*e pluribus unum*' is the only major element to survive on the obverse of the Seal, although it is still armigerous. Nowhere in the committee's papers is a bald-headed eagle holding arrows in one talon and an olive branch in the other (both incorporating the number 13). No constellation of 13 stars bursts through the cloudy heavens. On the reverse the eye of Providence in a radiant triangle survives, but has become the apex of an uncompleted pyramid. This (quasi-Masonic) imagery was to acquire two new mottos, both from Virgil: *annuit coeptis* (*Aeneid* IX, 625) and *novus ordo seclorum* from the 'Messianic' *Eclogue* (line 5).

Of the four members of the committee, Adams seems to have been least influential. His moral and civic allegory of the choice of Hercules offered as its icon a design merely copied from the third volume of Shaftesbury's *Characteristics* (1713). It was 'not original'. Since it was so swiftly expunged from national iconography, Adams's rejected design has received little attention. Yet it was not eccentric. Franklin, in 1782, was to suggest as the device for a medal commemorating American liberty the infant Hercules strangling snakes in his cradle, protected, on the one hand by Minerva (an emblematic representation of France) and attacked by a (British) lion. The extinguishing of two British armies, he wrote, 'gives a presage of the future force of our growing empire'. This medal was struck by Franklin on his own initiative and used by him to propagate the image of America as an infant Hercules at the Bourbon court. The device also forms part of the set of revolutionary-war medals struck in France under Jefferson's supervision with a motto from the Augustan panegyrist, Horace: 'the courageous child helped by the Gods'. Adams's Herculean icon, therefore, was a well-founded choice. As a mythic figure, traditionally interpreted as a type of heroic civic virtue, Hercules might be preferable to either of the other great role models from classical antiquity widely diffused in the symbolic history of the revolution: Cato Uticensis, admired by Washington in the recension of his story by Addison in his tragedy *Cato* (1713), and Cincinnatus, the patriot farmer who left his plough to save the state, and then returned to his plough again.[10] The problem with 'real-life' heroes is that they become contaminated with real-life problems. Cato lost his war against tyranny and committed suicide. The Society of the Cincinnati (of which Washington became President) was to become an instrument of the high-flying wing of the Federalist 'aristocracy'. Hercules, by comparison, as a mythic character from the realm of moral allegory was free from the contamination of local and partisan controversies (classic or American).[11]

There is nothing intrinsically inappropriate in Adams's Herculean icon, therefore. It may be textualised readily for it carried an extensive gloss. Gribelin's engraving was the frontispiece for an allegorical and aesthetic essay by Shaftesbury. As Adams's summary stated, the image shows the hero with his club (and lion skin) between two women. Seductive Pleasure (Adams called her 'Sloth') with the emblems of a feast, is rejected at his feet on his left (sinister) side. To his right the figure of Virtue, carrying an 'Imperial or Magisterial Sword' (as Shaftesbury describes it) points the attentive hero the pathway up a steep and rocky hillside. Read as a national icon, like Franklin's infant Hercules, this is 'young' America (in this respect the first of the 'young' national movements of the epoch). Shaftesbury's gloss is equally appropriate for the young nation since the choice of Hercules might be readily allegorised as the path of republican virtue: 'the way which leads to Honour, and the just Glory of Heroick Actions' in 'the deliverance of Mankind from Tyranny and Oppression' as Shaftesbury wrote. That 'way', pointed by Virtue, leads into a natural wilderness. The signifiers of culture (represented in the icon by the paraphernalia of the corrupting banquet of Pleasure) are to be rejected for a 'rough and rocky way' which leads from this 'solitary place' where (Shaftesbury writes) the divine reveals itself to man, up to the crest of a high mountain. Shaftesbury insists that this mountain also is without any of the signifiers yet of civilisation. There are no emblems here of '*Fortress, Temple,* or *Palace of* VIRTUE'. Hercules, in his lionskin, is a young man who chooses the hard life according to Nature, where with his simple weapons he will exercise primitive virtues. The wilderness is an appropriate *locus* for the liberty of America. As David Ramsay wrote, 'The natural seat of freedom is among high mountains, and pathless deserts, such as abound in the wilds of America.'[12] Hercules in the wilderness is in some ways the allegorical forefather of Fenimore Cooper's Natty Bumppo – a lion-killer rather than deerslayer, he of the long club rather than long carbine.

Adams had selected an appropriate image, therefore. But certain crucial elements distinguish it from all the other proposals. It is an emblem of *choice* for the new nation, and that choice is one that each moral individual must make for himself. Shaftesbury's gloss is insistent that Hercules, although he has turned to listen to Virtue, is still in the *process* of rejecting Pleasure and the corruptions of pleasurable Vice. The problem with 'the choice of Hercules' as a national emblem, therefore, is that the seductive lure of selfish Pleasure, leading to Vice, is always half of the picture. The young Man of republican virtue needs always to be educated for his salvation. Indeed, a pessimistic reading of the story might be that *only* the heroic individual – a demi-god like Hercules – is capable of making the right decision. Moreover, although Hercules in the wilderness was often allegorised as a type of Christ – who made the most significant of all choices – yet the Herculean story also had its darker side. For the classic hero was not always capable of acting according to his own heroic typology, as the subsequent labours tell. The national Seal, therefore, would have been, in Adams's design, a perpetual reminder of the difficulties of republican virtue. In a moral sense, this is a 'Federalist' allegory for the United States, if one accepts that one of the major distinctions between Federalism and Jeffersonian Republicanism is Federalist scepticism before the romantic claims of Jeffersonianism for the innate goodness or indefinite perfectibility of the new Man. On the contrary, in many of the major writers of Federalist persuasion, there still runs a strong element of eighteenth-century 'Tory pessimism' (or even a Calvinist sense of original sin). 'All men are men, and not angels', Adams claimed, adding that 'whoever would found a state...must presume that all men are bad by nature'. 'You will find all men substantially alike, and all naturally ignorant and wicked', claimed Timothy Dwight, rejecting the dangerous optimism of 'visionary philosophers' of the new age. So too Hamilton, who wrote of 'the ordinary depravity of human nature' or Fisher Ames on man as 'the most ferocious of all animals'.[13] Perhaps some of the Founding Fathers might have been saved the disappointments of romantic idealism, which Gordon Wood notes darkened their later years, if they had borne in mind this disenchanted view of the human animal.[14] But the role of Jefferson (like his fellows) on the Seal committee was not to be a doubting Thomas. Self-criticism was not to be a characteristic of the world according to the fourth of July. Hercules' choice of virtue had already been made.

There is another element in which Adams's problematic design differs from the rest. It alone raises gender as an issue. Woman is a major participant in the drama of choice. In this respect Adams's Virtue and Vice differ from du Simitière's female figures. For du Simitière the goddess Liberty was first the moral personification of the American soldier armed with rifle and tomahawk (who will defend her), and then, in the final proposal, the allegorical figure paired with the goddess Justice. The new nation has chosen both, and the goddess Liberty was to become the best known of all icons for the United States.[15] But for Adams, Man's relationship to Woman is intrinsically part of the whole *problem* of the allegory. The positive choice makes an armed woman, morally, the signifier of all that is virtuous in the new Man. This, *per se*, may seem straightforward, for this idealisation of Woman is not uncommon in romantic nationalism. Marianne was to become the embodiment of France (and the national anthem, the song of the women of Marseilles marching to water the fields of the motherland with the impure blood of aliens). Britannia in Britain, Cathleen ni Houlihan in Ireland, or the *figura* of Greece in Delacroix's 'Greece Grieving Over the Ruins of Missolonghi' are other common examples of the nation, victorious or oppressed, embodied in a female figure. But Adams's image (indeed the very story of Hercules himself) makes sexuality a central issue. His two women (Virtue and Sloth) are not supporters of the young nation, but represent a divisive dichotomy. Woman is both the nation in its ideal form, and the instructor of Man (Abigail Adams as allegorical type) but, conversely, she is also a slothful, sensual form of corruption which threatens the heroic male. Any document of the Founding Fathers sealed by Adams's device would, therefore, continually raise the gender issue of the relationship of masculinity to femininity in the nation. But the question of gender, like the question of moral choice, was to be totally expunged from the Seal. Woman, who is the dominant presence in Adams's device, was to have no place in the icon as we now know it.[16]

But Adams's presentation of his own proposal indicates that he expected it to make little progress. The concern of the committee was not with the problems of gendered morality and choice, but with the assertion of national will. This is clearest from one of Jefferson's icons. Firmly in Whig tradition, as he saw it, the signifier he chose to link the new nation to its *Urvolk* was the descent of Hengist and Horsa on the coasts of the decadent Celto-Romanic empire. These were 'the Saxon Chiefs, from whom We claim the Honour of being descended, and whose Political Principles and Form of Government We have assumed'. This is 'real' history moralised, and the reiterated 'We' is unselfconsciously confident. Jefferson was going back to the very origins of the so-called 'ancient constitution' invoked by Whig opposition to Stuart 'tyranny'. This was the constitution of the free 'Saxons' (or 'Germans') who, as Tacitus claimed, had successfully defended their ancient liberties against Rome. Hengist and Horsa, in this symbolic history, would be, for the United States, figures equivalent to Arminius (Hermann) in the development of German nationalism – *liberator haud dubie Germaniae*.[17] (His rout of the Augustan legions in the northern forests was the Germanic equivalent of Saratoga.) Jefferson's symbolic moment can be precisely located. The invading tribes of 'Saxons' (Jutes) fell upon the eastern seaboard of Celto-Romanic Britain in 449 and established their first colony at Ebbsfleet. Thus, the specific time and place of the landfall of the 'free' *Urvolk* is parallel to the landfall of the Pilgrim Fathers.

This is a violent signifier for the United States. There is good reason to suppose that this was Jefferson's intention. *The Summary View of the Rights of British America* (1774) had been explicit on one of the fundamental 'rights of man': the right of conquest:

> no circumstance has occurred to distinguish materially the British from the Saxon emigration. America was conquered, and her settlements made and firmly established, at the expence of individuals.... Their own blood was spilt in acquiring lands for their settlement, their own fortunes expended in making that settlement effectual. For themselves they fought, for themselves they conquered, and for themselves alone they have right to hold. (Viking edn, pp. 4–5)

There is a direct Machiavellian honesty about this statement. It is much blunter than Franklin's well-known letter to Lord Kames, 11 April 1767, about how the west was won. There is no universal claim here about the 'inalienable rights' of Man to life and liberty which make the Declaration of Independence so potent a romantic document. The *Summary View* states bluntly that the land and wealth won by bloodshed will be held by the conquerors. As the Saxons to the Celts, so the British Americans to the Indians (or any alien power). Hengist and Horsa (whom, one suspects, preferred the battleaxe to the ballot box) are appropriate signifiers on a Seal which imposes the forms of legality upon the conquests of war. Nor is there any reason to suppose that Jefferson ever abandoned this interpretation of the Saxon myth which paradoxically links conquest with law. We know that his Napoleonic imagination saw the *Einschluss* with Canada as an exercise for a mere summer's campaign; that the absorption of French and Spanish territories to the south and west were the objectives of his second term as President; and although he told Madison (27 April 1809) that subsequently the conquest of Cuba was the '*ne plus ultra*' of his territorial ambitions in the south (a project not without interest in the twentieth century), yet, in the fullness of time, who knows, the American people might spread south of Panama.... [18] In the symbolic order of things, one need only drop the word 'British' from the phrase 'British America' for the 13 colonies of the United States to metamorphose into 'one people' who identified their natural boundaries with that of the continent from Canada to Cuba, or beyond.

The icon of Hengist and Horsa belongs, thus, to the world of Machiavellian (or Bismarckian) *Realpolitik*. From a Machiavellian viewpoint, much of the subsequent history of the federal settlement might be interpreted as a series of exercises in duplicity, intended to conceal in the languages of law and liberty, civilisation and philanthropy, the simple, material, bloody fact: 'for themselves they fought, for themselves they conquered'. That would be a discomforting and crude reading of history. Conversely, therefore, one might equally argue, that the image of two Vikings storming ashore from their landingcraft is far too simplistic an image of the complex processes of colonial history. Jefferson's image obscures all sense of historical irony, of difficult moral choices to be made in real situations. *Mutatis mutandis*; that is what Adams had offered in his iconography, and what had been rejected as too divisive and divided. The rejection of Hengist and Horsa as a design, on the other hand, may be attributed to its ugly simplicity. Jefferson was too obviously bloody-minded.

The committee's agreement to use the commencement of the story of 'the conquest of Canaan' (to adopt the title of Dwight's epic, 1785) as a sign for the colonisation of America distanced in time and place and sanitised by religion the rights of conquest. The adoption of Moses as an American hero harnessed God's Providence to the establishment of the people in their chosen (promised) land. The mythos of the Pilgrim Fathers and the Mosaic analogy are so familiar that it is difficult to defamiliarise them, especially as the analogy between Pharaoh and George III is so apt. But the very archaism should arrest attention. Why should Jefferson select as a parallel to Hengist and Horsa, 'The Children of Israel in the Wilderness, led by a Cloud by day, and a Pillar of Fire by night'? His own ambience is not that of seventeenth-century Puritan allegorists, but that of Priestley and Paine; he was the close associate of revolutionary freemasons like La Fayette; and as an ethical Socinian he purged the Gospels of the corruptions of religious superstition. He even risked the future of his last, cherished project, the University of Virginia, by a determined secularism which clashed head-on with the religious fundamentalism of the new nation. His spontaneous choice of an Old Testament allegory is, in general, out of kilter with his mind-set. Moreover his Commonplace book had (albeit indirectly) criticised Moses for the 'exterminations of people' and for the propagation of an 'incredible' history (items 56, 58).

One must recognise, therefore, the power of that received tradition implicit in the very names of the committee: Adams, Benjamin, John and Thomas. The Biblical story is the basic foundational epic of European culture and Jefferson simply recognises the ineluctable fact and trades upon it as a unifying common currency of symbolic history. Indeed, in the Second Inaugural, his own symbolic history cast the President himself in the role of Moses at the head of a chosen people poised on the frontier of 'the Louisiana purchase'.[19] Perhaps, however, his own proposal for the Seal might be given at least a quasi-deistic gloss. The pillar of fire and cloud might be reconciled with the invocation of God and Nature in the Declaration of Independence. An understanding of God's purposes as revealed in his creation will guide the American frontiersmen in the wilderness (the tribes of the States) to the goal towards which Providential history manifestly guides them. The Divine Eye looking on, one element from the original committee which carries through to the present Seal, might be interpreted by some as a fundamentalist signifier, but would be read in Jefferson's circle as representing a Deistic or Masonic Supreme Being.

It was an easy step to meld Jefferson's icon with Franklin's more directly political image of a crowned and armed Pharaoh (George III) about to be swallowed up by the Red Sea (the Atlantic) while 'a Pillar of Fire in the Cloud, expressive of the divine Presence & Command' beams on Moses in the American wilderness. The motto: 'Rebellion to Tyrants is Obedience to God' makes Moses the first Whig, for he preserves the law even in rebellion. Who exactly is the American Moses might be unclear in 1776, but the foundation of states traditionally required a leader who was also a lawgiver (thus, Lycurgus and Numa from classical antiquity). The problem with such states, however, was that the *Führerprinzip* (as later theory was to describe it) was closely associated with national militancy – in classical antiquity in Sparta and Rome, and in Mosaic history with 'the conquest of Canaan' (to return to Dwight's American epic) and the 'exterminations of people' (in Jefferson's phrase). It may well be that both Franklin and Jefferson were seeking safer ground, therefore, by setting the tribes/States in the 'wilderness'. That place is primarily the *locus* of learning in which, in the fullness of time, the people will become a nation. Adams, likewise, had placed his moral individual in a wilderness, firmly emphasising that this was a region without the signifiers of culture represented by the architectural monuments of fortress, temple or palace. The advantage of this allegorical space is that there was nobody in the wilderness to be conquered. The historical presence of the recalcitrant Canaanites in Israel and the Indians in America is thus expunged from the image.[20] (Alternatively, when visible signs of an aboriginal people appear in Jefferson's *Notes on the State of Virgina* they are burial mounds and these, accordingly, can only represent a dead and departed people.) The iconography of the wilderness, as proposed by Adams, Franklin and Jefferson, avoids, therefore, the far more complex issues explored by Dwight in his foundational epic of conquest, or, to choose an example closer to Jefferson, by Joel Barlow in *The Vision of Columbus* (1787) and *The Columbiad* (1807). Columbus, at a crucial juncture in Barlow's mythic history, despairs at the ills his 'discovery' of the new world has provoked. But the evils of European invasion are transferred through 'the black legend' to the Iberian nations in South America. The role of the Anglophone colonists in the North, on the other hand, is to bring progressive civilisation (eventually for all mankind) in place of the savagery of the aboriginal settlements.

But that is letting the Seal Committee off the hook. Franklin's and Jefferson's linkage of religion (through the image of Moses in the wilderness) with nationalism (the establishment of Israel/the United States) is part of the wider cultural nexus of romantic nationalism. The fundamental use of religion is commonplace in the making of the romantic nation. The invention of the United States in this respect is no different from that of Greece or Ireland, for instance, in the same epoch (or the use of Islamic fundamentalism in national liberation movements in the twentieth century). Religion is a unifying factor for the new nation, and justifies too the separation of the chosen people (a separate 'race') from those 'lesser breeds without the law' (to adapt Kipling's phrase). The corollary in both cases was the 'cleansing' (to use a contemporary word) of the homeland. In the territories (of uncertain frontier) now called 'Greece' the extermination of the Muslim population was effectively carried through by the Christians, although elsewhere in the eastern Mediterranean the 'rights' of self-determination remain subject of contestation. In Ireland religious/racial mutual murder of Protestants by Catholics, or Catholics by Protestants, has likewise fuelled the drive to national separation. The ethnic cleansing of the Indian tribes who contested the Mosaic 'wilderness' (the western frontier of the United States) is merely part of the same genocidal pattern.

Seen in this wider context of religious nationalism, there is, accordingly, nothing surprising in the junction of the signifiers of militant Christendom with the religious fundamentalism of the republic in du Simitière's contribution to the Seal. The obverse of the Seal was to be formed from the heraldic devices of six European nations united as the 'Arms' of the United States (*e pluribus unum*) and surrounded by the 'scutcheons' of each of the 13 separate States, united by a Platonic golden chain. The invocation of Christendom through its feudal past – 'the return to Camelot' as it has been called – is a typical device confirming the history of the nation-state in Europe at this time, and the American committee envisaged their new nation through an iconography which would be familiar to Lady Morgan, Sir Walter Scott or Robert Southey. Even though du Simitière's device was (like the rest of the proposals) left 'to lie on the table' of rejection, the armigerous conception was sustained. The obverse of the present Seal is a clear example of European heraldry, adopted by the newest European nation.

The implications of du Simitière's proposal are substantial. The immediate purpose of the Seal was to signify the existence of a legalised government within the international sphere of treaty and conflict. In the world of great 'powers', what might be the signification of using du Simitière's obverse and Franklin's reverse to ratify a treaty, for instance, with the Ottoman empire (the nascent American fleet was shortly to be active in the Mediterranean)? The chivalric signs of armigerous and united European nations are linked to the Mosaic conquest of 'the holy land' under the all-seeing eye of God. This fundamentally divides (not unites) the world into two orders: that of Christendom on armed pilgrimage to liberate territories for God ('the empire for liberty' in a famous Jeffersonian phrase), and, on the other hand, the Satanic powers of anti-Christ which represent the evil empire of tyranny. The future foreign policy of the new nation is already implicit in 'the arms of the United States of America'.

What du Simitière's proposal reveals also is the spread of revolutionary nationalism in Europe. He thinks, it seems self-evidently, in terms of national identities. But the very names of the separate nations to which he gives armigerous identity would be highly provocative in Europe of the *ancien régime*. Scotland is split from

Britain; Ireland ('a nation once again') as an independent State might (as Franklin envisaged) follow the lead of the American colonists; what exactly is meant by invoking the national entities 'Holland' and 'Germany', and where might their national boundaries lie? What might be the reaction in the epoch 1776–1826 to the ratification of a treaty with the Court of St James sealed with the arms of Ireland; or a treaty with the Court at Madrid which excluded Spain from the nations which claim to be American? At Potsdam or Vienna, what might be understood by the idea of 'Germany'? Not even the victorious armies of President Woodrow Wilson after the European war of 1914–18 could satisfactorily resolve these issues of national identity among divided peoples or impose the custom of peace. It was good sense of Congress, therefore, to suppress du Simitière's national signs from the iconography of the Seal as now known. Why import European problems across the Atlantic? But erasure from the official record does not necessarily remove, but only conceal, the fundamental *Weltanschauung*. Nationality is a crucial category though which the order of things is organised among the peoples of European origin.

The motto which du Simitière gave to his nationalist device was the now universally known (then obscure) *e pluribus unum*. As used by the Seal Committee of 1776 it refers to the unification of separate European peoples within a new European power, the United States *in* America. But the coalition of emigrant peoples into another European entity was itself nothing new. After the breakup of the racial hotchpotch of the Roman empire, the history of Europe had been one of continual, and often massive, migrations of peoples both across the continent and across the oceans. The establishment of states within those complex currents of migration not infrequently required extraordinary acts of ethnic, linguistic or cultural elision – *e pluribus* if not always *unum*. These acts of elision were to make the ethnic cleansing (*Reinheit*) of romantic nationalism subsequently so difficult and bloody to effect. Since the United States originates from a 'British' (itself a contested word) template, one might use that collection of islands off the western coast of Europe as an example of a widespread historical process. The progressively 'united' Kingdom of Great Britain and Ireland (1707–1922) was a compound of four different 'national' entities (du Simitière forgot the Welsh), themselves established by successive waves of colonisation from east to west. The national language was a fusion of Anglo-Saxon and Norman French, originally incomprehensible, and often resisted, by peoples speaking variants of Gaelic derived from earlier Celtic tribal settlements. During this period the 'united' kingdom fought four civil wars: 1715, 1745, 1798, 1916–21. Key unifiers in Britain were the English language, the Protestant religion, the demonisation of an evil, competitive empire (the French), and the material opportunities provided by expansion at the frontier (the empire).[21] In the process some form of ethnic cleansing was effected by the spasmodically vicious maltreatment of Celtic/Catholic malcontents (the 'clearance' of the Highlands of Scotland after the civil war of 1745, and the 'voluntary' emigration of the Irish, for example). Britain and the United States were, thus, going through an analogous historical process (as the Hamiltonians understood). But in carrying through processes of national unification from heterogeneous elements, each nation claims to be different from any other. That is essential. Unless some principles of differentiation are found, or made, the desired coalition cannot be made. Unity will disintegrate into its constituent parts. Du Simitière's design, if adopted, by recalling what was a widespread historical process would have been a continual reminder of the national constituent parts of the new state and its involvement with European history. But what unity required in the United States was an emphatic rupture, and a self-generated sign of national being.

If these are the implications of the proposals of the Seal Committee of 1776 (and they are, of course, merely some of the ways in which the icons might be read) then it is not surprising that the proposals were left to lie on the table of rejection. They are too complex. The allegorical designs would be difficult to compress within the form of a seal (although the Revolutionary Medals with which Jefferson was concerned in Paris indicate that it was possible to compress *multa in parvo*). But the allegories themselves bring too much history with them. The more complex they are, the more open to diversity of interpretation. The audience for the proposals was the same audience for whom the *Federalist* papers were written, and if those papers are a guide to the way Congress viewed history, it was with a disenchanted eye. History taught by examples, as Bolingbroke argued, but those examples from the past were of repeated failure. The 'new world' (well-instructed by the failures of the 'old') was to break free from the corruption of the past – so the romantic rhetoric of revolution was to claim.

We know from the history of the Seal that a divide developed between the original committee who thought in terms of historical allegories, and those who preferred an 'heraldic' construction of word and image. An heraldic Seal, drawing upon a long-conventionalised iconography, would be less open to interpretation. In pursuit of a unifying simplicity, therefore, all the historical material of the proposals of 1776 was eventually expunged from what became (from a committee of 1782) the present seal (Plate 3). There is none of the Mosaic allegory (on which Franklin and Jefferson agreed); no Gothic history of the development of Whig liberty (Jefferson's suggestion); no European escutcheons reminding the new nation of its composite national origins; nor Liberty herself, nor Justice (and, of course, no crucial, individual moral choice). Instead, on the obverse, the bald-headed American eagle provides a national totem peculiar to the new continent. The battle-flag of the republic is incorporated into the shield over which the eagle is displayed. The eagle holds conventional emblems of peace and war ('Indian' arrows heraldically conceived and an olive branch), both symbols incorporating the number 13. Above, 13 stars burst in glory through circumambient clouds. The reiterated 13 alludes to the originary colonies, but their previous history has disappeared in an abstract, ahistorical emblem. Only one element from the original committee remains, the motto *e pluribus unum*, which the eagle holds firmly in its beak, but the plurality to which it alludes is not that of European peoples. From this device of 1782 the eagle (and the flag) have become the dominant national icons glossed in the obscurity of a dead language. The iconography (iconology) has become so familiar that it is no longer subject to interpretation (indeed, for most Americans, Latin is unintelligible). There is a point in the history of images when they lose problematical charges of meaning because historically trite. That ultimate triteness is manifest now in the dollar bill, for nothing could be less meaningful than the Seal inscribed there. All that is read of the bill is its numerical value (although it might be said that the reduction of the nation to a unit of commercial exchange – how many dollars are you worth? – is a bleak commentary upon the ideals of the Founding Fathers).

But what is dead iconography now was crucial then. The Seal of 1782 excludes one kind of (Mosaic and European) history, but it is not innocent of meaning. On the contrary, another kind of meaning is being inscribed, and the changes between 1776 and 1782 indicate how unfixed and open to interpretation was the process. The meanings of the new device, therefore, require exposition in the context provided by the rejected proposals. Even the one major element to carry through, the motto, although it uses the same words, has changed its signification. Congress contained good Latinists (and many were skilled lawyers). Changes of emphasis, recontextualisation of meaning, were unlikely, in that remarkable body of men, to slip by without notice. Since the motto is so familiar, and now so little subject to interpretation, how exactly might one read the one major common element between 1776 and 1782 which was used to explicate the national icon?

It is known that the committee of 1776 drew the phrase from *The Gentleman's Magazine* – which was far from a populist source.[22] In its origins, therefore, the motto belongs to the 'polite' world of civil discourse and civic humanism of the eighteenth-century British gentry. In this originary context the motto was an invitation to choose one (an essay from the miscellany) out of the diverse contents of the magazine. It therefore possessed exactly the opposite meaning to that presumably intended by its use on the Seal of the 'united' States. There, read in the context of 1782, the motto is strongly Federalist and appropriate for the widespread fascist iconography of the young republic. 'We' are 'one people', and there is one authority by which the people act. Plurality must yield to unity. That authority is represented now not by a bundle of rods (although they may be suggested by a bundle of 13 arrows), but by an eagle displayed – a conventional sign for imperial rule.

But intention does not control meaning, and the ambiguity of the motto is historically crucial. Read in its originary sense, separating an individual part from a plurality, the motto inscribes the right of 'one' to be separated from the 'many': the individual against the State and the States as against the authority of the Federation. Read in that way, the beak of the eagle, by separating the *e pluribus* from the *unum*, emphatically isolates the individual from the many. This dead Latin tag, therefore, incorporates the essential contradiction of the opening paragraphs of the Declaration of Independence between the 'power' of the nation to make 'one people' and the right of the individual entity to separate from that power.

But the unificatory gloss (the common way of reading the text) was the most apparent to the immediate devisers of the present Seal, Charles Thomson and William Barton, who (in 1782) referred the motto to Aristotle's *Politics* I.5: 'that some should rule and others be ruled is a thing, not only necessary, but expedient'. Since Aristotle was not a good democrat, it is not surprising that subsequent commentary has not explored the wider implications of what might well be read, in the context of the 1790s, as a Federalist party-political statement. It is more than Federalist, however. *Politics* I.5 is Aristotle's classic defence of slavery as a natural condition, and it is, thus, a passage readily amenable to racial or neo-Darwinian interpretation: it is necessary and expedient that there shall be masters as that there shall be slaves:

> But is there any one intended by nature to be a slave, and for whom such a condition is expedient and right, or rather is not all slavery a violation of nature? There is no difficulty in answering this question, on grounds both of reason and fact. For that some should rule and others be ruled is a thing not only necessary, but expedient; for from the hour of their birth, some are marked out for subjection, others for rule...the male is by nature superior, and the female inferior; and the one rules, and the other is ruled; this principle, of necessity, extends to all mankind...the lower sort are by nature slaves, and it is better for them as for all inferiors that they should be under the rule of a master....

In 1776 the motto *e pluribus unum* was coupled with Franklin's 'Rebellion to Tyrants is Obedience to God' – balancing unitary power against individual right. It is a gigantic step from there to a classic justification of slavery as 'natural'. But the options offered to interpretation in the ambiguities of language literally inscribe the perplexities inherent in the creation of the new nation. Out of the plurality of peoples in the north American continent contesting the being of the new nation both within and without, in what way is the 'one' constructed from 'the many'? Who is to rule, and who is to submit to that rule? Would that one could get out of that into something simpler such as, 'This was not the intention.' But it is not a matter of intention but interpretation and contestation. Disagreement about what was meant by the Union (and by the motto) tore the nation apart within a few decades and the Aristotelian interpretation of *e pluribus unum* may be found reiterated in 'Harper's Memoir on Slavery' at time of civil war: 'Man is born to subjection ...in all ages. It is the very bias of his nature, that the strong and the wise should control the weak and the ignorant...'[23]

Any humanist knows the slippery nature of text and interpretation. The elder Cato did not have to wait on Derrida. Perhaps the
meanings of three mere words have been turned in too many
directions. But the motto *e pluribus unum* is not the only text
inscribed on the medal of 1782. There is the reverse of the Seal.
It depicts an uncompleted pyramid to the completed by a triangular apex incorporating God's radiant eye. Two further Latin
mottoes gloss the icon: ANNUIT COEPTIS and NOVUS ORDO
SECLORUM. Conventionally, as President McKinley knew, the pyramid is a signifier of durability. The American republic will endure
forever. Its historical purposes will be overseen and completed by
God. The pyramid is also, in this context, a Masonic sign. This was
clear, at least as late as the Seal committee of 1884, although strenu-
ously denied by the current official history, and the Latin mottoes
would be as appropriate to the foundation of a new Lodge as a new
nation.[24] On the reasonable assumption that this was an open and
widely understood iconography (Franklin, La Fayette and Washington would all have known it), the pyramid and the Providential eye
in the triune apex allude to God as the First Architect; the universe
as the work of that architect; and the architecture of the Egyptian
world as directly derived from God either from the geometry of the
works of Nature or from Hermes Trismegistus (who in some recen-
sions taught his wisdom to Moses). The origin of the United States,
thus, is mystically linked with the origins of European civilisation as
expressive of God's intentions in Nature.

The Virgilian mottoes linked to the pyramid tell how God gave his
approval (nodded: *annuit*) to what had been begun; and how a new
millennium has commenced: *novus ordo seclorum* (lines read by
Christian exegesis as foretelling the birth of the New Man, Christ).
The introduction of Virgil contextualises the American eagle on the
obverse of the Seal. The American totem, associated now with the
language of Augustan and imperial panegyric, is a sign of *imperium*
and *auctoritas*. The conventional historical signifier is the legionary
eagle of the Roman State; the imperative, stated by Virgil: *tu regere
imperio populos Romane memento,/Hae tibi erunt artes: pacisque imponere
morem/Parcere subiectis, debellare superbos . . .*[25] – a triumphant march
from Plymouth Rock to the Philippines as President McKinley
would express it.

That is a straightforward gloss of icon and text in terms of a simple
intentionalism (although the official history of the Seal backs off
today from the more numinous aspects). In the context of the

debates of the original Seal committee, however, the iconography rewrites history as Franklin and Jefferson conceived it. Moses defying Pharaoh across the Red Sea has been replaced by a major symbol of the Pharaonic empire: the pyramid. Instead of 'Rebellion to Tyrants' signifying 'Obedience to God', the reverse of the Seal idealises as an American icon a monument to imperial vanity notoriously said to have been created by slave labour – perhaps even the slavery of God's own chosen people in the house of bondage. It was from that bondage Moses set his people free – the Biblical declaration of independence. In picturing Moses entering the unpeopled wilderness the original Seal committee was trying to suppress the idea of conquest. The wilderness was a region in which the people of God would, as it were, withdraw from the tyranny of Pharaoh to work out their own destiny; or, in Adams's conception, the wilderness was where Man finds God, and where he will eventually write the architectural signifiers of civilisation. But in 1782, on the contrary, it is the idea of imperial conquest which is emphasised. The two Latin mottoes, since they are drawn from Virgil, adapt the words of the major poet of imperial power and fascist *auctoritas* and apply them now as expressing the divine destiny of the new (Pharaonic) nation. The pun on *novus ordo*/New World is obvious. Our people have inaugurated a new millennium – the thousand-year empire as an alternative romantic nationalism expressed it in Europe:

> Ultima Cumaei venit carminis aetas:
> Magnus ab integro saeclorum nascitur ordo
> Iam redit et Virgo, redeunt Saturnia regna;
> Iam nova progenies coelo demittur alto ....

The last age of the world foretold by prophetic voice is come: the great order of time begins again; now Justice has returned to earth and the Golden Age; a new race of Man has come down from the heavens (Virgil, *Eclogue* IV, 4–8).

Thus, all that was left from 4 July 1776 was the Divine Eye (and the motto *e pluribus unum* on the obverse). In 1776 God's eye was on Moses; in 1782 (and on the present dollar bill) it is upon the empire. In 1776 Franklin and Jefferson wished to balance the unitary motto against 'Rebellion to Tyranny', divided, although undecided, between the right of resistance of each individual and the urgent need for mutuality in defence. In 1782 the motto *e pluribus unum* has become one Latin quotation among three, the others linking the United States with Roman imperialism and hence with the classic claim of European civilisation to universal government and authority within a unitary imperium.

If that iconography expresses the mind of Congress in 1782, it is not surprising that the Roman *fasces* should be one of the most commonplace signifiers of the new republic from Houdon's statue of Washington to the Capitol of Wisconsin. It would be historically naive to read the *Romanitas* of the new republic either in terms of the origin or teleology of that sign. No such easy alternatives are offered here. But there are implications in the drive towards national unity. The frontier is not so clear-cut as one might wish between 'the home of the free' and the imperatives of unitary power. Franklin expressed the national need in time of war with the words 'Join or die'.[26] The ambiguities of language make those words both an invitation, to those who come in, and a threat to those outside the romantic nation whether the 'savage men and beasts' of the barbarian wilderness, or those traitorous 'Tories' who preferred, at the loss of life, liberty or property, to remain citizens of another nation. To be 'unAmerican' was to be an 'alien' in 'the land of the free'.

3

Kennst du das Land?
Notes on the State of Virginia

> Every continent has its own spirit of place. Every people is polarized in some particular locality, which is home, the homeland. Different places of the earth have different vital effluence, different vibration, different chemical exhalation, different polarity with different stars: call it what you like. But the spirit of place is a great reality.
>
> D. H. Lawrence, *Studies in Classic American Literature*

Late in 1805 a detachment of the United States Army led by Captain Meriwether Lewis and Lieutenant William Clark, having crossed the North American continent, reached the Pacific Ocean. The auspicious moment was marked by an inscription. A tree was carved with the words 'William Clark December 3rd 1805. By land from States in 1804–1805.'[1] This apparently simple act has complex signification. Until inscribed the tree had no meaning for European culture. It was 'innocent of knowledge'. But inscription translates a sign without signification into an icon. It becomes, therefore, subject to commentary of which, in western hermeneutic tradition, there is no end. It is as if the use of language is like Eve's eating of the apple, and the American landscape which (in Chateaubriand's phrase) 'can alone give an idea of Creation as it came from the hand of God'[2] becomes paradise lost by precipitation into written history. Moreover, Clark's words are so complex in their implications that without a Rosetta stone to aid translation they might remain unintelligible outside the western hermeneutic tradition to which they belong.

The implicit process to which Clark's icon relates is that of foundational epic. The 'American' army, through their act of travelling 'by land' from the 'States' westward, had symbolically appropriated that land for the nation by what Ramsay claimed to be 'the right of prior discovery'.[3] It is an act reiterated on innumerable occasions in American history: by raising a flag, declaring a right to possession, naming a place or surveying and mapping. 'Westward the course of empire takes its way.' So that the epic act may be known, it must acquire name and fame. In European tradition the need to bestow fame by heroic commemorative utterance is as old as literature, and fundamentally associated with foundational acts. William Clark follows *pius* Aeneas, Romulus, or that Brutus from which the Britons claimed descent. So 'America' from Amerigo Vespucci (by way of the Latin form *Americus*), and the naming of the capital of the Americans from the leader of their armies, Washington. His body, it had been desired, should mingle with his native land in a mausoleum at the centre of the Capitol at the centre of the nation, while his sculptured image stands, as in life, on the floor of the great Rotunda, and his spirit is deified in the enskied apotheosis of the dome above. It is an act of national euhemerism. Mount Rushmore, in appropriating an Indian sacred place for the icons of a sequence of American presidents carved into the very land itself, was ultimately to link even the remotest west to the national capital and Capitol.

Like *pius* Aeneas, Captain William Clark, the American hero, has his attributes, signed in his name. By race he stems from the blood of the Anglo-Normans for he carries the Christian name of the Conqueror, and his family name indicates that by occupation his forefathers came from the clerisy, for they were clerks, and therefore, men of letters. The warrior and the writer are combined in this American hero. With him he brings the science and religion of his people. The system (part Arabic, part Roman) by which day, month and year are marked is determined from an originary point at which Clark, as a member of the Christian world order, would understand that the Saviour of mankind was born. Although Clark's inscription of the tree is about as simple an act of writing as could be found, it is a national proclamation so loaded with cultural implication that an immense body of predetermined assumptions and knowledge is required to comprehend it. It would, for instance, have no meaning for those illiterate people whom the Anglo-Americans called 'Indians' (after another land and continent). For them the tree would possess another (and to us unknown) signification. Their own heroic tradition, religion, sense of time and property, even their very names which determined cultural identity were all (irreconcilably) different from Clark's or ours.

If the 'homeland' (to use Lawrence's word from the epigraph to this chapter) is intrinsic in forming 'every people', that homeland, in western tradition, is a written place. It has its 'literature' of which Clark's inscription is part, and that literature gives the land its iconography. In this respect the 'new' world is no different from the 'old'. At the moment in which the land (unknown because unwritten) enters language, that naming involves the land with the entire history of the language. The land becomes at once as old, therefore, as the language. 'New' (as in 'new world') is merely an ideological assertion. This is not to claim that 'there is nothing outside the language' (*il n'y a pas de hors texte*). On the contrary, every *thing* (to use the Lucretian word) is outside language, and the experience of the thing shapes language as much as language shapes the thing. The experience of land as thing is (literally) vital. Their experience threatened Lewis and Clark with death, and it was because they were experienced in the land that they stayed alive by one of the great romantic triumphs of the will in young America. 'Different places of the earth have different vital effluence', as Lawrence phrased it late in the romantic tradition (and even different deadly effluence, as the American pioneers discovered). There is something, thus, beyond language which Lawrence called 'reality' and it shapes every 'people'. It is more than would be implied by a socio-scientific word like 'environment'. Different places have each their different 'spirit' – or what pantheistic religion in classical antiquity would have called the *genius loci*. The reality of the spirit is that it is a kind of categorical determinant universally true for all people, yet endlessly different in itself for each (national) people.

This is difficult terrain. There is an indeterminate frontier between writing the land as if there were a true 'American' language which could express an essential reality, (which is the position of a romantic nationalist like Whitman)[4] or, alternatively, treating experiential reality as if it were merely textual, as if there were some sort of determinant 'discourse' of which experience is a part. Thus Clark's inscription might be read merely as part of the 'discourse' of 'capitalist imperialism', and those real things, starvation and death in the land, disregarded. But there is a real difference between the experience of the red earth of Tara, the violation of which is a form of rape for Scarlett O'Hara, and the abstraction of a map; or between the dirt farm of Steinbeck's Grampa Joad – 'This here's my country' – and the profit-and-loss figures of an economist's America. Of course, in these examples, the experience of the O'Haras and Joads is textually mediated and culturally complex, for both are late fictional constructions from Jeffersonian ideology. Tara (like Monticello) belongs to the high culture of the slave villa; the Joads' dirt farm represents the Jeffersonian independent people: 'People is goin' on – changin' a little, maybe, but goin' right on', as Ma states, expressing the ineluctable Jeffersonian process. But the status of Tara and the Joads' farm as ideological fictions does not obviate the direct, experiential relationship of land to text. The feel, the smell, the taste of the land is real. It is a reality which shapes the people as much as the people shape the land. That is a fundamental argument of romantic nationalism, hence the idealisation of the *Volk* since they are closest to the land. It, the thing itself, makes them.

The point of entry here has been a moment in which that thing – the land – becomes textualised: Clark's tree as icon when first inscribed. It is what Wordsworth might have called 'a spot of time'. The third of December 1805, like the afternoon of 4 July 1776, when the Seal committee met, is a moment in which one looks for a sign to signify what it is that has been done. What was done on 3 December 1805, arguably, was more American than the sober-suited meeting of men of property in Congress iconised by Trumbull. Before such men of property could exist, property in the land itself must be won. But what has been done in this spot of time by the Lewis and Clark expedition is not something which can be 'sealed' effectively by closure. It is, rather, the inception of a process not yet defined. William Clark had reached the Pacific; he had yet to return by land to 'the States' (where he was, by some, presumed dead). The journals of the expedition (in various hands, from various viewpoints) were yet to be published, edited, and made subject to hermeneutic interpretation. Jefferson's elaborate brief to the expedition as to what they were to survey (what they were to see and how they were to see it) initiated a process which was to reach a culmination in the great railroad surveys of the later nineteenth century. But the history of 'the West' (or 'the wild west') and 'the frontier' radically diverges from the scientific parameters of Jeffersonian enquiry. The very terms 'West' and 'frontier' would not (could not) carry Frederic Jackson Turner's signification for him.

For Jefferson, 'Louisiana', into which he sent his military expedition, was initially an area without even a map, an imaginary space where the mammoth or the megalonyx roamed, a blank piece of paper over which ink and ruler might spread, inscribing the geometry of new clones of the United States: Polypotamia, Pelisipia, Saratoga, Metropotamia, Assenisipia, Sylvania – to name some names forgotten to history. All that was offered subsequently to Congress in the Special Message of 19 February 1806 was a map of the course of the Missouri and a 'statistical view' of 'the Indian nations' – an 'interesting communication' as he lamely called the report of the expedition in the Sixth Annual Message. It was a lame message to Congress because the enormity of the thing out there was resistant to his textualisation. For Jefferson the laws of God and Nature had offered him an America of the imagination geometrically symmetrical and therefore geographically unified. As the land was east of the Mississippi, so would it be to the west. What the all but lost vanguard of the American army had found in an epic journey almost *übermenschlich* in its heroism, was another 'new' world of oceanic 'prairie' (English had no word for it), of 'desert' and the gigantic barrier of what are called 'the Rocky Mountains'. The explorers had run for their lives before a hostile party of 'Sioux', and even fled from the grizzly bear. Had it not been for the help of friendly Indians, they would not have been able to recross the mountains. When Clark inscribed his tree on reaching the Pacific, the scratched lettering is both a sign of an indomitable will to survive, and also, in its laconic transience, a sign of the insignificance of one man in relation to the enormity of the otherness of things.

There is, thus, a recalcitrance in things to the processes by which they are culturised. The easy reading of romantic nationalism is one in which 'Nature' (itself a cultural concept) is benign; Man enjoys 'communion' with Nature as a form of the divine; and the homeland, endowed with its unique manifestation of Nature, provides what Wordsworth called a 'deep, abiding place' in which identity has been and is determined by processes which are intrinsically good. The mountains of the English Lakes, the forests of Germania, Bohemia's woods and fields, or the American prairies each produce, in Whitman's phrase 'the representative . . . man', and for Whitman the representative American man was an ideal embodiment of 'the race of races'[5] – a view appropriated for itself each in its own way by numerous other national cultures. But this is to step back from the experience of land as thing into a form of 'transcendentalism', and, thus, from the initiatory moment of writing the icon – Clark's epic inscription of his tree. For Clark the making of the land as icon is part of a continuing struggle, or, to adopt a Germanic word, *ein Kampf*. Indeed, it is difficult to think of anything greater than Clark's struggle to reach the moment of inscription, and even the very act of inscription is marked by force and resistance as the knife, necessary to the explorer, incises the bark of the tree.

To illustrate that *Kampf*, textual examples of more complexity than Clark's inscription are needed. Two passages may serve from texts close in time to Jefferson's own *Notes* on the land of Virginia: William Bartram's *Travels Through North & South Carolina, Georgia, East & West Florida* (1791) and Charles Brockden Brown's *Wieland* (1798). In their time Bartram's and Brown's texts belong to the most contentious period of the forming of the nascent nation, when neither a national teleology, discourse or theory had acquired form. Unlike the writings of the Lewis and Clark expedition, neither of these texts are Jeffersonian in ideological intent. They are 'free' texts, and, unlike Clark's laconic inscription, they are also highly articulate, for Bartram and Brown are masters of the language of the Anglo-American people. Their language is operating between the extreme poles of what is not culture – the land as thing discovered by Bartram – and what has been culturised (by Brown) through the operations of the highly symbolic mode of self-evident fiction. Bartram's American land is, as far as language permits, the unmediated experience of an explorer. Brown's novel reveals the way land has changed into 'landscape'. The reader's attention in the fiction is directed to the way in which culture has been written into the landscape historically, aesthetically and in terms of race, class and gender. The two texts, therefore, may be seen as 'ranging shots' falling each side of Jefferson's *Notes on the State of Virginia* (1781/7) which are a mediation somewhere between land as discovered (as in Bartram) and land as fictionalised landscape (as in Brown).

'How shall I express myself so as to convey an adequate idea ... to the reader, and at the same time avoid raising suspicions of my veracity?' Bartram asks, in his account of his battle with the alligators/crocodiles (II, V). Let us pick up the story on the second day of his running battle as he fights his way through the infested swamp:

> The noise of the crocodiles kept me awake the greater part of the night; but when I awoke in the morning, contrary to my expectations, there was perfect peace; very few of them to be seen, and those were asleep on the shore. Yet I was not able to suppress my fears and apprehensions of being attacked by them in future; and indeed yesterday's combat with them, notwithstanding I came off in a manner victorious, or at least made a safe retreat, had left sufficient impression on my mind to damp my courage; and it seemed too much for one of my strength, being alone in a very small boat, to encounter such collected danger. To pursue my

voyage up the river, and be obliged every evening to pass such dangerous defiles, appeared to me as perilous as running the gauntlet betwixt two rows of Indians armed with knives and firebrands. I however resolved to continue my voyage one day longer, if I possibly could with safety, and then return down the river, should I find like difficulties to oppose. Accordingly I got every thing on board, charged my gun, and set sail, cautiously, along shore. As I passed by Battle lagoon, I began to tremble and keep a good look-out; when suddenly a huge alligator rushed out of the reeds, and with a tremendous roar came up, and darted as swift as an arrow under my boat, emerging upright on my lee quarter, with open jaws, and belching water and smoke that fell upon me like rain in a hurricane. I laid soundly about his head with my club, and beat him off; and after plunging and darting about my boat, he went off in a straight line through the water, seemingly with the rapidity of lightning, and entered the cape of the lagoon. I now employed my time to the very best advantage in paddling close along shore, but could not forbear looking now and then behind me, and presently perceived one of them coming up again. The water of the river hereabouts was shoal and very clear; the monster came up with the usual roar and menaces, and passed close by the side of my boat, when I could distinctly see a young brood of alligators, to the number of one hundred or more, following after her in a long train. They kept close together in a column, without straggling off to the one side or the other; the young appeared to be an equal size, about fifteen inches in length, almost black, with pale yellow transverse waved clouds or blotches, much like rattlesnakes in colour. I now lost sight of my enemy again.

This is only one of the many ways in which Bartram seeks to find words for the land. He is elsewhere in the *Travels* the scientist who catalogues; the picturesque tourist; the Ossianic recorder of the deaths of past people; the Rousseauesque celebrant of the Noble Savage and the Golden Age restored, and so on. The *Travels*, for the student of 'discourse', are a kind of American compendium of ways of writing the land. Here the language in which the fight is described has the immediacy of the mode of *Robinson Crusoe* or Franklin's *Autobiography*. It is, perhaps, even simpler than these in its attempt to convey unmediated experience, for the larger religious parameters of Puritanical pilgrimage are not present. There is only the fight. The *Kampf* so obviously fills the verbal frame that it may seem redundant to emphasise its significance. But it is not Divine Providence which works its darker purposes through Bartram's pilgrimage (or destiny). What saves him is his ability in battle. That ability to survive at this time, in this place, is the originary experience of the land. Although the language is not ostensibly seeking to culturise that experience, Bartram's survival depends upon the European technology he has brought with him: his boat, his gun. He is, in this respect, an archetype. This is how the European came. Read, thus, archetypically, even this simple passage acquires a kind of iconographic signification. If Bartram is the type of European man, his deadly opponents were one of the earliest icons of the continent he is exploring. Not only is America the home of the alligator, but America is signified by the beast.[6] It is the very antithesis of the Golden Age idea. In Hobbesian terms, this is the state of Nature which is the war of each upon each, or, to look forward into the construction of the romantic nation, Bartram's fight is an experiential example of the Darwinian and Spencerian idea of the survival of the fittest. As in Nature, so with the nation or the race; those who fight best are destined to survive and conquer.

One may wish, with Bartram, that these things were not so, but speculations on Utopian policy are not much use in an alligator swamp. In a state of war, those who cannot protect their own territory die. Clear evidence of that is written even into the land of the 'new' world. Bartram has already told how the nation of the Creeks migrated across the continent, subjugating, killing, even exterminating weaker peoples. Thirty mass graves in three acres are now the only signs that remain of the defeated Yamasees. But the Creeks only practise what 'all other nations of mankind' do also (Bartram claims), and older even than the mass graves of the Yamasees are the great tumuli of some other dead people without record, whom Bartram can only call 'the ancients'. Later historical examples of the policy of the Creeks would not be difficult to find.[7]

But why is Bartram (a solitary white, European man with a boat and gun) in the alligator swamp? What has impelled him with a force so strong that he will put his life at risk rather than turn back? The passage does not even pose the question. Bartram merely writes, 'I resolved.' It would be an evasion of the mystery to supply secondary causes here. Elsewhere in the text both mercantile and scientific imperatives are obvious. Bartram sees the land as future colonial territory; and, as a scientist, he is meticulous to inform future inhabitants of the land of what is there. These are strong motives. But there is something else operative in the alligator swamp. The statement 'I resolved' is essentialist and existentialist. It is expressive of a (manly) determination to challenge the alligator on and for its own territory. It is the will of the beast against my will, and my will shall triumph. This is the simple imperative of the Homeric hero: a man has to do what a man has to do.

Perhaps that imperative is a thing that is 'natural' and thus prior to 'culture', for the alligator has a similar will also; or it is as old as culture, for the Creeks have the same will as Bartram. But whether this be fact or fiction, the telling, by entering the web of words, becomes culturised. The fight is involved with an originary act of 'naming of places' (to use the Wordsworthian phrase) for this is now to be known to history as the fight of what Bartram has called 'Battle lagoon'. The place is categorised as separate, therefore, from the ineffable wild. It has its name, its date in the calendar, even its cartographic coordinates. So Lewis and Clark wrote American nationhood into the Rocky Mountains with the rivers called Gallatin, Jefferson, Madison. Thus, too, the foundations of nations are commemorated by the names of victorious battles. Jefferson would have called one of the spaces he drew on the map of the north-west territories, Saratoga.

Even in battle, Bartram is scientist as well as originary warrior. He notes of the 'young brood of alligators' (recalling emotion in tranquillity):

> They kept close together in a column, without straggling off to the one side or the other; the young appeared to be an equal size, about fifteen inches in length, almost black, with pale yellow transverse waved clouds or blotches, much like rattlesnakes in colour.

The most obvious elements in this categorisation are mensuration ('about fifteen inches'), generification ('much like the rattlesnake') and colour ('almost black, with pale yellow transverse waved clouds'). But the science depends also upon anthropomorphism and metaphor. The word 'column' suggests that the alligators operate in their own military formations, for in the struggle for survival, battle formation is instinctive and essential. This is not an anarchic Hobbesian state of war of each against each, but a primitive society. The family is a unit of survival, and one 'race' – the alligators –

competes against another – Man. That is the order of things. Paradoxically, even in the killing-field, there is, from the human viewpoint, an aesthetic in things. Indeed, that may be one element which
distinguishes human civilisation from that of beasts. Bartram's
phrase 'pale yellow transverse waved clouds' suggests a correspondence between the skin of the alligators and the circumambient
sky above. In another context, if Bartram were not fighting for his
life, the skin of the beast would be beautiful. (So Coleridge's ancient
mariner on the beasts of the sea.)

A wider context is offered by the anthropomorphic simile with
which the battle begins:

> To pursue my voyage up the river, and be obliged every evening
> to pass such dangerous defiles, appeared to me as perilous as
> running the gauntlet betwixt two rows of Indians armed with
> knives and firebrands.

As alligators, so Indians. Both are natural enemies. But the Indians,
in one respect, are worse than the animals. Whereas it is natural for
alligators to eat men, the Indian gauntlet is cultural. It is a gratuitous
act of cruelty practised by them on their enemies. Their knives
suggest the teeth of alligators, but their firebrands are the attributes
of the furies of hell. There is a familiar paradox behind the simile.
Men and women are worst than beasts in their cruelty to their own
kind. But the paradox is now linked specifically, and experientially,
to the war for this land, here between alligators and Bartram, more
generally between Europeans and Indians. What Man in Battle
lagoon knows is a state of war, and for those defeated in the war
of survival there is gratuitous cruelty in store. That is, here, the
Lawrentian 'spirit of place'.[8]

The Indian simile is the more disturbing because this is not the
way the *Travels* usually represent Indians or the relations between
races. Bartram, like George Catlin, is a sympathetic observer of
aboriginal culture at first hand. When he returns to civilisation, the
Indians he meets, acculturised by their proximity to a (rare) good
white man appear like the noble savages of Amadas's and Barlowe's
first voyage of discovery (1584): 'most gentle, loving, and faithfull,
voide of all guile and treason, and such as live after the maner of the
golden age'. Bartram's account of these 'happy people' rises to
rapture: 'O divine simplicity and truth, friendship without fallacy
or guile, hospitality disinterested, native, undefiled, unmodifyed by

artificial refinements'. Then, from the idealising distance of a high prospect, he celebrates 'the enchanting Vale of Keowe, perhaps as celebrated for fertility, fruitfulness and beautiful prospects, as the Fields of Pharsalia or the Vale of Tempe'. We are not offered the usual Virgilian irony – too happy people, if they only knew their own happiness. But the reader familiar with European culture will recognise another kind of irony in the reference to 'the Fields of Pharsalia'.[9] It is the nature of the Golden Age and of Paradise to be lost.

But if there is irony in Bartram, it is marginal. America is both the alligator swamp *and* the land of the Golden Age. The *Travels* sometimes tell it one way, sometimes the other. By comparison land as landscape in Brown's *Wieland* has become subject to a deeply complex symbolism. The writer's manipulation of language is so self-critically self-knowing that knowledge itself becomes doubtful since language itself may be an instrument of deception rather than the means to truth. In terms of mere plot, the novel begins by telling how the elder Wieland, a German mystic (now established in the archetypal role of an American farmer) erects a belvedere on his estate as a retreat, as a place of prospect over the landscape and as a sign of his worship of the God of Nature:

At the distance of three hundred yards from his house, on the top of a rock whose sides were steep, rugged, and encumbered with dwarf cedars and stony asperities, he built what to a common eye would have seemed a summer house. The eastern verge of this precipice was sixty feet above the river which flowed at its foot. The view before it consisted of a transparent current, fluctuating and rippling in a rocky channel, and bounded by a rising scene of corn-fields and orchards. The edifice was light and airy. It was no more than a circular area, twelve feet in diameter, whose flooring was the rock, cleared of moss and shrubs, and exactly levelled, edged by twelve Tuscan columns, and covered by an undulating dome. My father furnished the dimensions and the outlines, but followed the artist whom he employed to complete the structure on his own plan. It was without seat, table, or ornament of any kind.

This was the temple of his Deity.[10]

'My father's temple, as his son names the patriarchal structure, is derived from one of the great topographical commonplaces of European picturesque tradition: the circular temple of the Sybil on its precipitatory eminence at Tivoli (sometimes known as the temple of Vesta – the domestic hearth – or of Hercules). As an originary commonplace it is, thus, related to the widely diffused symbolism of fortress, temple or palace on a high place to which Shaftesbury alluded in his allegorisation of 'the judgement of Hercules' (discussed in Chapter 2 above). First, there is the wilderness where Nature is closest to God; then civilisation signifies its presence by writing architecture into Nature so that 'furst buyldynge and habytacion' makes 'A memory perpetuall!':[11] thus the Acropolis in Athens, the Capitol on the Capitoline Hill in Rome, Jefferson's domed villa on his little mountain at Monticello; or, in darker mode, Cole's cycle of paintings 'The Course of Empire' in which civilisation writes its architectural presence into the Arcadian and savage wilderness, but declines and falls back into the wilderness again.

Although Brown's symbol is not ostensibly nationalistic, the symbol of the temple on a hill was readily adaptable for national purposes. In Cooper's *The Pioneers* (1823) it is Judge Temple whose name is associated with the high place of prospect named 'Mount Vision' (the allegory is nothing if not obvious). The reader is given an overview of the Susquehanna Valley (so attractive to the Pantiosocratic society of the English lake poets) which in architectural palimpsest represents the progress of American civilisation from Indian burial-site through pioneer cabin to comfortable farm, village church and school, and thence to whatever unlimited vision of the future which a mind like Temple's might contemplate with philanthropic pleasure. The 'view' which Brown offers is open to the same ideological construction, for the eye is directed from a steep and rocky eminence (the virgin land direct from the hand of God) and led by the 'transparent current' of the undefiled river to 'a rising scene of corn-fields and orchards'. It is a method of landscape composition derived from Claude and thence by way of Turner's picturesque England (ideologically glossed by national Georgic) which was to be variously repeated and nationalised by the Hudson River School and its followers. As Cole wrote: 'Without any great stretch of the imagination we may anticipate the time when the ample waters shall reflect temple, and tower, and dome, in every variety of picturesque magnificence.'[12] In paintings of this 'School' the eye is frequently led from some high eminence, signifying 'Nature', to the signs of advancing prosperity and civilisation in America represented by farm, village or, even, distant glimpse of manufacturing industry: witness Cole's *View of Monte Video, the Seat of Daniel Wadsworth, Esq.* (1828), and the *Oxbow* (1836); Durand's *Progress* (1853), Cropsey's *Valley of Wyoming* (1865) or Woodward's *Connecticut Valley from Mount Tom* engraved for the widely diffused *Picturesque America* (1874).[13]

In the creation of this national landscape nothing is more characteristic of the new nation than the adoption of the architectural signs of the old world to signify the civilisation of the land. If Gothic abbey or ruined castle might have spoken of superstition and tyranny, classical antiquity had originary authority. Even now a tourist of Washington by night (when the prime national monuments are floodlit) is transported back to an imaginary Rome frozen in stone at some moment of triumphal *auctoritas*. Obelisk and Pantheon, Temple and Villa, like some classical House of Loretto, have taken transpontine wings and settled in their new and rightful place as signifiers of American *Libertas* and *Imperium*. In this tradition (and initiating the tradition in the same epoch as Jefferson chose the Maison Carrée as the model for the Capitol at Richmond) Brown's American farmer, the elder Wieland, erected a classical temple to signify the coming of civilisation to the land. That civilisation arises out of Nature. The airy and circular form of the temple mirrors the heavens themselves (made by the divine geometrician), and the prospect in all directions imitates the panoptic eye of God. The twelve Tuscan columns belong to one of the simplest of the architectural orders, appropriate therefore for this rustic temple, and in Christian culture the meaning of the number 12 is inescapable. These are Christ's disciples whose 'city' is built upon this hill. The temple of the Sybil is Christianised. The floor is levelled rock, without seat or ornament. The virtue of the simple American husbandman needs no ostentation. If this is also the temple of Vesta, the simplicity speaks also of hearth and home. If Hercules is present also (a remote allusion), Christian piety and homely *pietas* are heroic virtues.

This is merely to sketch the place of 'my father's' temple in the national landscape tradition. But the function of the temple within Brown's darkly obscure symbolic fiction cannot be contained within this simple, nationalistic matrix. The temple is not a spontaneous manifestation in the land. It is the product of material wealth, and the material base of that wealth is spelled out by Brown. It comes from the cheap acquisition of the land of the dispossessed Indians, and that land is worked by 'the service of African slaves.' The deeply religious elder Wieland intended to turn these evils into good by the conversion of the heathen to Christ. But he failed in this Quixotic aim, and the temple is his hermitage of retreat from that failure:

> His exhortations had sometimes a temporary power, but more frequently were repelled with insult and derision. In pursuit of this object he encountered the most imminent perils, and underwent incredible fatigues, hunger, sickness, and solitude. The license of savage passion, and the artifices of his depraved countrymen, all opposed themselves to his progress.[14]

What happens then, suddenly, unexpectedly, inexplicably, is the striking down of the founding father by some form of spontaneous combustion in the precincts of the temple itself. This is followed by hideous putrefaction, delirium and death. Such is the prelude to the entry into the world of classical Georgic of the 'daemon' Carwin, the ventriloquist whose deceptions with language induce madness, fanatic murder and suicide into the once-happy family circle. The complications of the plot need not concern us. Read allegorically, the tale tells how the enlightened axis God–Nature–Man, iconised as the universal order in the simple classical temple, self-destructs and opens the way to acts of violence which defy rational analysis. The savage, thus, is not an alien to be expelled from the land and then converted by a superior culture. Darkness, disorder and mental disease are within, and released by the malignity of Carwin's deception. His ventriloquism subverts the correlation between word and thing, or thing and interpretation. The 'American dream' in *Wieland* has become an American nightmare.

Brown's marginal position in the canon of American literature (or its peculiar subsection: 'early American literature') has obscured his relation to one of the major preoccupations of European romanticism: the failure of the Utopian expectations of the self-characterised 'Enlightenment'. But if one were to read *Wieland* as a text of the same mythic significance as, for instance, Mary Shelley's *Frankenstein*, the 'Gothic horror' has the same ideological signification. Mary Shelley's novel has become the classic example of the hubris of the enlightened mind. The revolutionary new order in

Europe produced a 'new' man, but that man was a monster. The monster represents a displacement of something evil which the Enlightenment had disowned in itself, and at its own peril. It is difficult to be more specific than that 'something evil', because the mode of Gothic fiction is symbolic, and symbolism is a way of going round and about the hegemonic discourse of triumphalist rationalism. The 'sleep of reason' (to use Goya's phrase) breeds something monstrous which is ineluctably part of the mind of Man, but that monster is so deeply buried in the human psyche that it can be seen only indirectly in the projections of the symbolic imagination. Brown, like Shelley, through his fiction is embodying the dark 'other' of revolutionary Utopianism. The difference between them is that whereas Shelley is invoking the Faustian myth of the European scientific superman, Brown's novel challenges one of the mythic archetypes of the American revolution. The American farmer – 'my father' – is the revered national type who self-destructs.

These interpretations both of Bartram and Brown are, of course, allegorical. The simple, basic elements in the exemplary texts have been read as fundamentally national. They are about the relation of *Volk* to *Land*. In the American formulation, the pioneer (Bartram) yields to the farmer (Wieland). Land becomes landscape as it acquires the signifiers of civilisation (of which God's temple is the highest expression) and through territorial possession *Land* becomes native land/State/nation. In that progression the two texts have been seen as representative of two poles of discourse: one being that of attempted scientific empiricism (this is what the pioneer has found), the other that of imaginative and symbolic fiction. What is common in both the exemplary texts is that the land (whether empirically or imaginatively narrated) is a site of violence turned outward (in the act of conquest) or turned inward (into the heart of darkness in civilisation itself). These exemplary texts are not necessarily typically 'American', of course, and the hermeneutic complexity with which they have been invested, like all textual commentary, is problematical. (But what would be a typical text, and would any text necessarily yield a simpler and truer 'America'?) But Bartram and Brown have been selected as exemplars because the polarities of their discourse are Jefferson's polarities in the *Notes on the State of Virginia*. They are, as it were, 'ranging shots' to locate his interpretation of the Land. Their themes are his themes; their problems, his problems, as will be seen.

Ostensibly the *Notes on the State of Virginia* are outside the problems of hermeneutics raised by Bartram and Brown. In so far as the discourse belongs to the kind of scientific, empirical language represented by Sprat's *History of the Royal Society* (1667) – 'as many things in as many words' – then the writing is a transparent window on reality. The facts about the land are verifiably correct. 'Truth' may be distinguished from 'Error'. The model is Robert Boyle's *General Heads for the Natural History of a Country, Great or Small; Drawn out for the Use of Travellers and Navigators* (1692) supplemented by the methodology of question-and-answer developed by the Royal Society's international correspondence.

More specifically, in national context, the *Notes* are part of a substantive literature of 'histories' of States in North America, given impetus by the revolutionary war. Jefferson's text belongs with such works as Jeremy Belknap's *The History of New-Hampshire* (1784), Thomas Hutchins's *An Historical Narrative and Topographical Description of Louisiana, and West-Florida* (1784) and *A Topographical Description of Virginia, Pennsylvania, Maryland, and North Carolina* (1778), Gilbert Imlay's *A Topographical Description of the Western Territory of North America* (1792), Samuel Williams's *The Natural and Civil History of Vermont* (1794), David Ramsay's *A Sketch of the Soil, Climate, Weather, and Diseases of South-Carolina* (1796), and le Comte de Volney's *A View of the Soil and Climate of the United States of America* (translated 1804). As David Ramsay wrote, such histories would make Americans 'a homogeneous people' and 'unite as one people'.[15] This was to be the ostensible purpose of Jedidiah Morse's continually evolving *American Geography* (a work which drew extensively on Jefferson's *Notes* both for matter of fact and for ideology).

In that kind of context Jefferson's *Notes* might appear generically secure and assured in discourse. They have a particularly central position, furthermore, among the histories of the States of the 1790s. Virginia, for Jefferson, is *the* American heartland both politically (for this is the State which gave the nation four of its first five presidents), ideologically, for this is a model of the agrarian republic he desired, and geographically, for 'God and Nature' had declared for the Potomac as the seat of government and a major artery of trade. It was a reasonable (though false) assumption that the future of the United States would be the progressive cloning of Virginia.

Yet it is well known, as a matter of biographical fact, that Jefferson was unwilling to publish the *Notes* or to see the work widely circulated. Nor was it a work he ever saw as properly completed. Like

Wordsworth's *The Prelude* (another work which the writer was reluctant to publish), it both reveals too much and yet is too indefinite. Textual scholarship is complicated by ongoing revision; finally revision itself was abandoned of subjects treated 'imperfectly' or 'scarcely touched on' at all. Jefferson wrote to John Melish, on 10 December 1814, 'I consider... the idea of preparing a new copy of [the *Notes*] as no more to be entertained. The work itself indeed is nothing more than the measure of a shadow, never stationary, but lengthening as the sun advances, and to be taken anew from hour to hour. It must remain, therefore, for some other hand to sketch its appearance at another epoch, to furnish another element for calculating the course and motion of this member of the federal system.' Rather than describing a 'state' in the political or physical sense of the word, the *Notes* are seen here as descriptive of a process, and the metaphor strangely mixes optimism and pessimism, for if the advance of the sun suggests progressive enlightenment, Virginia itself is nothing but a shadow (which language vainly seeks to fix). Whatever it is that exists between the light and the shadow has disappeared. Jefferson's metaphor ultimately derived from Plato, and in Plato the shadows perceived by the eye are the signs of an unknowable reality beyond human apprehension.

The eye, therefore, in Platonic myth, is an uncertain organ, whereas the convention of scientific empiricism is that the rational eye is objective, certain and panoptic. Rational science, thus, might report on the state of Virginia from some sort of detached height in which the geography, history, and peoples of the land are, as it were, spread out cartographically below. As a work of enlightened science the *Notes* accordingly begin with the famous map of Virginia drawn by Jefferson's own father. This is how the land might appear represented from some satellite in outer space. There follow a series of mathematical coordinates and a history of the derivation of the State lines represented by those coordinates. But even in setting out the scientific facts, something else intrudes. The mathematical coordinates are derived from the imperial meridian at Greenwich; the State lines were themselves the product of historical dispute. This is not, therefore, ideology-free science. It cannot escape its own cultural history and cultural conventions. It is the science of western imperialism. But that is an obvious commonplace, requiring no elaboration.

What is more perplexing is the unreliability of perception itself as Jefferson moves from the allusive space of panoptic vision into the actual land itself and centres himself subjectively at the lofty vantage-point of Monticello: his temple of vision,

> Having had occasion to mention the particular situation of Monticello for other purposes, I will just take notice that its elevation affords an opportunity of seeing a phaenomenon which is rare at land, though frequent at sea. The seamen call it *looming*. Philosophy is as yet in the rear of the seamen, for so far from having accounted for it, she has not given it a name. Its principal effect is to make distant objects appear larger, in opposition to the general law of vision, by which they are diminished... at Monticello it is familiar. There is a solitary mountain about 40 miles off, in the South, whose natural shape, as presented to view there, is a regular cone; but, by the effect of looming, it sometimes subsides almost totally into the horizon; sometimes it rises more acute and more elevated; sometimes it is hemispherical; and sometimes its sides are perpendicular, its top flat, and as broad as its base. In short it assumes at times the most whimsical shapes, and all these perhaps successively in the same morning. The Blue ridge of mountains comes into view in the North-east, at about 100 miles distance, and, approaching in a direct line, passes by within 20 miles, and goes off to the South-west. This phaenomenon begins to show itself on these mountains, at about 50 miles distance, and continues beyond that as far as they are seen... (Query VII)

There is an epistemological problem here, and it is one which is raised also in Brown's *Wieland*. Seen from Monticello (as if from Wieland's 'my father's' temple) the landscape should be expressive of order. But, just as in Brown's novel, events seen by the eye deceive, so here too the land does not obey what Jefferson calls 'the general law of vision'. A mountain changes from cone to square; it rises and sinks above the horizon, undergoing what Jefferson later calls continual and rapid 'metamorphosis' even in the same morning. The process is not only beyond the cognizance of 'Philosophy', it has not even been named by philosophical language. But if the simplest empirical observation by the sense is unreliable, and beyond naming by science, on what then can one base knowledge of the land? If this were Wordsworth writing, the interchange between inner perception and outward form would be a familiar subject, for this is one of the great romantic topoi. Wordsworth makes explicit in 'poetry' what is implicit in Jefferson's attempted

1. Monticello: the garden front.

2. The University of Virginia: the Jeffersonian campus.

3. The Seal of the United States of America (as displayed on the one-dollar bill).

4. Monticello in the Virginian landscape.

5. Chiswick Villa, London.

6 Monticello: the entrance front.

7. Monticello: the hall.

8. Houghton Hall, England: the Stone hall.

9. Plan of the ground floor of Monticello.

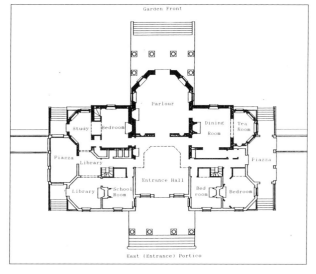

10. Monticello: Jefferson's bedroom.

11. Monticello: the tearoom.

12. The temple of Ancient Virtue, Stowe, England.

13. Monticello: the dome-room.

14. The Jefferson Memorial, Washington, DC.

15. Monticello: a staircase.

'science'. For the landscape seen from Jefferson's 'elevation' becomes, in the medium of descriptive language, instinct with the writer's own personality. The solitary eye is looking at 'a solitary mountain', informing it, thus, with human personality, and then with animation for the hill subsides and rises, and then the whole Blue ridge moves, first coming into view, then approaching, passing, and going off to the South-west. At the same time the landscape composes itself into a merely fanciful, cubist geometry in which it is constructed from regular cones, hemispheres and squares, dissolving thence into 'whimsical' shapes – as though to write of a hill as a regular cone were not itself a whimsy. Like Carwin's ventriloquism, the way the words work shifts the signification of things; but the things themselves are constantly shifting. All is in constant 'metamorphosis' before the solitary, subjective eye.[16]

The same subjective metamorphosis informs the famous passage in which Jefferson describes 'the passage of the Patowmac', and the land changes into American landscape in the description:

The passage of the Patowmac through the Blue ridge is perhaps one of the most stupendous scenes in nature. You stand on a very high point of land. On your right comes up the Shenandoah, having ranged along the foot of the mountain an hundred miles to seek a vent. On your left approaches the Patowmac, in quest of a passage also. In the moment of their junction they rush together against the mountain, rend it asunder, and pass off to the sea. The first glance of this scene hurries our senses into the opinion, that this earth has been created in time, that the mountains were formed first, that the rivers began to flow afterwards, that in this place they have been dammed up by the Blue ridge of mountains, and have formed an ocean which filled the whole valley; that continuing to rise they have at length broken over at this spot, and have torn the mountain down from its summit to its base. The piles of rock on each hand, but particularly on the Shenandoah, the evident marks of their disrupture and avulsion from their beds by the most powerful agents of nature, corroborate the impression. But the distant finishing which nature has given to the picture is of a very different character. It is a true contrast to the foreground. It is as placid and delightful, as that is wild and tremendous. For the mountain being cloven asunder, she presents to your eye, through the cleft, a small catch of smooth blue horizon, at an infinite distance in the plain country, inviting you, as it were, from the riot and tumult roaring around, to pass through the breach and participate of the calm below. Here the eye ultimately composes itself; and that way too the road happens actually to lead. . . . (Query IV)

Every 'thing' here is in process of change in the vision of the super-elevated eye (which encompasses the land as landscape) and in the imagination (which constructs the visible scene as an icon of historical change). The solitary reader, who shares Jefferson's vision, is incorporated into a lived experience of the signification of the river. As a 'picturesque' scene, the way the land is constructed here has obvious general affinities with the landscape as seen from 'my father's' temple in *Wieland* and, in general, with the process by which Claudian tradition was nationalised in romantic art. 'We' (Jefferson and the reader as kindred spirit) are set on a high and wild elevation; height gives elevation to the mind as well as 'the comprehensive and equal eye' – Washington's phrase (in his Inaugural); the eye is led by the flow of the river from the wild frontier into the plain country beyond which is the civilised State of Virginia. Since this is ostensibly a landscape picture, 'we' (who share Jefferson's sensibility) read it as if it were a prospect poem. The scene is an historical allegory, expressive of a 'quest' (a pregnant word for American culture).[17] The natural forces of the river are a kind of allegory for that quest of the human mind, dammed up for aeons by resistant forces, which now has forced a 'passage' and then found a 'road' through obstruction into a future, fertile, civilised countryside: 'placid and delightful'. This is nature's purpose, and nature herself is a landscape artist schooled in the sublime and the beautiful. It is she herself who has given 'the distant finishing . . . to the picture'.

Despite this evocation of natural process, the 'passage' belongs to the symbolic order of fiction and not to the discourse of science. Sprat or Boyle would not write like that (although Bartram might, or Timothy Dwight in the Miltonic romanticism of the *Travels in New England and New York*, 1821–22). But if the landscape is read here as a literary construct and as an historical allegory, what kind of history is this? The significant moment recorded by the vision is when the mountains were broken through. That breakthrough is the *locus* of cataclysmic violence. At this moment the rational mind is switched off: 'the first glance of this scene hurries our senses' into a conviction that this is a place of catastrophe. There is no rational consideration of other alternatives – for instance, the gradual erosion of the land over aeons of time. Jefferson, instantly, stops thinking and yields to the most sensational scenario. First there is resistance, then the dam is broken. The waters rush together, they rend the mountain asunder, tearing it from its summit to the base, leaving in the passage the clearest marks both of disrupture and animated 'avulsion'. This is what he calls elsewhere in the *Notes* a 'convulsion', and it is at this place of 'riot and tumult' in the roaring breach that we stand. The 'road happens actually to lead' on from this place, but the intense terror of the sublime scene for Jefferson is being located at the very place of convulsion itself.[18] (It is the same Niagara-like force of the sublime which elsewhere in the *Notes*, he tells, prostrated him on his knees, his head pierced by pain, on the dizzy heights of the natural bridge.) If this is an historical allegory, and it is difficult not to read the landscape that way, then the writer's senses have been hurried away by the *Sturm und Drang* of revolutionary conflict, by the great struggle (*Kampf*) which has torn things apart from summit to base. As Ramsay wrote of the revolutionary war, 'it was like the letting out of waters'.[19] This is the Jacobinism of the picturesque. But the excitement at violence itself suggests too something of the psychosis of *Wieland*.

This is not a common apprehension of landscape. A taste for the revolutionary sublime, developed beyond the aesthetic of Longinus and Burke, is an elite, cultural acquisition; a taste for the prostrating excitement of fear is a special kind of (Gothic) sensibility. The *Notes* were not a text intended to be clapper-clawed by the palms of the vulgar but written for the kindred spirit. Presumably the 'aristocracy of virtue' of whom Jefferson wrote to John Adams were also an aristocracy of sensibility. Beyond that small circle of leaders are other, ignorant people who would not even stir six miles to share the view of 'the passage of the Patowmac'.

> This scene is worth a voyage across the Atlantic. Yet here, as in the neighbourhood of the natural bridge, are people who have passed their lives within half a dozen miles, and have never been to survey these monuments of a war between rivers and mountains, which must have shaken the earth itself to its center.

It was to keep one sublime part of the landscape from contamination by these kind of people that Jefferson bought the natural bridge and added it, therefore, as a great *fabrique* of Nature to his private estate.

Jefferson's landscape, in fact, both at 'the passage of the Patowmac' and for 'the Spectator' at the natural bridge, is empty of 'people'. This is not because Jefferson is uninterested in the actual details of the land itself – as if he were always in the sublime mode of visionary generalisation. On the contrary, the *Notes* are rich with an intimate sense of the relationship of Man to land which makes the very sensation of home so potent a force in national feeling. He is as aware of the winds as they blow, for when the wind sets in from the north-east in Virginia the houses built from bricks of the native clay sweat inwardly; as a woodsman he perceives the spread of settlement by the coming of the honey-bees; he feels the weather change through the ecological processes that come from the felling of the woods; and, of course, the man who wrote of 'looming' at Monticello had his eye constantly on the play of light over things.

But 'the people' (as in 'we, the people') are never present in the landscape as percipient and participant as they are in a great spiritual socialist like Wordsworth. Wordsworth walked the landscape with his sister, and they talked with common men and women. Jefferson's social position in the landscape of Virginia placed him on high, either on the hill-top of Monticello, or astride his horse, overseeing his overseers. He is an aristocrat and his view of 'the people' is sublimely patrician. Witness his letter to the Marquis de La Fayette 11 April 1787 instructing the Marquis on how to acquire democratic knowledge:

> to do it most effectually you must be absolutely incognito, you must ferret the people out of their hovels as I have done, look into their kettles, eat their bread, loll on their beds under pretence of resting yourself, but in fact to find if they are soft. You will feel a sublime pleasure in the course of this investigation, and a sublimer one hereafter when you shall be able to apply your kno[w]-ledge to the softening of their beds, or the throwing a morsel of meat into the kettle of vegetables.

But the *Notes* do not people the landscape of Virginia even with that kind of 'sublime' knowledge, and the kind of people glad of a morsel of meat would not be the readers of the *Notes*. (Nor did Jefferson in Paris have any real dealings with *sans culottes*.) Instead, when Man and land are brought into relation in Virginia it is by means of symbolic abstraction. At a climactic moment in the text Jefferson bursts into a visionary effusion:

Those who labour in the earth are the chosen people of God, if ever he had a chosen people, whose breasts he has made his peculiar deposit for substantial and genuine virtue. It is the focus in which he keeps alive that sacred fire, which otherwise might escape from the face of the earth. It is a mark set on those, who not looking up to heaven, to their own soil and industry, as does the husbandman, for their subsistance, depend for it on the casualities and caprice of customers. Dependance begets subservience and venality, suffocates the germ of virtue, and prepares fit tools for the designs of ambition. This, the natural progress and consequence of the arts, has sometimes perhaps been retarded by accidental circumstances: but, generally speaking, the proportion which the aggregate of the other classes of citizens bears in any state to that of its husbandmen, is the proportion of its unsound to its healthy parts, and is a good-enough barometer whereby to measure its degree of corruption. (Query XIX)

Although this is ostensibly an excursus into 'enlightened' sociology, the real drive of the historical vision arises from the mystic evocation of 'labour', not Jefferson's own, but that of the people who work 'their own soil' and 'in the earth'. The roots of the symbolism are in the Augustan ideology of Livy and Virgil (Cincinnati-ism), and this has blended with a quasi-Mosaic nationalism (of the kind revealed by the Jefferson/Franklin imagery of the Seal of the United States). The 'chosen people of God' alludes to those Americans/Israelites who, having crossed the Atlantic/Red Sea into the wilderness, are to become the inhabitants of the promised land. They are also the people called in one, pervasive, romantic theory, the *Volk* – whose purity comes from their proximity to their own land and 'the face of the earth'.[20] The land is the place of hearth and home, and it is a 'sacred' fire which burns there in the breast of the 'husbandman'. It is the masculine virtue and generative seed of the husbandman which in the 'mass' represents what is 'healthy' in contradistinction to what is 'unsound' in the nation. As Jefferson wrote for the *Encyclopédie*, 'The cultivators of the earth are the most virtuous citizens and possess most of the *amor patriae*.' The 'unsound', on the other hand – merchants, the *canaille* of great cities – are 'marked' like Cain. Although 'the American farmer' is a commonplace of nationalist ideology, the mystic quality with which the soil is invested here by Jefferson, and the abruptness of the division between what is healthy and what is corrupt, are extreme.

Jefferson's concern here is with something later romantic theory called *Reinheit*: the purity of the native stock. The *Notes* are deeply concerned with the threat both from without and from within to that *Reinheit*. In this romantic context the word 'corruption' (used in the account of 'the chosen people') shifts radically from its old Whig association (where it means 'bribery' and 'subservience'). Now 'corruption' comes also from the alien peoples of Europe, and thus the Europeans (except those 'useful artificers' who may join those who 'plough and hoe') should be excluded by 'native Americans' – by which phrase Jefferson means those white people born in America. His fear is that emigrants

> will bring with them the principles of the governments they leave [absolute monarchies], imbibed in their early youth; or, if able to throw them off, it will be in exchange for an unbounded licentiousness, passing, as is usual, from one extreme to another. It would be a miracle were they to stop precisely at the point of temperate liberty. These principles, with their language, they will transmit to their children. In proportion to their numbers, they will share with us the legislation. They will infuse into it their spirit, warp and bias its direction, and render it a heterogeneous, incoherent, distracted mass. I may appeal to experience, during the present contest, for a verification of these conjectures. (Query VIII)

Equally strong is the language with which Jefferson ended his account of 'the chosen people of God'. A Europeanised urban 'mob', carrying with them 'their manners and principles', threaten to bring a 'canker' of 'degeneracy' to eat up 'the manners and spirit' of the uncorrupted husbandmen. The republic is in danger.

Given these principles, it becomes clearer why du Simitière's original design for the American Seal had been rejected. His emphasis had been upon the European diversity of the peoples of the United States. But the historical, Jeffersonian, movement of the *Notes* is towards a self-generative, self-sustaining unitary *Volk*, purified by their proximity to the land, protected by the Atlantic from foreign corruption (a watery, rather than iron, curtain). What outsiders threaten is to bring both alien manners and their alien 'language'. They are not of the land, and they do not speak English (which, in material fact, Jefferson was shortly to impose as the official language for the alien peoples incorporated in 'Louisiana').

The result is that what was unitary in the *Volk* would become heterogeneous, incoherent, distracted, cancerous and, as the aliens breed, degenerate.

It is urgent that this should be prevented at the very inception:

> In every government on earth is some trace of human weakness, some germ of corruption and degeneracy, which cunning will discover, and wickedness insensibly open, cultivate and improve ... Our rulers will become corrupt, our people careless.... From the conclusion of this war we shall be going down hill.... the people ... will be forgotten. They will forget themselves, but in the sole faculty of making money.... The shackles, therefore, which shall not be knocked off at the conclusion of this war, will remain on us long, will be made heavier and heavier, till our rights shall revive or expire in a convulsion. (Queries XIV & XVII)

These sentiments are conflated from different parts of the *Notes*. Elsewhere, in more optimistic vein, Jefferson claims that 'the people' in America, afer all, will prove too numerous to be corrupted by bribery. But these 'chosen people of God' who, somehow, will not go the way of the others down the path of corruption into 'shackles', are merely a symbolic abstraction. The mythic *Volk* are never embodied, as de Crèvecoeur sought to embody a 'new race of men' in himself as the 'American farmer' (and failed in the turmoil of civil war post-1776); nor are the agrarian people the subject of the kind of elaborate economic and social analysis offered, for instance, by John Taylor in *The Arator* (1813). One must confront, therefore, the implications of Jefferson's language itself, for there is little else, and what the language is expressing is an intense fear of 'degeneration', or, to play with the word, of a de gener nation. There has been a unique moment of foundation 'while our rulers are honest, and ourselves united' – the moment of escape from the 'shackles' of the tyranny of the old world by the crossing of the symbolic Red Sea. At this spot of time the entire nation is one people, uncontaminated by a new breed of aliens from Europe ('a wolf' to be kept 'out of the fold' in another Jeffersonian image) and thus by miscegenation. But given the visionary force of Jefferson's rhetoric, there is no mistaking the alarm of his prediction that if the *gener* (the race) is corrupt, it will either 'expire' or need to 'revive' in a 'convulsion'. That word 'convulsion' belongs to the symbolic language of the historical landscape of the passage of the Potomac, where nature works by cataclysm. Either great force is dammed in by great power, or bursts through with its own avulsive power. The word 'convulsion', therefore, belongs to an interpretative matrix of revolutionary violence. Merely to distance this by some sort of phrase like 'agrarian republicanism', or relate it to physiocratical philosophy entirely misses the emotive urgency of the language.

This is, of course, a not unfamilar romantic revolutionary discourse in its language of freedom and shackles, rights and tyranny. One perceives Jefferson hovering at that extraordinary cusp in time when the intense heat of expectation raised by romantic revolution confronts the darkness of disappointment should those hopes fail. That is common ground for many idealists in this epoch. But there are 'darker' areas associated with the idea of de gener nation which must be addressed. When Jefferson writes of keeping 'the wolf' out of the fold, Jeffersonians will already have picked up a far more famous (or notorious) image of potential degeneration (and 'convulsion'): 'we have the wolf by the ears, and we can neither hold him, nor safely let him go. Justice is in one scale, and self-preservation in the other.' This is from much later in his career, when 'the chosen people of God' had already expanded westward into those lands which were intended to preserve their agrarian purity. Jefferson's letter to John Holmes, 22 April 1820, concerns the Missouri compromise which he perceived as a fatal first step towards the destruction of the unity of the States. The 'wolf' held by the ears was the negro; the matter at issue was slavery; and the question of negro slavery was fundamentally involved with *Reinheit*: the purity of the white race.[21]

If the United States was, in some measure, protected by the *cordon sanitaire* of the Atlantic Ocean from 'corruption' by European aliens from without, the racial issue *within* the North American continent was local and acute. There were 'three races' (to use de Tocqueville's phrase) which might equally claim proximity to the 'land' by which the nation lives and moves and has its being: the 'aboriginal' people (as Jefferson called them); the white colonists; and the black slaves who actually worked the very land of Monticello. Since this is an emotive issue one needs to approach it with as little prejudgement as possible. One of the intrinsic factors in forming the romantic nation is that there should exist an idea of difference precipitated round an ideal national type. Our people are different, and exceptional – how else can we separate ourselves from others as a nation? This is not a matter of science – did the negro possess an ape-like skull or not? – that, at present, is a view of race which stands on shaky ground. It is rather a question of the 'natural' perception, or cultural invention, of something which can be construed as 'different'. In that respect 'white, 'red' and 'black' (the 'three races') are, in the simplest sense, natural perceived differences in Jefferson's America. The very existence for the white of those who are red and black, self-evidently, provides an essential visual sign by which the whites might forget their own diverse origins and define their unificatory selfhood against those who are different. In the process they become *e pluribus unum*. In different contexts (in Europe, for instance), whites defined themselves against each other by different criteria – likewise the aboriginal tribes in the Americas and in Africa. (Thus Bartram found evidence in mass graves of genocidal tribal warfare among the 'red' inhabitants of North America who had other categories of 'racial' discrimination.) But at the initiatory moment of 'convulsion' in which Jefferson sets the *Notes*, at the time of 'the birth of a nation', unity is essential in order that a war may be fought and won, and an ideal of difference ('race') is essential if 'we' are to continue to cohere after the war. That is the Machiavellian fact, to which Darwinism was shortly to add the apparent authenticity of natural history. Or, to put the matter metaphorically, multiculturalism, in Bartram's alligator swamp, was not an option.

Jefferson's thinking about 'race', therefore, is linked with white survival. The three major historical options for national formation in the United States were genocidal clearance of the land (the Mosaic solution, as Jefferson had noted), separate development, or 'multicultural' intermixture. What is ideologically curious about Jefferson's thinking about these options is that the 'reds' and the 'blacks' do not occupy the same place in his thinking. Given his fear of miscegenation and degeneration, but his commitment to human rights, separate development would have been the obvious policy for all races (an idealised Herderian solution, although open to obvious corruption). But, in the text of the *Notes*, a misty kind of nationalist fantasy involving the 'reds' as 'aboriginals' separates them radically from the 'blacks' imported from Africa. The aboriginal peoples are in substantial measure idealised. The Monticello slaves, notoriously, produce in Jefferson revulsion and fear.

Perhaps this difference is a matter of absence or proximity. The 'aboriginals' exist only in the memorial of textuality in the *Notes*. They have become a significant absence from the State of Virginia, known only to Jefferson as picturesque visitants and orators in unknown languages. In terms of the foundation of the romantic nation these are the *Urvolk* – those whose 'rights' are derived from 'immemorial occupancy' (as Ramsay wrote).[22] There is no need to associate Jefferson here with some of the more extravagant of Germanic theories. The idea of an originary people is directly derived from eighteenth-century British romantic nationalism in general, and from Jefferson's favourite poet Ossian in particular. National history is long history, relying, in Lincoln's words, on 'the mystic chords of memory'. The further back in time *Volk* and *Land* are associated, the more deeply rooted the national culture. The defeated Celts were, therefore, not written out of British romantic nationalism but, on the contrary, absorbed into the symbolic history of landscape painting and literature. The 'translation' of Ossian from Gaelic gave Britain a native Homer; the novels of Scott sentimentalised and sanitised the culture of the rebellious clans; the wearing of the plaid and the plaintive music of the pipes were the signs of a liberal multiculturalism. These things followed the extermination of the Highland army at Culloden and the obliteration of the real clan system by systematic clearances of the aboriginal tribal lands. First security, then sentimentality.

For Jefferson, the Virginian, that security already existed. The land had already been cleared and the aboriginals had melted away from the landscape (seemingly through some unexplained process apparently marked by the coming of the bees which are the sign of the approach of the agricultural settlements of the whites). The Indians in the *Notes* are now merely textual signs: a gazeteer of names; a vocabulary (lost) of lost languages; a culture devoid of architectural or literary monuments, recordable in its primitive (even Homeric) purity and savagery only by succeeding culture. Since the aboriginals are slow to breed (compared with the whites), natural process itself points to the inevitable conclusion. In the past, lamentably, war also had taken its toll. Hence the famous passage in which the Indian warrior and patriarch, Logan, laments the extermination of his *gens* by the whites:

There runs not a drop of my blood in the veins of any living creature. This called on me for revenge. I sought it: I have killed many: I have fully glutted my vengeance. For my country, I rejoice at the beams of peace. But do not harbour a thought that mine is the joy of fear. Logan never felt fear. He will not turn on his heel to save his life. Who is there to mourn for Logan? – Not one. (Query VI)

The Indian is wrong in believing himself unlamented. Every sentimental reader of Ossianic fiction would shed a tear. One admires the brave when the brave is no longer a threat. Genocide has seen off this clan; but the defeated *Urvolk* are safely lamented, memorialised and incorporated. Logan's evanescent oratory has been written down in the language of the white nation. Logan belongs with what Chateaubriand called *les restes des Natchez* and Cooper 'the last of the Mohicans', or, since Ossian was in Jefferson's mind, he is the 'last of Fingal's race'. Since no one shares Logan's blood, fortunate peace has now replaced war. *Ubi solitudinem faciunt, pacem appellant* (They make a wilderness and call it peace).

So much for the past. For the future, the continuation of the process will be without pain. Jefferson told Démeunier, 'Not a foot of land will ever be taken from the Indians without their own consent. The sacredness of their right is felt by all thinking persons in America as much as in Europe.'[23] Jefferson's Indian strategy, for those removed west of the Mississippi, was that loss of their tribal grounds would reduce warriors to small farmers. The *Urvolk* would then intermarry with the frontiersmen, and they would, thus, blend with the chosen people of God. The Indian problem would have reached its final solution.[24] Meanwhile, in Virginia the delightful tale of Pocahontas blended the blood of an Indian princess with Jefferson's own family, for tradition held that the Randolphs of Tuckahoe were connected with her bloodstock. As a Welshman, Jefferson was also connected with another tradition, that of 'Prince' Madoc and the lost tribe of Welsh Indians yet to be found in the west. These charming stories of ancient Princesses and Princes belong with the Irish novels of Lady Morgan or Southeyan epic. They unite a dominant caste with a lost aristocracy preserved yet among the *Volk*.

So different is this romantic view of Indian culture from that of the 'blacks' in the *Notes* that an explanation of Jefferson's relation to the 'three races' as merely 'racial' would be imprecise. The writing on slavery in the *Notes* is the most passionate and most uncertain anywhere in Jefferson's work. The hatred of the institution of slavery (now inscribed on 'tablets of stone' in the pantheon of the Jefferson Memorial in Washington, DC) is matched by an intense revulsion and alarm at the actual physical presence of the slaves themselves. They are the most powerful human presence in the text (far more than 'the chosen people of God'). It is the Monticello slaves who are the people actually transforming land into landscape, the wild (or wilderness) into civilisation. Jefferson, as American farmer, designed a plough; these people put their hands to it. But these slaves already are only partially 'black' because degeneration had been produced on two sides: from the orang-outans who had in Africa descended from the wild and raped the black women (so Jefferson believed), and in America from the white men who emulated the orang-outans (not least at Monticello, as Jefferson's slavebook shows). Biologically, therefore, miscegenation is producing a breed of mulatto semi-apes.[25]

Jefferson's desire (in theory) to find a solution to the black question was matched equally (in fact) by a continuing inability/refusal to act. This is a notorious matter of biographical controversy. But any analysis of how Jefferson addresses the problem through language in the *Notes* must work at an extraordinary textual interface where the ostensibly objective discourse of analytical science becomes involved with ideological and material self-interest (indeed the *Notes* here are a classic example of this dilemma). But, ultimately, language seems to be failing before something else which Kurtz in *Heart of Darkness* was to obfuscate in the cry 'Oh the horror!' There are elements in Jefferson's writing on his slaves which suggest some form of deep inner psychosis.

In the context of romantic nationalism, the 'blacks', in contradistinction to the aboriginal *Urvolk*, represent the racial 'Other' – those against whom 'we, the people' define ourselves. But it is something powerful and atavistic which is more than an issue of self-evident 'colour'. If the 'blacks' are functioning in Jefferson's imagination as a kind of self-defining 'Other', then we may be confronted with a typical instance of that 'Other' being used as a form of scapegoat projection in which everything we would wish to disown in ourselves is seen as mirrored in the alien. In that mirror, in which we would not choose to look, there exists a monstrous image of ourselves. This is not unfamiliar theory.[26] In general, we are looking at those processes in which enlightened rationality breaks down before an inherent darkness within the mind of Man: what Goya depicted in the icon of 'The Sleep of Reason' or Gothic fiction in the stories of the *Doppelgänger*. The great problem, and tragedy of romantic expectation (putting 'the enlightenment' into practice) was that Man, liberated by romantic revolution, did not behave like a Shelleyan Prometheus unbound, but with the ferocity of a beast.

Frankenstein made a new man, and he was a monster. This was the experience of which Jefferson had seen the inception in revolutionary Paris; and which was the ongoing problem across the Atlantic in the multiracial genocidal conflict of Haiti. It was the 'wild' which Federalist pessimism foresaw in 'the west' in the United States once men were outside the rule of law.

Thus, in the wider context of this symbolic history, the presence of the huge slave population (rapidly multiplying) in the State of Virginia was not an issue of United States politics alone. It is part of the fundamental problem of romantic liberationism, of which the Declaration of Independence, in its proclamation of universal 'rights', was an initiatory document. Rousseau had written that Man was born free and was everywhere in chains. What happens when you knock off the chains? Bring that matter home to one's own backyard in Mulberry Row, and there is an ineluctable link with the Terror in Paris which was far from the abstraction of romantic discourse. It is in this context one should read the words inscribed in stone in the Jefferson Memorial (now radically torn from context for later political purposes):

> I tremble for my country when I reflect that God is just: that his justice cannot sleep for ever: that considering numbers, nature and natural means only, a revolution of the wheel of fortune, an exchange of situation, is among possible events: that it may become probable by supernatural interference! The Almighty has no attribute which can side with us in such a contest.... (Query XVIII)

This is reinterpreting the signification of the Providential Eye of the Seal of the United States with a vengeance, and this kind of apocalyptic and prophetic writing belongs far more with a world seen, for instance, by Blake rather than eighteenth-century Whiggery. He 'hopes', Jefferson continues, that this contest between masters and slaves will not come to pass, and he 'hopes' that by abatement and mollification there is 'preparing, under the auspices of heaven [but not of Jefferson] . . . a total emancipation', but the conclusion of this enunciation (almost as famous as the Declaration of Independence) was written on the eve of the Terror in France:

> I hope . . . that this is disposed, in the order of events, to be with the consent of the masters rather than by their extirpation.

There is no reason to doubt the threat expressed by the word 'extirpation', and the threat to the very 'order' to which Jefferson belonged which a servile war would pose. He called such war, to Démeunier, 'exterminating thunder' – a phrase too apocalyptic for the *Encyclopédie* to adopt. If one is to understand Jefferson's text one needs to understand the experiential nature of the fear that you are to be killed because you are white, or because you own property.

> It will probably be asked, Why not retain and incorporate the blacks into the state. . . . Deep rooted prejudices entertained by the whites; ten thousand recollections, by the blacks, of the injuries they have sustained; new provocations; the real distinctions which nature has made; and many other circumstances, will divide us into parties, and produce convulsions which will probably never end but in the extermination of the one or the other race. (Query XIV)

Just as the landscape of Virginia was marked by cataclysmic 'avulsion', so too history is threatened by genocidal 'convulsion': the dammed-up servile flood will destroy the barrier imposed by the masters. If further European 'importation' from *without* the new nation was to be resisted, so too the final and utter separation of masters and slaves, *within* the nation is an essential corollary. Jefferson's traumatic vision of history may indicate why the emancipation of his own slaves was not an option he chose to pursue, for it would merely exacerbate the problem. The solution could only be that total separation which the Voortrekkers in another continent called *apartheid*, and which by American reformists was given a nationalist dimension in the invention of another national entity and invented identity: the new State named 'Liberia' by the Reverend R. R. Gurley in 1824. Romantic nationalism, therefore, hoped to see the diaspora of African peoples terminated in the same way as, a century later, the Jewish diaspora was ended.

But the problem is that the very existence of the alien within has already introduced corruption. Master and slave are symbiotically related. The 'Other' has become the 'Self'. The slaves' situation induces race and class hatred, criminality, and irrational sensuality. But their masters are likewise contaminated by the habits of despotism and sloth.

> The whole commerce between master and slave is a perpetual exercise of the most boisterous passions, the most unremitting

despotism on the one part, and degrading submissions on the other.... With the morals of the people, their industry also is destroyed.... And can the liberties of a nation be thought secure when we have removed their only firm basis, a conviction in the minds of the people that these liberties are the gift of God? (Query XVIII)

This is at that very foundational moment in which, Jefferson had argued, corruption must be excluded lest the wellsprings of the chosen people be contaminated. But if what he writes here of the 'commerce' (a word with sexual overtones) between master and slave is true, the writer himself cannot escape. 'The man must be a prodigy who can retain his manners and morals undepraved by such circumstances.'

It is unpleasant to spell out what Jefferson implies by 'depravity' here, but the *Notes* are graphically clear what he sees and fears in the slave. To enter the slave camp of the State of Virginia (Query XIV) is to descend from the world of rational order (as it were from 'my father's' temple in *Wieland* to the world after the extermination of the father). Without the restraint of reason here 'the imagination is wild and extravagant, and, in the course of its vagaries, leaves a tract of thought as incoherent and eccentric, as the course of a meteor through the sky' (so too it had been an 'incoherent' mass which Jefferson had feared from Europe). It is unsurprising that the slave, being an unreflective and incoherent animal, is sensual. The male is 'ardent after their female: but love seems with them to be more an eager desire, than a tender delicate mixture of sentiment and sensation.' Otherwise this animal is sunk in natural sloth, for 'an animal whose body is at rest, and who does not reflect, must be disposed to sleep'. This lustful animal is ugly also. Its odour is offensive. One would not risk miscegenation with such people: 'when freed, he is to be removed beyond the reach of mixture'. Black men must not breed with white women. If such separation does not take place, the alternative is genocidal war.

The most disturbing observation on the slaves, however, is, paradoxically the passage in which Jefferson seeks to retract what, ostensibly in the language of panoptic scientific objectivity, he has written about 'a whole race of men':

let me add, too, as a circumstance of great tenderness, where our conclusion would degrade a whole race of men from the rank in the scale of beings which their Creator may perhaps have given them.... I advance it therefore as a suspicion only that the blacks, whether originally a distinct race, or made distinct by time and circumstances, are inferior to the whites in the endowments both of body and mind...

But it follows, thus, that if the slaves are not distinct by race, nor inferior because created so, then that degradation which Jefferson observes is intrinsic in human nature itself. This is worse than the 'corruption' threatened in the body politic by the intrusion of the alien from without, for it is a corruption of the very body itself. Its relation to sexuality is obvious, both in the reference of the 'commerce' of the master with the slave, and in Jefferson's perception of negro sexuality in terms of the 'ardent' male. It is a matter of national *Reinheit*, therefore, but it is also a question of personal moral purity. Since master and slave are symbiotically related by their commerce, the frontier between self and other is violated, and those things which the self seeks to disown are reflected in the inescapable and monstrous mirror of the other. It is the kind of symbiosis depicted in *Prometheus Unbound* where Jupiter, the master, and Prometheus, the cursing and tortured slave, are alternative selves. But Shelley, even in the pure symbolism of poetry, no more has a solution to the problem than Jefferson. The ending of the master/slave relationship by 'Necessity, demand no direr name' is an explanation by Shelley where nothing is explained. Why 'Demogorgon' in *Prometheus Unbound* should be a power for good rather than evil is obscure.

The dire question for romantic optimists was, what if self and other were inextricably corrupted by their symbiotic relationship? It was an issue which Jefferson (like Shelley) preferred not to pursue. The darkest passages of all in the *Notes* are accordingly marginalised, and are frequently suppressed in popular editions. They are to be found in the Appendix of 1800. It is in the Appendix that 'the people' emerge from the generalisations of Jeffersonian archetypes ('chosen people', 'aboriginals', 'blacks') and for the only time in the *Notes* speak directly in their own voice and not by Jeffersonian ventriloquism. We know these people by name: Harry Innes, John Gibson, Ebenezer Zane, William Huston, Jacob Newland, John Anderson, James Chambers, David Reddick, Charles Polke.... Ostensibly they are reporting on a matter of fact: who killed the family of the Indian chief Logan? Jefferson, as impartial judge, merely collects evidence to correct and supplement his own text. The issue was highly contentious, for what the long Appendix documents as matter of fact is the deliberate extermination of racial blood-stock – what Jefferson called the 'extermination of peoples' and the twentieth century calls 'genocide'. What could not be achieved in fact was carried out symbolically. Hence the whites disembowelled and impaled (on a death-giving phallic stake) a pregnant Indian woman from Logan's family (as told by William Robinson). The Indians understood the ritual language of the whites, thus the cry of the chief of the Wabash: 'The whole crop shall not be destroyed; I will have seed out of it for a new crop' (as told by John Heckewelder). The symbolic genocide was mutual. Hence the Indians cut to pieces (and presumably castrated) and scattered (repeatedly) one of their victims, thus denying a dead enemy sepulchre in their land. If one asks, what caused these atrocities, Sappington's apologia for the whites reports that it was the putting on of white men's clothes by Logan's brother, and his calling a of white 'the son of a bitch' which provoked the whites to homicide. In Sappington's view, the whites were justified. Symbolically, it seems as if the perceived threat was that the alien had taken on the form of the self, and dishonoured the white man's race. At a deeper level, perhaps, the white perceived his own savagery concealed by the garb of civilisation, and determined to kill the savage as scapegoat. But, however interpreted, this is American history returned to the inter-racial conflict of Bartram's alligator swamp.

As Jefferson told the story in his main text, all his sympathy flows to Logan, who is now powerless – indeed, shortly after the events related, he suffered a mental breakdown and died, providing a classic instance of the destruction of selfhood which follows the loss of cultural identity. But by focusing in his text on Logan's Ossianic eloquence (Logan's own language was unintelligible), Jefferson avoided the depiction of the real, graphic violence and its signification for his own race. These named white men whose own voice intrudes upon the text in 1800 are not the *canaille* of Paris, nor the corrupted lackeys of capitalistic commerce (the 'merchant' class). On the contrary, these real-life frontiersmen are the *Sturmabteilung* of those chosen people of God who will settle in the promised land. What sort of Americans (the 'new race of men') are these who disembowel a pregnant woman, and shoot a man for putting on another's coat? Or what kind of 'empire for liberty' is it, when it is contested by mutual racial murder in 'a country whose frontier was drenched in blood'?[27]

That contest (*Kampf*) is for the very possession of the land. It corrupts the whites on the frontier just as much as the ownership of slaves corrupts the master of Monticello. Although the discourse of enlightened science, to which the *Notes* aspire, seeks to rise panoptically above such things, the thing outside has its own power beyond the control of writing. What has been stressed here is the 'darkness' of that power. At the heart of that darkness is, as it were, the alligator swamp: that Darwinian nature where you eat or you are eaten. One stands at the very point of 'convulsion' and 'avulsion'. That moment of historic change involves 'the three races' each intimately, experientially related to the land, and each in potentially lethal conflict. 'Extermination' (to return to Jefferson's word) is the issue. It is a national issue, because 'race' (perceived difference) is intrinsic in separating 'we, the people' (for whom this is the natural, or divinely given land) from those who are alien. But that distinction between self and other cannot be sustained. For all that is dark within the self and projected on to the alien outside is intrinsic in the very imagination which creates the alien. We make our own monsters out of ourselves. That is why the Terror in France, and Jefferson's own terror of his own slaves, are related 'romantic' experiences. The temple of reason, to use Brown's icon, by an act of spontaneous corruption, is destroyed. There remains some *thing*, malignantly destructive, unsettling all confidence in the relation of word and image. Like the landscape of Virginia itself, word and image 'loom'.

4

The Villa on a Hill

In a country changing from licentious barbarity into civilized order, building is an object of perhaps greater consequence than may at first be apparent. In a wild, or but half cultivated tract, with no better edifice than a mud cabin, what are the objects that can impress a love of order on the mind of man? He must be wild as the roaming herds; savage as his rocky mountains; confusion, disorder, riot, have nothing better than himself to damage or destroy; but when edifices of a different solidity and character arise; when great sums are expended, and numbers employed to rear expensive monuments of industry and order, it is impossible but that new ideas must arise, even in the uncultivated mind; it must feel something first to respect, and afterward to love...

Arthur Young, 1776[1]

The European visitor to the International Center for Jefferson Studies at Kenwood, Virginia, can still enjoy something of the imaginative and symbolic experience of the pilgrimage to Monticello taken by La Fayette on 4 November 1824. For the European it is a remote experience. The journey, even now, has been long and arduous across the Atlantic – even if not 'romantic' in the economy-class of a 747. The romantic dimension may be added, however, by walking the terrain of Monticello. On foot, leaving the garden of the Kenwood estate behind, one may still select a pathway which returns to the primeval forest. The land here, and for tens of thousands of acres in the Blue Ridge mountains to the west, remains as it was in the beginning, without culture, a space of infinite silence and of alien being, of animal and vegetable life unknown to the European, even now of some potential danger from poisonous ivy, insects and snakes. But the most dangerous enemy of all, aboriginal Man, is no longer here. To the east, at the plantation settlement of Carter's Grove, the signs of the massacre of 1622 have been revealed in the very grounds of a great country house. 1622 was the year when the aboriginal Indians came out of the woods to exterminate once and for all the settlers on the James River, and failed.

To walk in the woods now is to avoid Man, not to risk war. The present American settlers arrive at Monticello by car, or in a continual fleet of coaches, among which the homely yellow American schoolbus is prominent. 'The machine in the garden'[2] separates the folk from the aboriginal forest – there is even a bus to drive the people from their bus. The size of the car park carved out among the shading trees indicates the importance of the site. Monticello is big tourist business. It is also, as the presence of the schoolbuses signifies, part of the business of national education. At the house the admirably informed and objective guides tell the story of the founding father through the home he built for himself. The tour to Monticello is part of a national tourist circuit which, in the same State, includes Washington's Mount Vernon, the Capitol and the White House. Architecture is intended to instruct the mind through the eye.

But a European romantic, on foot, has passed by the well-bussed route. That choice of a different pathway carries iconographic signification. The 'wood' through which this discourse has led the reader is closer to Dante's *selva oscura* than that of primeval paradise. It is dark and perplexed. Or, if America is still a *paradeisos* for the Blakean innocence of youth spilling off the schoolbuses (or would that be too great a stretch of imagination?), the solitary European tracking through the woods is like Milton's Satan, refusing the proper gateway into paradise. Experience has replaced innocence, as it had for La Fayette in 1824 after half-a-century of post-revolutionary disenchantment.

But not to come to Monticello by the metalled road is a means, at least, to recover the essential surprise of an extraordinary work of art. Whatever one expected on the long, steep climb up the hill on foot, it was not this experience. Familiarity now with one of the most common American icons – on every nickel with the aureole – *e pluribus unum* – should not obscure the shock of coming out of the forest on the top of a high hill into the charm of a garden, and suddenly perceiving, surrounded by a lawn, flowers and flowering trees, a low and miniaturised recension of the Pantheon in Rome. But not quite the Pantheon, for the temple has changed into a kind of angular, brick bungalow, decorated with rococo Chinese lattice-work and gleaming in the greenery with the white paint of recent and loving restoration. Walk round the bungalow, and each apparently symmetrical, neoclassical facade is different. Even the famous dome comes and goes. In English country-house tradition, the inaccessible, steep hilltop would be the site of some extraordinary folly – some remote *fabrique* designed for retirement or to make some iconographical point in the design of a great estate. But Monticello is the great country-house itself, the signifier of culture and power (Plate 4).

The shock of this difference – the meaning of which is deferred – is a matter of relativity. To see the difference, one must first know the country-house ethos which is disrupted by Monticello. To have walked here from the International Center for Jefferson Studies at Kenwood is itself a first step in that knowledge (quite different from the trip in the schoolbus or the journey by automobile). For Kenwood is another country house, built by Franklin D. Roosevelt's aide, General Watson, and used by the President himself as a country retreat away from the *fumum, et opes strepitumque* (smoke and wealth and noise) of Washington.[3] The country house seemed a natural location for those great men – general or president – who exercise power. Now, transformed to an educational centre, Kenwood, in its naturalised park, has become the place where the ideology of country-house culture is transmitted between national generations. Here the study of Monticello is Centered. To the European visitor this is a familiar historical process. One thinks, for instance, of Lord Cobham's great powerhouse, Stowe, become a school. The great house is now divided into the 'house' system in which the schoolchildren of the rich still learn their social *mores*; the vast, iconographical gardens have now become part of the estates of the British 'National' Trust.

For La Fayette, in 1824, his own journey to Monticello had also begun at a symbolic country house, La Grange in France, and he was to leave Monticello for another house deliberately built to culturise power, President Madison's Montpelier. The meeting on the lawn of Monticello with Jefferson, and the subsequent movement from villa to university, made public, for all eyes to see, what both men were already practising within the walls of their country houses. Their life 'at home' preserved, for the instruction of the new generation, the ideology of what both believed was the true revolutionary nation. And, like Monticello, La Grange was a site of 'pilgrimage'. So Lady Morgan, Irish nationalist, liberal Whig, and romantic novelist, described her journey to La Grange as if it were through an enchanted forest, and she made her journey to the house, she wrote, 'with the same pleasure as the pilgrim [who] begins his first unwearied steps to the shrine of some sainted excellence'. Nor did La Fayette disappoint her. She found a hero dedicated to high thinking and simple living, rich in books and the experience of history. 'To have conversed with him, and listened to him, was opening a splendid page in the history of man.' She found in La Fayette a politician happiest now as a farmer, a new Montaigne (or, she might have written, Cato or Cicero), a 'philosophical agriculturalist'. Hence, he was the antitype to the self-centred political ambition of Napoleon. It was an image La Fayette was carefully to cultivate: for James Fenimore Cooper (and with a profound influence upon Cooper's *Notions of the Americans*); for Destutt de Tracy (whose post-revolutionary commentary on Montesquieu was intended to translate Whig theory to the new generation in Jefferson's America), and so too for Benjamin Constant, Mary Shelley, Stendhal and Heine.... La Fayette at La Grange was an icon, and the house was, so Remusat wrote, 'the empire of the patriarch of liberty'.[4]

There is nothing in the iconography of La Fayette at La Grange which would be out of place in the life of Jefferson, a 'philosophical agriculturalist' of the new world.[5] To journey from La Grange to Monticello was, thus, in many ways to come home again for La Fayette. The same would be true at Madison's Montpelier, or, had Washington still been alive, at Mount Vernon, even if there, in Jefferson's view, the first President had been contaminated by the 'forms' of Toryism. This idealisation of the life of virtue at home at one's country house is as much a 'Koine' of Jefferson's private circle as is the discourse of romantic nationalism in the public world in which La Fayette's visit is involved. It is derived from the villa culture of the Roman republic and empire; transmitted through the agricultural writings of Cato, Varro and Columella; idealised in the lives of Cicero (republican statesman and philosopher) and Pliny the younger (civil servant and aesthete); and poeticised by Horace, Martial, Statius and Sidonius. This is a well-established tradition.[6]

The power of the tradition lies in its historical diffusion and complexity, for it might equally be drawn upon to idealise the life of a great man like Lord Cobham at Stowe, or the petit-bourgeois Pope, piddling with little, in his suburban villa at Twickenham, or even to justify the Wordsworthian cult of the cottage. It would be unwise to simplify that complexity. But, in general, it is a tradition in which proximity to what is 'natural' in the life of the countryside, and in the practice of agriculture, is idealised in contradistinction to the corruption of 'Rome', the city, its politics and commerce. It is at home in his villa that the wise man (and it is a masculine tradition at its inception) can be 'free' (as Stoic and Epicurean discourse would phrase it) and 'independent' (as Whig ideology rewrote the tradition). This is a dignified leisure – *cum dignitate otium*[7] – and in that leisure the wise and happy man is able to cultivate the philosophical mind and his estate, enjoy his library and the artefacts of culture, and with suitable modesty entertain his friends, not for self-interest but for the greater interest of finding philosophical wisdom.

It is an ideal especially adopted into the Whig villa tradition via the classic status given to Palladio's *Four Books of Architecture* (1570). The ancient sages, Palladio wrote, used to retire to their villas, where

> The body will more easily preserve its strength and health, and...where the mind, fatigued by the agitations of the city, will be greatly restored and comforted, and be able to attend the studies of letters and contemplation.

Here, being attended by virtuous friends and relations, the ancients, by cultivating their house, their garden and their virtue, 'could easily attain to as much happiness as can be attained here below'.[8] That word 'happiness' has, of course, a special Jeffersonian resonance. Another favoured Jeffersonian exemplar, Lord Bolingbroke (whose writings crowd Jefferson's early commonplace book), expended a fortune in making Dawley Farm a symbolic *locus* for virtuous philosophy (in opposition to the tyrannical tendency of the commercial empire of Hanoverian London). He decorated the walls of his country house with replicas of those agricultural instruments whose virtue was in their symbolism. It was *otium* which was dignified, not *labor*. George Washington, at Mount Vernon, was to employ the same symbolism. But it is needless to multiply examples. The neoclassical, neoPalladian tradition is everywhere diffused through Whig culture, by works like Robert Castell's detailed reconstructions of *The Villas of the Ancients Illustrated* (1728), Conyers Middleton's *Life* of Cicero (1741), or works of graphic art, such as Richard Wilson's great villa landscape 'Cicero' showing the statesman discoursing on the laws with his friends in the landscape garden of his villa. Jefferson's own most characteristic statements about Monticello are the commonplaces of the tradition: his weariness with the world of affairs, his hostility to commerce and his love of agriculture, his desire to shut himself up with his books and to open his house to family and friends. This is the correct image of the wise man.

It is a tradition which culturises and, hence, naturalises power. The private world of the villa becomes public and national because it is only the 'independent' man of property who is properly 'free' (in material substance and in mind) to make the equal and wide prospect by which the greater interest of the nation may be understood. Other interests are 'factions'. Those who threaten the independence of the man of property represent the worst of all factions: that of 'tyranny'. These too are the commonplaces of Whig philosophy. They underlie the English revolution of 1688, and the American. In so far as those who owned country houses also owned the very land of the nation, or the greater part of the land, then they might represent 'the people'. This was natural, for the land was not only the source of wealth, and thus of power. It was also the signifier of 'Nature' and therefore closest to God. Power was religiously mystified.

As a cultural ideal, inextricably involved with power, the country house is thus the major signifier in this symbolic history of an emergent national culture. It is the goal towards which the upwardly mobile aspired, and the model from which national culture descended downwards. Thus George Washington progressively changed Little Hunting Creek Plantation, already pretentiously renamed Mount Vernon after Admiral Edward Vernon. Washington inherited a frame farmhouse a storey-and-a-half high, a traditional 'Sabine' home, four rooms square, around a central passageway. He transformed it into a mansion appropriate for the President of the United States of America. It was refaced with a simulacrum of stone, and extended with a banqueting hall lit by a Venetian window. The porch became a neoclassical portico; neoPalladian courtyard wings set off the approach to the house; and a belvedere rising above the edifice (imitating the Governor's Palace at Williamsburg) was graced by a dove of peace (won by successful war). Likewise, at President Madison's estate at Montpelier, under Jeffersonian influence, a simple farm was ingested and disappeared within a Palladian villa announcing its cultural (and hence political) correctness by a classical portico (got right at the second attempt). That villa itself was subsequently ingested into the home fit for the Du Ponts. Their entrée into country-house tradition spread the gilded splendours of the *nouveau riche* through 77 rooms, 14 bathrooms and a private hippodrome. Only at Highlands/Ashlawn (among the country houses of the four Virginian presidents of the Jeffersonian period) has something of the simplicity of a 'Sabine' farmstead survived, at least in outward form, for Monroe, despite Jefferson's persuasion to join him in forming a choice society in the vicinity of Monticello, rarely resided there. Family necessity demanded closer proximity to Washington, DC. Something else of the Sabine life is clear at Highlands/Ashlawn. The slave quarters dominate the farmyard and crowd upon the farmstead. That too is a tradition from classical antiquity intrinsic, and redefined, in national culture.

To place Jefferson and Monticello in this context is a 'reactionary' interpetation of the American revolution. It drags against the romantic enthusiasm of the millennial leap into the future of the emergent republic:

> We can no longer say there is nothing new under the sun. For this whole chapter in the history of man is new. The great extent of our Republic is new. Its sparse habitation is new. The mighty wave of public opinion which has rolled over it is new.... (to Joseph Priestley 21 March 1801)

It was for this 'new chapter in the history of man' that the great Jeffersonian statements about human rights and liberty ring out like a clarion call, or, set in tablets of stone in the Jefferson Memorial, have been used as quasi-sacred texts in the promulgation of what are seen as the universal truths of the 'free West'. To see, instead, Jefferson rooted, as it were, at Monticello in Whig country-house tradition would be a great check to enthusiasm. It would also be reactionary in the sense that it would return Jefferson to an originary and explanatory source. Even a *lumpen* Marxism might seem to be ill-concealed behind the arras. Might one hesitate the suggestion that Jeffersonian culture (and Jeffersonian libertarian rhetoric) are mystifications of something as (banal) as class interest or as ill-defined as 'power'?

But that is not the intention of the argument – neither to backtrack to classical antiquity, nor to make the great leap forward into another kind of revolutionary society. Monticello occupies the inbetween. It is a Whig country house translated to a new place and time. 'Power' in this new context is that empowerment which comes from the idea of universal rights, from the independence of property, and from education. That is the Jeffersonian ideal, and that ideal, put into social effect in the revolutionary nation, frees the individual to enter into the realm of 'culture' which Monticello represents. The villa is the product of empowered individualism. It signifies and embodies that classical, European and western inheritance into which the individual, once freed, may enter in a process of illimitable growth. In this context the abstract idea of 'liberty' acquires the quality of life itself. This is the way the free individual should live.

As pure symbol – and Monticello is an ideological rather than practical plantation house – we are at an extreme level of idealism – *tamquam in republica Platonis*. There is in Jefferson's imagination an extraordinary America in which the *Volk* are each man a Cincinnatus, as if the charming historical fictions of the first books of Livy were become real in 'the American farmer' – the patriotic minuteman with a plough at one hand and his long carbine at the other. The Jeffersonian variant envisages an ideal American nation of self-sufficient small farmers, an empowered democracy in which each man (white male) would be independently enfranchised by the possession of 50 acres. From this broad base Jeffersonian agrarian society would taper sharply upwards by universal, progressive and highly selective education to produce that 'aristocracy of virtue' which both Plato and Jefferson called the Guardians: 'the future guardians of the rights and liberties of their country...endowed with science and virtue, to watch and preserve the sacred deposit'.[9] The University of Virginia, which Jefferson founded, indicates how narrow that (white, male) aristocracy might be. The students were to be self-selected by the rich, supplemented by ten scholarship boys 'raked from the rubbish annually'[10] (a Jeffersonian phrase which reveals his own aristocratic position), and taught government by a politically correct republican professoriat from Jeffersonian texts.[11] The full complement of this university (which, in practice, Virginia could not make up) was 218 students. It was the (ostensibly reluctant) duty of this 'aristocracy of virtue' to submit to election for the atrabiliar cares of office, although each man (following the typology of Washington) would long to retire as soon as duty permitted to cultivate philosophical retirement on his country estate – *O rus, quando te aspiciam...?*[12] Hence, it may be, the omission of Jefferson's presidential role from his obelisk at Monticello, for in this tradition, to seek office (and no one sought it eventually with more vicious ruthlessness than Jefferson) was a distraction from the improvement of man's estate upon his estate. Office was not something, therefore, in which the virtuous aristocrat would admit that he looked for happiness. As for atrabiliar care, that Jefferson certainly found.

Stated thus baldly, the ideal Jeffersonian republic appears a mere product of *Schwärmerei*, or what he called 'Quixotism' (letter from Edmund Pendleton, 11 May 1779). But this was the imaginative base of his practical politics. The educational base was never achieved in Jefferson's lifetime (for it was seen as too Jacobinically liberationist), but the material superstructure of the university was created. Seen as symbolic architecture for a Platonic ideal republic, 'the Lawn' (as the campus is known) designates the university as a cultivated extension into Nature of the country house.[13] The Lawn is encompassed by an exercise in 'correct' neoPalladian architecture which through the eye would teach each student true principles (Plate 2). One of those principles is that there is an aristocracy even within the aristocracy of virtue. The Lawn is hierarchically organised in a gradation from student cell to professorial neoPalladian mansion, to Rotunda. The Rotunda closes one end of the Lawn, but the other end is open, for its 'indefinite' extent, Jefferson wrote, was the symbolic counterpart of the 'indefinite' extension of human learning (*Report of the Commissioners for the University of Virginia*, 1818). It is a typical expression of the revolutionary leap into futurity by the romantic nation.

It is difficult to conceive, however, to what extent those neoPalladian colonnades might go on extending into Nature. The intention was that they should never be closed (the campus, Jefferson envisaged, would clone itself sideways). In practice, the future terminated the Lawn by Cabell Hall,[14] and beyond the tiny jewel of its Jeffersonian heart the university now spills out into the architectural anarchy of an unstructured campus hooked on to a city without a centre ringed by an interminable movement of automobiles. Each citizen of the republic now exercises his (and her) inalienable right to drive on the 'free' way. But even the Lawn, notoriously, at the beginning soon became a centre not for reduplicating order but for anarchy as the self-governing, rationally free academic community Jefferson envisaged dissolved into violence and even murder. The song of the 'Wahoo' is a remote, but logical derivative from Jeffersonian principles: 'From Rugby Road to Vinegar Hill/We're gonna get drunk tonight/The Faculty are afraid of us/They know we're in the right.' The Wahoo exercises an inalienable right to pursue happiness (by getting drunk), opposition to which by the Faculty would be tyranny. *Ça ira.*

This is merely to play with Jefferson's *Schwärmerei* – the 'Utopian dream' of which he wrote to Joseph Correa de Serra (25 November 1817). But, in essence, his 'American dream' is a nationalised version of country-house culture projected as a model into a recalcitrant present and an indefinite future. The present generation had no ultimate means to determine that future for, in Jefferson's notorious 'Jacobinical' phrase, 'The earth belongs... to the living' (to James Madison, from Paris, 6 September 1789). By a peculiar Laputan mathematics, Jefferson gave each generation to whom 'the earth belongs' eighteen years and eight months to work out its destiny. But in the Paris of 1789 from which Jefferson wrote to Madison, in practical fact a generational time-span of eighteen years and eight months was utterly beyond the revolutionary horizon. The revolution was to consume its own children on a daily basis. Jefferson vainly believed that his acolyte La Fayette and his liberal circle could stabilise the revolutionary process in France at some halfway stage between America and Britain (the old world having some catching-up to do). But, had Jefferson belonged by nationality to the French aristocracy of virtue, he would have been fortunate to escape with La Fayette to prison at Olmütz, and the guillotine might have been a more merciful end than that which met a dinner-companion like La Rochefoucauld, stoned to death before his family ('a little blood' to water the tree of liberty). When the revolutionaries halted the 86 boxes of the Jeffersonian household *en route* back to America it was because they seemed like the property of an *émigré* in flight. It was a reasonable supposition. At no time in his life was Jefferson more at home than in the society of the liberal Parisian 'aristocracy of virtue' in happy interplay between the salons of the great and semi-rural excursions to the Bois de Boulogne, Mont Calvaire, Marly and the Désert de Retz, made doubly charming by the presence of Maria Cosway. It was from this base that he returned to his own cultural origins in the long tour of 1786 of the country houses and gardens of the revolutionary Whig aristocracy in England. In comparison, 'dear' Monticello at this stage of his career was the remote (Marie-Antoinnesque) pastoral fantasy of the 'heart and head' letter to Mrs Cosway.

But, as 'the Atlantic revolution' post 1789 spun out of control, what was at threat was not 'republicanism' *per se*, but rather an entire culture: that of the country-house order in Europe and America – an order of things which Jacobinical republicanism totally rejected. The post-revolutionary meeting of La Fayette and Jefferson on the lawn at Monticello in 1824 was thus a reactionary event for it was a celebration that the worlds of La Grange and Monticello still existed to influence the future of their respective nations. For Jefferson especially the building of the *new* Monticello, the villa begun *after* his return from France in 1789, was to be as ideological as La Fayette's concurrent use of La Grange. There was nothing like Monticello in America, Jefferson believed, and the purpose of this architecture, new in context for the new world, was to teach the emergent nation right principles by embodying those principles in the permanent signs and forms of architecture. Although the earth belongs to the living, a great country house, rooted in that earth, was to be a permanent sign of the continuity of the deep roots of the people, and thus a check to the anarchical flux of a revolutionary world running off the rails. Jefferson's Monticello, therefore, is not just a place in which to live the good life; it is an anchor in a storm.

The hope, even the theoretical certainty, was that the permanence of architectural form and its importance as the *locus* for human activity, would rightly form the new citizen for the new nation. Here French theory supplements English Whig politics and the exemplary models of the English country-house tradition. As Kersaint argued: 'let us unite the energetic language of monuments to verbal instructions; the confidence which it is so necessary to inspire in the stability of our new laws will establish itself, by a kind of instinct, on the solidity of edifices destined to conserve the laws and to perpetuate their duration'. Or, in more visionary mode, as Ledoux argued: 'examples and models persuade the multitudes, more than the sentences of Socrates and Solomon'.[15] This is Jeffersonian by analogy and a characteristic part of revolutionary *mentalité* – as the Pantheon in Paris and the Capitol in Washington, DC indicate. A key text expressive of that *mentalité* is Ledoux's *L'Architecture considérée sur le rapport de l'Art, des Mœurs et de la Législation* (1804), where laws, morality and the forms of art and architecture are seen as intrinsically one. Revolutionary neoclassicism in France saw architecture both as 'speaking' to man (*parlante*) and also as morally instructive (*édifiante*). It possessed what both Ledoux and Boullée called *caractère*. It possessed this power because it was founded upon the primary truths of Nature divinely ordained. This was an argument which, in its extreme theoretical expressions, became a quasi-mystic (or Masonic) appeal to God as the originator of light: 'God created light. Art, following his example, centralizes it. How fine it is to construct temples that would have to be invented if

Nature herself had not founded them!'[16] God is also the maker of a geometrical universe. The primary architectural forms, therefore, are the circle, the square and the pyramid. But there was a correspondent appeal downward from the Creator to the creature. Revolutionary architecture claimed universal validity because founded on a doctrine of sensation (part Lockean, part Kantian) in which the perception of symmetry and variety are intrinsic categories of human perception. Behind all is the humanistic figure of Vitruvian Man, the patriarchal order inscribed within the primary forms of the square and circle.

One illustration from Jefferson's practice may exemplify complex theory in practice. Jefferson's (unrealisable) scheme for an administrative centre for Richmond was a visionary project like that of Ledoux's design for La Saline de Chaux. Only the Capitol was completed, derived from the Maison Carrée at Nîmes, but now devoted not to religion but to the secular needs of government in the new nation. In Jefferson's ideal scheme there was 'In the middle...a room thirty-six feet square, of the whole height of the building, and receiving its light from above. In the centre is a marble statue of General Washington, made at Paris by Houdon....The statue is made accurately of the size of life...' (*An Account of the Capitol in Virginia*). The room, thus, combines two fundamental geometrical forms, the square and the circle, at the centre of which, in the centre of the Capitol, is set an heroic human figure (Washington as Vitruvian Man, and as the founder of the nation). His iconographical signifiers (as given by Houdon) are his sword, the plough and the American commonplace, the *fasces*. The room is lit by God's light from above, and Art and Nature thus combine to celebrate Man and God, and to teach the nation. Jefferson also desired that the room should be surrounded by a peristyle of columns. (These were not realised.) Since he was well-read in theory he would know that the classical orders were derived from the trees of the forest from which the first buildings were reared, so that the native woodland of America, expressed in the peristyle, surrounds Washington, and supports the entrance to the chambers above. To those who had eyes to read, the edifice, thus, would edify.[17]

This sketch of architectural history is merely a framework: an approximate placing of Monticello. It has moved by ellipsis from Monticello as the inheritor of the power culturised of the neoPalladian villa to the villa as model for the new nation. It is a developing ideology underpinned by that peculiar blend of utilitarian instruction and mysticism which permeates visionary revolutionary architecture in France. It is a summary which is as imprecise as the evocation of 'romantic nationalism' at the meeting of La Fayette and Jefferson where these essays began – and for the same reason. The purpose is to open up possibilities and to widen the enquiry here so that Monticello, as signifier of national culture, may be seen somewhere in a spectrum which extends from (for example) the declared Whig ideology of Lord Cobham's Stowe to the romantic mysticism of the Désert de Retz and the unrealisable revolutionary projects of Ledoux or Boullée. That is Jefferson's visual and ideological world in which he was a time-traveller, spectator and embattled participant. The centre of this spectrum is what has been called here (but not defined) 'the country-house order'. That order of things, at Monticello, brings together the historic culture of the villa and the romantic nation in an *architecture parlante* and an *architecture édifiante*. (Thus the yellow schoolbuses in the car park today, and every day.) If the triad of land, folk and culture are essential elements in the idea of the romantic nation (the originary hypothesis of these essays), then this country house materially and symbolically involves, organises and interprets that relationship. By an act of synecdoche Monticello (a part) becomes the whole (the nation); hence the signification of the aureole *e pluribus unum* around the emblem of the domed villa on the national coinage: this one thing expresses plurality. Or that, at least, is the Jeffersonian ideal: America fixed in architecture as Jefferson wished to define it and embody it in correct and historically rooted symbolism.

But, of course, the ideal form is subject to alternative interpretations, to change and to decay. It is as controversial as the emblems for the folk on the American Seal, and as likely to 'loom' as the very land itself, or even to become 'the measure of a shadow'.

First the ideal.

In John Adams's design for the Seal of the United States, Virtue pointed Herculean man the way up a steep hill. In Shaftesbury's gloss on the allegory, the meeting of Hercules and Virtue took place in a wilderness, because here Man was closest to God.[18] The high hill, yet to be climbed, was innocent of architectural signifiers, temple, fortress or palace. Virtue would create these. This portrayal of Herculean man as a type of emergent civic virtue is an ideal, and commonplace signifier, familiar in art and landscape design. In the English Whig garden of the eighteenth century it provides, for instance, the dominant conceit for Henry Hoare's moral allegory at Stourhead. The Pantheon in the garden there is a temple of Hercules from which a pathway leads up a steep hill to the Temple of Apollo as the summation of the visitor's pilgrimage through Nature. At Monticello, Jefferson's 'little hill' may be read as a variant of the same *topos*. It too is the hill which virtue must climb. The villa on the summit represents a moral as well as physical summation within the natural scene. But in America there is a living 'Hercules' embodied in the civic virtue of Jefferson himself.

Perhaps Monticello improves morally upon Stourhead because the natural context in America for the Herculean choice was closer to God than the landscape garden in England. To create a garden in America, Jefferson claimed, one need only to cut out 'the superabundant plants'.[19] The land was 'virgin'. Here is Nature, then, as it was first formed by God. From the trees like these the first architects built their primitive huts, from which the classical orders derive.[20] An American villa, therefore, is closer to the Maker of the universe. Into the purity of the primeval forest, had wealth and opportunity permitted, Jefferson would have crowded architectural signifiers. Early and late in his career he planned an imaginary programme which would have turned the estate at Monticello into a complex iconographical scheme possibly improving on the moralised circuit of Stourhead, or purifying the Whig politics of Stowe (which Jefferson had visited in 1786), or even making real in the new world the visionary realm of the Désert de Retz (seen in his enchanted weeks with Mrs Cosway). His imaginary projects are rich with unrealised symbolism. There would have been a pyramid of the 'rough rockstone'; a 'turning' Tuscan temple of the 'proportions of the Pantheon' (the masterpiece of 'spherical' building); and 'a model of cubic architecture' such as the Maison Carrée. The garden would thus have exemplified the divine geometry of the universe. Extending the bounds of culture, Greece would have been signified by Demosthenes' lantern, and China by an imitation of the Chinese pavilion from Kew. Returning, at the end to Nature, a grove of 'ancient and venerable oaks' would have marked a melancholy burial-ground with 'Gothic temple of antique appearance'. Beyond the confines of the microcosmos of the garden itself, on an eminence overlooking Monticello, on what Jefferson called the 'high mountain' (Montalto), he planned a variety of observatories, one of which would have been a column of 200 feet with a spiral staircase twisting from bottom to top. From here the virtuous philosopher would scan God's heavens above. ('Get thee up into the high mountain.') For some of these *fabriques* Jefferson planned suitable epigraphs. Some of these recall the most poetic of English gardeners, Alexander Pope. Pope's filial celebration of his mother, inscribed on the obelisk at Twickenham, seems to have lingered in Jefferson's mind. It is the basis for his memorial for his sister ('Ah! Joanna puellarum optima!'). So too Jefferson remembered Pope's lines 'Nymph of the grot, these sacred springs I keep....' For these he sought an appropriate *locus* at Monticello. At Stourhead the inscription forms part of the moralised movement up from Nature to God. The nymph, as a power of Nature, presides over a spring of pure water in her subterranean grotto on the visitor's pilgrimage to the Pantheon and Hercules and the Temple of Apollo. Water springing from the rock of America would have been purer yet.[21]

These are 'mere dreams' (in Yeatsian phrase) and belong only to an imaginary landscape. But they indicate a desire to introduce a 'speaking' and 'edifying' architecture into the virgin land (with 'proper inscriptions'). God's purposes would have been realised in forms of architecture imitating divine intentions; Nature would have been idealised; family piety recorded. The range of monuments suggest an encyclopedic desire to centre the whole world into the microcosmos of the estate. Had the schemes been realised, Monticello would have become the greatest *jardin anglais* of the newly 'independent' nation. In actuality only two forms were realised. They are the pyramid and the pantheon and they came to dominate the symbolic order of the estate. Although Jefferson did not have the resources to build a pyramid in stone, he insisted that it was 'out there' in Nature and was visible to the directed eye. He showed it to visitors in the form of Willis's mountain. The 'pantheon' was the place from which the pyramid was seen, for the pantheon, of course, is the fundamental form expressed by the second Monticello.

The symbolic pyramid is part of the standard nineteenth-century 'Jeffersonian image'. Henry S. Randall's *The Life of Thomas Jefferson* (1858) may serve as a major example. Randall's account of Monticello set the villa in a visionary landscape in which America is 'stretched out like a map' before the visitor. Remarkable in the landscape was Willis's Mountain, 40 miles distant to the south. 'Mr. Jefferson was wont to call the attention of visitors to it, as presenting a pretty correct idea of the appearance of the pyramid of Cheops at the same distance. The latter is stated by Stevens, we believe, to be eight hundred feet square at its base, and four hundred and sixty-one feet high. Older writers make it much larger.'[22] Randall's account derived from Jefferson himself. Thus, Francis Hall recorded in 1817 that Jefferson took him round the estate to indicate his 'improvements': 'during the walk, he pointed out to my observation a conical mountain, rising singly at the edge of the southern horizon of the landscape: its distance, he said, was 40 miles, and its dimensions those of the greater Egyptian pyramid; so that it accurately represents the appearance of the pyramid at the same distance; there is a small cleft visible on its summit, through which the true meridian of Monticello exactly passes....' Henry D. Gilpin was to repeat the story (with variation), reporting that Willis's mountain ('at a distance of eighty miles') presented 'as Volney told Mr. Jefferson exactly the appearance of the Great pyramids of Egypt seen from that distance; it gives you an idea of the immensity of those structures beyond anything that can be imagined; on a point of the mountain commanding this prospect... Mr. Jefferson had erected a little Grecian temple & which was a favourite spot for him to read & sit in....'[23]

Obviously it was Jefferson's intention to read culture into nature in this imaginary landscape. But the obvious was, in fact, not obvious. The great pyramid needed to be pointed out. As part of this constructed image, Jefferson himself became part of the edifying landscape as philosopher (in the widest sense of the word) reading in a Grecian temple and gazing out across the 'map' of America to the form of the originary pyramid. It is only by his own philosophical reading, and by the report of another philosopher, Volney, that he is able to decode from Nature the signification of Willis's mountain. This product of the literal imagination, as it descends to us textually, is invested with a strange apparatus of quasi-scientific exactitude: of miles (Willis's mountain is forty or eighty miles away), of feet (the pyramid is eight hundred square by four hundred and sixty-one high, though 'Older writers make it much larger'), and even of global location, for it is claimed that the meridian of Monticello 'exactly passes' through a cleft of the summit. The villa and the pyramid seem to be united, thus, by the Divine Geographer himself, whose purpose has been revealed to the philosopher reading in his temple. Ultimately, the name given to this natural pyramid draws it into the realm of private property and of the independent country estate. The natural pyramid in some sense 'belongs' by name to a man called Willis.

This creation of the associative imagination links back to one of the dominant motifs of the originary Seal for the new nation. The pyramid was appropriated there as a national sign. Its traditional association was that of perennial permanence – it is, as it were, the man-made equivalent of a Wordsworthian mountain. Here the divinely created mountain declares that the forms of Nature are the basis of architectural order. The Palladian commonplace that Art imitates Nature is manifestly demonstrated in the Monticello landscape. (The 'Natural Bridge' was a similar *locus* for Jefferson, who bought it. Like 'Willis's' mountain, the signifier was appropriated as personal property.) The pyramid, as manifest on the Seal, was invested with quasi-Masonic signification. God was the first architect, who taught Hermes Trismegistus, who taught Moses, from which sources western architecture has developed. This myth was appropriated for the invention of the nation, linked, through Virgil, with the divinely sanctioned creation of a new order of things. That is the penumbra of American signification around the pyramid. For Jefferson, reading in his Grecian temple, looking out over the land beyond his estate, the originary architectural form is linked to the architecture of Monticello by process of historical development. This process extends chronologically from the primitive forms of Pharaonic empire, through Hellenistic culture (which was philosophical and democratic, building upon and superseding Egyptian experience) and thence, via Vitruvian Rome and Palladian Italy, to the Whig country house, first in Britain, now on a high mountain in America. Monticello is the summation of this divinely originated process, standing metaphorically as well as in scientific fact on the exact meridian of Willis's mountain.

This natural pyramid was a raw form, as it were Nature struggling to express what Culture will realise. Monticello, as the pantheon *redivivus*, alludes to the formal perfection of achieved culture. The Pantheon was the acknowledged masterpiece of spherical building (as Jefferson's imaginary garden scheme stated), and it is the *fons et origo* of those seminal buildings: Palladio's Villa Rotunda at Vicenza, and Lord Burlington's Chiswick. Monticello, as the summation of the tradition, is a recension of all three. The signification of the pantheon in humanist culture is, therefore, both central and complex. Serlio's five books of architecture (1537–47) are a convenient point of entry. III, iv begins (in the Peake translation of 1611):

Among all the ancient building to bee seene in Rome, I am of opinion, that the Pantheon (for one piece of work alone) is the fayrest, wholest, and best to be understood; and is so much the more wonderfull then the rest, because it hath so many members, which are all correspondent one to the other, that whosoever beholdeth it, taketh great pleasure therein, which proceedeth from this, that the excellent workeman, which invented it, chose the perfitest forme, that is, the round forme.... And it may be, that the sayd workman, considering all things proceeding orderly, have a principall and onely head, whereon the nether parts depend, was of opinion, that this piece of worke should have only but one light, and that, in the highest part thereof, that it might spread abroad in all places alike.... For that the Pantheon seemeth unto me to be the perfectest peece of worke that ever I saw, therefore I thought it good to set it first in the beginning of this Booke, and for a principall head of all other peeces of worke. The founder of this Temple (as *Plinie* writeth in more than one place) was *Marcus Agrippa*, to accomplish *Augustus Caesars* last will, who being intercepted by death, could not finish it: and so it was built about fourteene years after the byrth of our Lord, which is about 5203 yeeres from the beginning of the world.

Serlio's association of the Pantheon with Augustan Rome (it is modern scholarship which dates it from the reign of Hadrian) placed the most perfect of forms at a crossroads of history. This was the epoch of revolutionary transition in the Roman state between republican virtue and imperial splendour, in which, architecturally, Augustan culture found Rome (republican) brick and left it (imperial) marble. The Pantheon, as a temple to all the gods, is also associated with that epoch when a greater God than the pagan deities chose to be born, and a spiritual empire superseded a material order. Virgil's Augustan *novus ordo seclorum* and his allusion to the divine sanction of the Augustan regime, *annuit coeptis*, had been readily appropriated by Christian eschatology as prophecies of the coming of Christ long before they were mystically reappropriated by American nationalism. But as Serlio describes the Pantheon, it emerges out of the particular matrix of Augustan and Christian history to acquire, for him, a universal signification. It has 'the perfitest forme' for all time for it is spherical (like the heavens themselves) and is 'more wonderfull' than other architectural forms 'because it hath so many members, which are all so correspondent one to the other': *e pluribus unum.* That 'perfitest forme' of the circle, in Vitruvian theory, contained the human form itself. It would be in accord with the allegorial temper of the Renaissance for the reader of Serlio to perceive an analogy between architecture, the body of man and the body of the state. Serlio's description of that perfection which consists in having 'a principall and onely head, whereon the nether parts depend' has clear political connotations. There is a plurality of parts, but one guiding principle: 'this piece of worke should have only one light, and that in the highest part thereof, that it might spread abroad in all places alike': *unum, pro pluribus.*

This symbolic form was secularised by Palladian villa culture. But many of the originary allegories still remained vital and are pertinent at Monticello. The motif *e pluribus unum* is, perhaps, the most obvious, but the historical and religious elements derived from Augustan history are equally strong. It remained a fundamental tenet of the American revolution that the *novus ordo* in America marked the transition between imperial and republican orders, although here the Augustan revolution was reversed. It was a *ritorno* (to use a Machiavellian term) to an earlier purity, and, for some, a puritanism deeply embued with religious mysticism. It was an equally fundamental tenet of Jeffersonian liberalism that all forms of religion might coexist within the state. That liberalism, in the Pantheon of Augustan Rome, had been based on a profound philosophical scepticism about any form of religion. The wise statesman saw the utility of belief in a divine order, but looked down upon the forms of local superstition (Gibbon's interpretation – which is close to Jefferson's own). But there is also in Jefferson's thinking a clear distinction between 'Truth' and 'Error' and, thus, an implied higher source of light. Multiplicity of belief is subordinated to a single source of illumination and to a single head. The 'oculus', which letting in divine enlightenment illuminates all parts of the human pantheon equally, is both a liberal and a fascist signifier, enlightening multiplicity, but one in its quasi-divine authority.

There is one major difference, however, between the ancient temple and its modern recension. In the pantheon the one true God (so Christianity believed) was originally excluded from the pagan shrine (later rededicated to Christianity). But, in the villa, the entire culture of the secular temple was centred upon the unifying figure of its owner as Vitruvian man, the centre of the house and the estate. This extends to the owner something of a mystic authority. 'Thy lord dwells', wrote Ben Jonson, initiating the long tradition of country-house poetry in English, and the word 'lord' is both secular and divine.[24] Accordingly, a religious motif runs through Monticello, for the internal architectural decoration is consistently religious in origin. The hall derives its frieze and mantel decorations from the Temple of Antoninus and Faustina in Rome; Jefferson's bedroom draws upon the Temple of Fortuna Virilis; the parlour, rising to the Corinthian order, alludes to the Temple of Jupiter, chief of gods, and the dome above, derived from the Temple of Vesta, alludes, thus, to the palladium of the Roman republic. The details of the stucco reveal signs of fertility in flowers and children, emblems of sacrifice in the heads of oxen, of victorious war in shields and helmets, and of vigilance and courage in the griffins in the hall. If some of the allusions are recondite, yet even an elementary reading of architecture must recognise the pervasive religious motifs. Even for those totally ignorant of culture, there can be no doubt that the villa exists only as a manifestation of the will of one master, and to serve that will only. Although the spasmodic and complicated history of the building of the villa denied Jefferson a correlation between his own central authority and the centre-point of the architectural design, the omission was clearly in his mind. It was a motif he was to manifestly establish at Poplar Forest, the last great *fabrique* constructed on his estates. There the villa is built within a series of concentric circles extended through the garden, and at the centre of the villa itself is the cube room (the dining room).[25] The square is set within the circle, as Vitruvian theory required. At the centre of the square is Vitruvian man, Jefferson himself, at the head of his dining table, supported, in proper hierarchy at Poplar Forest, by his admiring granddaughters, served by those he called (perhaps biologically as well as metaphorically) his wider 'family' – the negro slaves. 'Thy lord dwells.'

There are, thus, many elements at Monticello which would have been easily 'read' by an Augustan Roman, by humanist culture in Renaissance Italy, or by Lord Burlington, or any builder of a Whig mansion in Britain. The Pantheon is the archetype; Palladianism the intermediary. But Jefferson, on his only visit to Italy, preferred not to see any actual example of Palladian architecture, which remained, therefore, a purely imaginative stimulus. In 1786, however, in the company of John Adams, he had made at first hand a long and detailed study of the architecture of Whig Palladianism in England, including the *fons et origo* of the English movement, Lord Burlington's Pantheon *redivivus* at Chiswick. These examples were the only material signifiers of the country-house order he knew, just as earlier architectural exemplars derived from the English country house and its estate had been, of historical necessity, the models for the pre-revolutionary colonial plantations of Virginia. The salons of urban Paris and the palaces of Bourbon absolutism, which Jefferson also knew at first hand, have no real social or historical relation to the culture of Monticello.[26]

It has been taken as 'self-evident' in this argument, therefore, that Monticello belongs to Whig Palladianism – that English recension post-1688 of the villa culture derived from the ancient world. But the iconographic signification of the country house is changed by its transplantation out of the 'metropolitan' culture of the originary colonial power. The house is set in a different 'land' and among different 'races'. It thus is a sign of a different nationality, hence the epigraph to this chapter from Arthur Young writing about Ireland. For Ireland and America were parallel Whig colonial plantations among an alien people, in a raw, undeveloped land, threatened by racial conflict, uncertain of national identity. Hence, for Young, the importance of architecture as the manifestation of a superior culture. The difference between Whig villa culture in Anglo-America and Anglo-Ireland is that the plantation aristocracy in Ireland, as a minority among an indigenous and hostile helot race, clung to its metropolitan roots, whereas those roots were torn up in the post-revolutionary United States. In the emergent nation, therefore, it was necessary to establish a new identity for the white majority (the helots and the indigenous race were, as in Ireland, equally hostile, but were to become a minority). In Jefferson this desire to produce a new identity leads to an almost pathological Anglophobia, and a hypersensitivity to anything which was called 'Tory' (that is, derived from English metropolitan roots). Hence, in the forms of architecture, his almost total dismissal of Anglo-American colonial building and, thus, of some of the most beautiful exemplars of colonial villas from which he might have learned simplicity, functionalism and grace. Compare the great flying staircase at Shirley with the mean backstairs clumsiness of Monticello, or the subtle beauty of the plasterwork of Kenmore, with the quasi-barnlike starkness of the hallway at Monticello. But Jefferson's aesthetic blindness (and ignorance of colonial architecture) is part of his attempt (in vain) to disown his own affiliation to the imperial power rejected (as its 'Other') by the postcolonial nation. It is a familiar phenomenon, for which Ireland again provides an immediate parallel where Georgian architecture was eventually to stand to Celtic nationalism as colonial Virginian architecture to Jefferson's nationalism.

Hence the attempt by Jefferson to avoid the 'Other', or the rejected 'father' culture in which one does not wish to see either one's own origins or reflection. Instead he returned to older, purer roots. He bypassed Britain for (in historical regression) Palladio, Vitruvius, Grecian forms and ultimately Egyptian originals derived from the First Architect himself. These are 'mystic chords of memory' and this mysticism and memory is intrinsic in the formation of the romantic nation. If one cannot claim immemorial settlement in the land, one settles in the land immemorial signs. In this respect the grammar of Monticello's architecture, which formally is 'neoclassical', is in its expressive quality 'romantic'. In comparison with what was in the land before it is also (in a romantic sense) utterly 'original'. It is radically new (in the context of colonial architecture, which Jefferson rejected) and is *ab origine*, from Nature itself. Thus, it is in the beginning of things that the immemorial origins of the American people lie.

To demystify this subjective function of Monticello one needs to supply what is ideologically denied, but everywhere present: the English Whig country house which Jefferson romanticised out of existence, but which, in fact, has been nationalised for postcolonial purposes. If language is intelligible because it is a system of differences, the differences between Monticello and the key signifiers of Whig culture seen by Jefferson (with John Adams) on his English tour of 1786 elucidate the iconography of both. The Jefferson/Adams tour itself, moreover, is expressive of the postcolonial dilemma. For there would have been no reason to make the tour if the *architecture parlante* of Whig Palladianism was not of immense signification to both men. Why, otherwise, make the tour? Yet the claim is that it is not an *architecture édifiante*. Jefferson, meticulously following the standard guides such as Whately, was largely silent on what he saw (his Memorandums are, in the main, banal jottings of facts and figures), but Adams's record of his peregrination, in his diary, is, in large measure, a standard republican diatribe against the lost revolutionary tradition in England.[27] 'Ostentations' and 'vanity' mark the estates. 'Jobs, Contracts, Salaries and Pensions' have drained the commonwealth to 'procure all this Magnificence' and the 'Pillars, Obelisks &c.' erected to the monarchy. At Edgehill and Worcester, Adams harangued 'the People': 'Tell...your Children... all England should come in Pilgrimage to this Hill, once a Year' (a pilgrimage to be institutionalised in America in climbing the little hill of Monticello). Adams concluded his tour:

> It will be long, I hope before Ridings, Parks, Pleasure Grounds, Gardens and ornamented Farms grow so much in fashion in America. But Nature has done greater Things and furnished nobler Materials here.

There is nothing in Adams's diatribes at variance with Jefferson's own view of the corruptions of 'the vaunted scene of Europe' and his romantic preference for Nature in his native land. It would be redundant to supplement the Koine of republicanism of Adams's diary with parallel passages everywhere diffused and widely known in Jefferson's works. The silence of the Memorandums is, as it were, pregnant with Adams. That may be taken as 'read'. But Jefferson returned from the tour of England and from Europe to destroy the first Monticello and to spend the best part of the next two decades creating a new house which is, in its formal grammar, a recension of the Whig Palladianism he had seen in England. But in its ideological language (its iconography) Monticello enters into a kind of dialogue with those great Whig models Jefferson had seen at Chiswick and Stowe, Blenheim and Hagley, and thus with the very architecture he sought to avoid by a return to ancient and mystic origins. One architectural model (in imperial culture) is reinterpreted for postcolonial and nationalist ends. That dialogue, therefore, requires close analysis.

'Look here, upon this picture, and on this.' (Plates 1, 5 and 6)

Closest of all to Monticello among the Whig country houses which Jefferson saw was Lord Burlington's Chiswick: the domed villa on the model of the Pantheon intended both as a declaration of the Palladian revival and, as scholarship has gradually revealed, a complex enunciation of an elaborate iconography.[28] Compare the facades of Chiswick and Monticello as Chiswick was on 2 April 1786, the date of Jefferson's visit, and Monticello when completed in 1809.

What Jefferson saw at Chiswick was a domed neo-Palladian villa still attached by a long hyphen to an older manor house (since demolished). The approach to the villa had been lined with sculptured sphinxes; the villa itself presented two entrances; one for common use in the rusticated ground floor, the other by way of a double, ceremonial staircase and through the Corinthian columns of the portico. Interpreted in terms of what Jefferson called 'the monarchical aristocratical system', the villa is iconographically linked to the older feudal order by its direct physical link with the old manorhouse. Whig culture acknowledges its 'Gothic' roots and historical continuity. But only the learned will understand the full significance of Burlington's icons. Hence the sphinxes along the driveway. They indicate that this approach should only be for initiates learned in mysteries – *procul, o procul este profani* (as the garden at Stourhead was inscribed).[29] Whether the Theban riddle represented by the sphinxes was aesthetic and playful, Masonic and spiritual, or even contains a latent allusion to the divinity of kings, is problematical – Chiswick invites diverse readings of no concern here – but such mysteries are the province only of an elite. The two-storey structure of the house, with a lower and upper entrance way, accordingly separates the learning and ceremonies of aristocracy from the mundane and terrestrial affairs of the commonality. The Corinthian order of the upper entrance was associated by Palladio with nobility, elegance and beauty.[30] It is appropriate for what Lord Burlington intended to be a temple of the arts.

Compare the redefinition of Chiswick at Monticello. Seen from the eastern approach (from Europe towards the western frontier), the dome of this neoPalladian villa is not apparent. Nor is there a *cour d'honneur*. This has been removed and turned inwards at Monticello to become the platform for Jefferson's garden walk. There is no ceremonial staircase outside (nor, eccentrically, within, for the interior stairs are notoriously cramped and difficult to climb – Jefferson did not use them). Thus, by comparison with Chiswick, Monticello seems to be merely a single storey high, which signifies a democratic equality between the owner and the American people. The house is simple of access (notoriously too simple as the pestered sage of Monticello discovered). It stands unattached within a picturesque garden directly in visual relation with the natural Virginian countryside. The Doric portico is two grades down the hierarchy of the classic orders from Chiswick's Corinthian entrance. Compared with Chiswick, the political iconography declares the owner's (and the nation's) allegiance to Nature (and Nature's God) rather than to feudalism (represented by the old manor house at Chiswick). At

Monticello there is a domestic familiarity between the house and the folk, not the sybaritic values of the wealthy and sensual Corinthians. But this is within a hierarchical gradation. Jefferson did not go as low as to use the Tuscan order and, in fact, like the orders of architecture, the villa has its own internal gradation. Monticello is in fact divided between four floors, each with a separable function. The external façade presented to the visitor, therefore, is a form of mystification. It makes an ideal statement about the republican nation, but it conceals the order of class, gender and race within. For those who live or work in the villa, the gradation extends from the symbolic dome room above – which becomes fully visible to those who enjoy the domestic freedom of the garden – and down to the slave-quarters below – concealed within the slope of the hill. Just as at Chiswick, therefore, the superstructure has a base. Lord Burlington made that clear in England in the doubled storey of his façade which is a manifestation of power. In America, power is concealed. What seems ideal at Monticello, seen from outside, may, therefore, experienced from within, generate stresses located in the imperative of idealism to suppress potential contradictions. To enter the villa (as it was at the end of Jefferson's life) is to become involved, thus, with a complex act of structural analysis. The signification of the icons depends both on their relationship to the implied other of the Anglo-Palladian Whig tradition, which Jefferson ideally rewrites in the interests of national culture, but also on the tensile relationship between the purpose of the villa to conceal tensions, or even fractures within the ideal order. In this, Monticello is like any complex work of art which seeks to resolve generic or ideological paradoxes, ironies and even contradictions by the synthesis of form.

The point of entry, the hallway, initially, serves its usual function in the Palladian villa. It is the waiting and reception area for visitors thence to be divided between the various areas of the house (with their distinct functions). Within this Palladian tradition the hall at Monticello might be said to be ostentatiously simple (Plate 7). An extreme example from Whig Palladianism may reveal the range of the spectrum. Colen Campbell's Houghton was not on the Jefferson/Adams tour of 1786, but as Sir Robert Walpole's 'home' (and the possible original of Pope's satire on Timon's villa) it is a *locus classicus*. The Stone Hall at Houghton is a perfect cube (one is tempted to add, 'of course') (Plate 8). The geometrical order of God's universe is reflected in the social order of the country house. But the word 'hall' (an English rather than American designation) hovers between two social orders. Although the architecture is classic, the word 'hall', as in Houghton Hall, is Gothic and a synecdoche in which the part had once represented the whole. A Gothic hall would have been the centre of the community of house and estate; the place where meals were taken in common by the household and where, on special feast days, the tenantry of the estate would be hospitably welcomed. It was the place where 'all come in' as Jonson wrote in *To Penshurst*. It would have been, thus, a sign of 'community', and was to become even a signifier of 'socialism' (in the imagination of Pugin or Morris).[31]

Obviously this is no longer so at Houghton Hall. This is a power-house. The hall, as vestibule to the rooms of state, reveals the dynastic grandeur of Sir Robert. That is the essential function. His bust, by Rysbrack, dominates what should have been a communal hearth in the Gothic order. It is virtually deified by its setting, for the chimneypiece becomes a kind of sacrificial shrine to wisdom armed and to statecraft. In the ceiling above, supported by angelic putti, is Sir Robert again, his wife Catherine, his son George (George for England, agriculture and the Hanoverian monarchy), and George's wife, a Devonshire heiress (dynastic marriage enhances wealth and power). One expression of wealth and power is the ability to buy the signifiers of taste everywhere manifest in the hall. The connoisseurship of the language of the twentieth-century guidebook exemplifies this perfectly:

> The chandelier is noteworthy – also the bronze 18th Century copy by Girardon of the Laocoon group in the Vatican – Kent of course made the fine stand. The bronze on the centre table is a copy of the Persephone group, now at Versailles, and is attributed to Benvenuto Cellini. The carpets are exceptional....

Had John Adams recorded the house in his diary, his apoplectic comments on this display of wealth may be readily imagined.

By comparison, the republican simplicity of the hall at Monticello is manifest. It is, of course, only by comparison. Monticello's modest entrance would swallow many a pioneer cabin. This remains a gentleman's villa. Those whose insignificance in the social hierarchy made it their business merely to wait in the hall would be seated upon simple, vernacular 'Windsor' chairs – the word 'Windsor' indicates how difficult it is to shake off the legacy of the language of the colonial power. Simplicity, however, was not carried as far as an affectation of pioneer crudity. The vernacular woodwork of the chairs was painted. Those familiar with the iconography of national history would recognise that these are the same kind of home-made chairs upon which the revolutionary nationalists sat in Robert Edge Pine's *Congress Voting Independence* (1796). If one might doubt the signification of this, compare Trumbull's *Declaration of Independence* hanging in the Capitol. There the artist has elevated the revolutionaries to gentlemanly *fauteuils*. At Monticello, the attendant visitor would have to reach the parlour before being thus accommodated with the upholstered comfort of the *ancien régime*. Since Jefferson was acutely aware of the signification of 'forms' this hierarchy within simplicity is not accidental.

Two national icons in the hall are already familiar. On the south wall stood a model of the Great Pyramid, the base of which contained a portion of Egyptian sand and a pebble from the desert. Since Monticello stands upon the same meridian as Willis's mountain (the natural representation of divine architecture) it was fitting that the house should contain a simulacrum of the Great Pyramid itself which, by some kind of mystified science, is given added authority and authenticity by the presence of real Egyptian sand and a real Egyptian pebble. On the ceiling above there was (probably) displayed then (as now) the American eagle. The national symbol has now acquired a halo of 18 stars (rather than the 13 of 1782) which would date it between 1812 (when Louisiana was admitted to the Union) and 1816 (Indiana's admission). It would seem, therefore, to be a triumphalist allusion to 'the Louisiana purchase' by Jefferson and to the extension of the 'empire for liberty'. In its claws, instead of a *fasces* of arrows for war and an olive branch for peace, Jefferson's eagle holds the central light of the hall. America, thus, illumines the entrance to the villa and occupies the place of the divine oculus in the Pantheon.[32]

Compared with the dynastic ambition and grandeur displayed by Sir Robert Walpole at Houghton, Monticello dedicates its hallway to the nation by incorporation in eagle and pyramid of two of the fundamental icons from the national Seal. But they are, inescapably, linked to the owner of the house. The hall prominently displays the bust of Thomas Jefferson by Ceracchi, and if it is not set in the heavens like the dynasty of Sir Robert, it was placed on a broken green marble column inscribed: 'To the Supreme Ruler of the Universe, under whose watchful care the liberties of N. America were finally achieved, and under whose tutelage the name of Thomas Jefferson will descend forever blessed to posterity'. The column (a gift from Madame de Tessé) was decorated with the ten lost tribes of Israel (the chosen people of God) and decorated with the signs of the zodiac (representing God's heaven). This was set in direct contradistinction to a bust of Jefferson's arch 'Tory' rival, Alexander Hamilton. The visitor should not forget that it was Jefferson's 'revolution of 1801' which preserved the almost lost virtues of the revolution of 1776. Perhaps this is modestly stated compared with the ostentation of power at Houghton, but it is not an insignificant assertion of power.

Where power is more obviously displayed is in the Indian artefacts which crowded the space. Jefferson called the area his 'Indian hall', and it was crowded with bows, arrows, quivers, lances, clubs, pipes of peace, clothes and domestic utensils, devotional objects, Tecumseh's belt and shot pouch, an Indian painting on buffalo hide of a battle, and an Indian map on buffalo hide of the Missouri and its tributaries. These were displayed among a multiplicity of other objects – the thigh-bone and tusk of a mastodon, minerals, maps, eleven religious paintings, a statue of Ariadne, busts of Turgot and Voltaire, and Jefferson's bizarre clock whose works disappear into the invisible nether regions. Visitors overwhelmed by all this referred to it as a 'museum'. But, in the creation of the icon of the romantic nation, it is the 'Indian' presence in the museum which is of foundational signification. These are the *Urvolk*.

They form part of Jefferson's project in the villa to record American history (portraits of early explorers hung elsewhere in rooms higher in the hierarchy; the library was rich in texts of national history, law, geography and other sciences). By becoming part of what visitors interpreted as a 'museum' (a designation also used today by the Center for Jefferson Studies) the *Urvolk* in the Indian Hall have acquired a special place in American history. They have become part of what is shown here to be a superseded past. The primitive religion of the ancient culture, with its crude idols, is set first against the higher religious faith of Christianity (represented by the religious paintings Jefferson displayed in the hall) and then compared with the philosophical Enlightenment which (Jefferson believed) had superseded Christianity. The busts of Turgot and Voltaire signify the Enlightenment, and their incorporation in the hall unites the owner of Monticello with the great figure of Franklin as the summation of progressive philosophy. (It was Turgot who had said that Franklin had taken Jove's thunderbolt from the heavens, and the sceptre from tyranny; and Voltaire, in a famous, public embrace, had welcomed the American to the bosom of the new philosophy). Compared with the busts of enlightened Man, the artefacts of the Indians are the detritus of the inter-tribal conflicts of warrior peoples. In contradistinction, no weapons of the white man are in evidence (even the eagle displayed on the ceiling has lost its heraldic armaments). The crude Indian map of the Missouri region (again the Louisiana purchase is alluded to) is contrasted with western maps showing, scientifically, the cartography of Virginia (drawn by Jefferson's father), the United States and the whole world. The Indians fought within territories they hardly knew; under Jefferson that territory has been geographically determined and then legally 'purchased'.

It is an idealised progressive scheme. It derives from the Whig ideology of property rights. The national homeland is seen as a kind of extended estate, first mapped out by surveyors and then purchased by a contract between equal and consenting peoples as part of the processes of developing civilisation. The concept represented by the phrase 'the Louisiana purchase' has become such an historical cliché (and cause of national celebration as one of the great Jeffersonian achievements) that one hesitates to turn upon it a sceptical eye. But what Jefferson, in fact, bought from Napoleon Bonaparte was a tract of territory which no one possessed, and, therefore, which no one could sell. The boundaries of the 'purchase' were unknown, and therefore could not be consensually agreed. To this 'purchase' no inhabitant of the territory – Indian, Spanish, French or British – had given assent. The whole thing was an imaginative fiction where the acquisition of national *Lebensraum* by the direct application of force (present or future) is masked by paper legality. Hence the significance of the one Indian named in the hall: Tecumseh, represented not in *propria persona* (he is not that important) but by his belt and shot pouch. Tecumseh is a figure of the same importance as Pocahontas for the invention of the new nation, but is weighted with a different meaning. He is a major example of an Indian leader who opposed, by force of arms, the policy of forced 'purchase'. He joined with the former imperial power (the so-called tyrannical British) in the war of 1812. He saw *Realpolitik* for what it was, and what was threatened in future for his own race. The Indian Hall recognises this irritant in the progress of national history; but it reduces him to a mere anthropological artefact and, as it were, incorporates him into what is past like some out-of-date Scottish clansman in a novel of Sir Walter Scott (or 'Indian John' in Cooper's *The Pioneers*). There are, thus, two things which the 'Indian Hall' does to the *Urvolk*. By making them part of museum culture, it fits them into that process of cultural unification by which the new nation seeks to organise its past history as a common inheritance: *e pluribus unum*. It is also a death warrant. Museum culture is dead culture.

This use of a Palladian hallway is uniquely Jeffersonian. There is not another house quite like this, although it appears that Madison's Montpelier (closely influenced by Jefferson) was also themed as an expression of nationalist culture.[33] But even Montpelier had no 'Indian Hall'. From one perspective, therefore, the Jeffersonian villa is individually eccentric and a radical departure from the conventions of colonial plantation culture. But in the larger perspective of romantic culture at this time, the involvement of the *Urvolk* within the progressive development of the romantic nation is a commonplace (as has been argued earlier). This applies, therefore, in the country house as much as elsewhere. Accordingly, at Monticello, Anglo-American relates to Indian as Anglo-Norman to Celt or Saxon in the British country house. Jefferson on his tour of 1786 would have seen at Hagley how the iconography of the garden establishes a sorites from the neoclassical house back to the Anglo-Saxons – in Alfred's Castle in the gardens – and outwards into Nature and immemorial time represented by the vistas of the Welsh mountains – the signifiers of the superseded (and conquered) Celtic *Urvolk* lingering on the horizon. Lyttelton's library records that he made the appropriate tour of the Celtic homeland: *antiquam exquirite matrem*.[34] During the revolutionary wars against France the return to national and British 'roots' became more urgent. The 'Gothic revival' provided a national symbolism in contradistinction to the continental tyranny of Napoleon. The 'Gothic hall' (as reconstructed at Belvoir) or a themed house, like Sir Walter Scott's Abbotsford, are British equivalents of Monticello. The conflicts of racial identity of past history are nationally unified in opposition to an alien force without and by reconciliation within through the imaginative forms of architecture.

But, as in a novel by Scott, at Monticello the world of the primitive tribesman is a phase through which national development has passed. It is retained in symbolism (the peace-pipe at Monticello, from Jefferson's 'friends'; the wearing of the tartan in Scotland by the now-friendly clans). The visitor passes through to the penetralia of the villa and from the history of America, as it was, to the ideal formulation of western culture in the country house perfected in the 'parlour'. This is situated directly under the cosmic signifier of the invisible dome room above. It is that point of focus where the entire community of the villa come together in their common room. This is, for those within the culture, the equivalent of the old Gothic hall where 'all come in', and Jefferson accordingly preferred the domestic nomination of 'parlour' to the more formal appellation of 'Salon' (by which the equivalent room is often designated in the Whig Palladian villa). The democratic equality of the parlour is further signified by the absence of any indication of a staircase – one need only compare the progression from the 'Roman hall' at Holkham by ceremonial stairway upwards. Jefferson rejected within the house, as well as without, any sense of hierarchical progression. But this democratic equality, paradoxically, is also highly exclusive. That exclusivity is marked by the practical difficulty (when use demands) of actually moving either up or down from this level. The Monticello staircases, tucked away out of sight in a passage, would be inadequate as backstairs even for servants. The bedrooms, with their bizarre floor-level fenestration and cramped accommodation, suggest rather the sleeping quarters of some undermaids. Jefferson did not go there. Conversely, to go down is made more difficult yet. Since this would be a descent from the white world to the black, no white would make that Avernine descent. Instead, Jefferson's famous dumb waiters delivered fine French cuisine and fine French wines from the invisible subterranean terraces below the level of culture. Major sacrifices of utility have been made to maintain the external illusion that this is a house upon one level only.

The ground floor of Monticello, therefore, is a Palladian *piano nobile* denying its own nobility (Plate 9). Within that 'democratic' area Jeffersonian culture is represented by the material display of the contents of the 86 boxes of fine furniture, pictures and *objets* which he brought home from the *ancien régime* in France. These are supplemented by his major library, the modern catalogue of which extends to five substantial volumes. By the time the villa was completed about 1809 the furnishings of the house might be seen, from a European perspective, as already somewhat conservative and old-fashioned (like La Fayette's visit to Monticello in 1824, signifying past history), but otherwise they represent what one would expect in 'villa culture' within the European tradition at this time. Here and there Jefferson supplemented his European purchases with an indigenous piece of simple furniture made on the estate (a touch of 'arts and crafts'); his collection of books and pictures possessed an American bias; but compared with the didactic eccentricity of the Indian hall, the rest of the furnishings at Monticello would pass as unexceptional in any home of the aristocratic classes.

A visitor to Monticello would, however, experience some differences within the inherited culture which Jefferson was seeking to redefine for national ends. Great Whig didactic villas like Chiswick, Houghton, Hagley or Stowe were designed as some sort of cross between a 'theatre' (which displays) and a 'hotel' (which entertains). They were intended to serve as the *locus* for 'the country-house party' (whether the retreat of a weekend or of weeks) and the country-house party was the major social institution through which 'the monarchical aristocratical system' functioned. It was at such parties, for instance, that Sir Robert Walpole planned politics at Houghton, and the index of who was 'in' or 'out', or to which family, faction or party one belonged, might be derived from inclusion (or exclusion) from the guest-list. But although Monticello retains the function of a 'theatre' (it is an epideictic house) and of a 'hotel', its uses meld in unusual ways. The country-house party was no part of the function of Monticello. The house was a 'hotel' only in the sense that the old ('Gothic') tradition of 'Virginian' hospitality meant that a gentleman would offer accommodation to other gentlefolk on the road (consider the primitive state of Virginian inns, where they existed!). But the visitor was entertained in order to be instructed. Part of that instruction was to teach the lesson of virtuous domesticity and philosophical retirement as manifest in the life of Jefferson at Monticello. As the head guide to the house today correctly announces on the threshold: 'Welcome to Mr. Jefferson's home.' Monticello, which in its display of purchased taste resembles a villa like Houghton, yet, in its emphasis that 'there's no place like home', seeks, in function, to resemble a quasi-Wordsworthian cottage.

The intricate design of the ground floor at Monticello results, therefore, from Jefferson's intention to use the villa as 'theatre', 'hotel' and 'home'. He needed to blend his role as philosophical statesman in retirement but on display, with the desire to entertain and instruct the transient visitor, and to emphasise the use of the villa as a family residence. From the axis of the hall and parlour there are divergent routes: south to Jefferson's personal realm (his study/bedroom and library); north to a continuing suite from parlour to dining-room and to what Jefferson called the 'most honourable' room (more domestically called 'the tea room'). Or, backtracking to the east, through the cross-axis of a central passage-way, one reaches either the family schoolroom on one side of the hall, or what was, presumably, the best bedroom for guests on the other side. It is an intricate design.

Ideologically, domesticity has been elevated to the same level as philosophical statesmanship. We know that Monticello was crowded with Jefferson's extended family as well as with visitors. The schoolroom is joined to Jefferson's library and to the entrance hall, so that it was as likely for a visitor to meet grandchildren on their way to instruction by the daughter and housekeeper Martha as to be greeted by the sage himself. Or, moving in the other direction, the rising republican generation would be tempted by the sweets of learning in their grandfather's book hoard. This emphasis upon the family is what ancient Roman republican virtue would have called Jefferson's *pietas* and is part of his image promulgated to posterity through Randall's biography and that charming work of familial hagiography, Sarah N. Randolph's *The Domestic Life of Thomas Jefferson*. We see how the sage loved to play with children, and how he unbent even to supplement maternal instruction. This places Jefferson within the same didactic world as the novels and stories of Edgeworth or the ideal educational schemes of Rousseau's Émile or Sophie. His domesticity is also part of the cultivation of the instructive simplicity of image which developed after his return from France in 1789. He abandoned the dress of a gentleman for what became either a careless or deliberate slovenliness. At the White House, as part of the same image-building, he refused to give formal dinners. All were invited to come in 'pell-mell'. A similar pell-mell was not uncommon in the overcrowded spaces of Monticello.

Jefferson's domesticity is one of the most charming elements of the man, and still strongly emphasised in the accounts of the villa given to the parties of American schoolchildren touring Monticello. Its iconographical function is equivalent to having one's portrait painted. It is part of the image constructed for the public and for posterity in the way, for instance, the younger Pliny's letters on his life in his villas constructed an ideal Roman image of the 'good' life (*beatus ille...*).[35] Jefferson acts, as it were, as his own Parson Weems to establish an image of what it is to be a virtuous American. At the root of that virtue are the home, domesticity, children, instructive simplicity. Others, like Washington, celebrated their greatness with Augustan pageantry (witness his inauguration); Jefferson will be remembered walking in his flower garden with his grandchildren. This mythos of Monticello is so well-established it needs no elaboration. The iconography of space at Monticello, however, is not as simple as that. In the usual forms of circulation in the country house, the library is one of the major common rooms. Instruction (or entertainment, for the house is a 'hotel') was available in common to all those who had the social status to justify use of the *piano nobile*. This was not so at Monticello. On the contrary, the quartet of rooms comprising library/cabinet/bedroom (with Jefferson's bed set midway between library and cabinet) constituted a private domain denied to visitors (as they complained), access to which was a special privilege. Jefferson controlled the library as a personal space, as, indeed, he controlled the domestic rhythm of the day at Monticello (and with the punctuality of a General Tilney, at Poplar Forest, as his granddaughters tell)[36] This is part of the well-known biographical icon, and needs no reiteration. But, if Monticello is a *locus* of inherited culture for the new nation, that culture is disrupted. The ostensibly equal community is divided by the reimposition of a hierarchical order which is strictly patriarchal and exclusive. Since the sage actually sleeps among the instruments of philosophy, neither the family, nor the visitor, is going to profane these intimate (even revered) penetralia. Although Jefferson's famous bed is not the bed of state for some great man's *levée*, it is, nonetheless, a signifier of the essential exclusivity of his studies (Plate 10). As the story tells, the philosopher always arose before the sun to pursue his labours for his country and mankind. The implication is that others, far removed from Jefferson's books, continued to slumber. That icon is part of the mystique of the sage of Monticello. It is, thus, exclusive to Jefferson. No one else in the villa could live in that way, and the family house, paradoxically, could not be a dynastic house. It could not function in its Jeffersonian order from generation to generation of family inheritance. When that bed in Jefferson's domain no longer had its incumbent, it is not possible to imagine another generation utilising his space in his way. Jefferson's culture, therefore, dies with him.

Biographically considered, this is part of Jefferson's bachelor eccentricity. The house reflects the man, as William Howard Adams has persuasively argued.[37] But iconographically and ideologically the study/library/bedroom is both Jacobinical and nationalist. It is Jacobinical because its undynastic status is part of Jefferson's aristocratic denial of his own aristocracy. Since 'the earth belongs to the living' and no generation lasts even twenty years, everything is always in revolutionary flux. There are, therefore, no Burkean deep roots uniting generation to generation by dynastic and spiritual continuity, and Monticello is functional only for Jefferson for Jefferson's lifetime. Or, put another way, whereas the *ancien régime* in Britain venerated old oaks as signs of national continuity, the American nation-builder, confronted with a tree, reached for his axe and cut it down. That is the way gardens are built in the new world, as Jefferson claimed. But Jefferson's personal realm is also national because it was *his* library which he construed as forming the basis of national culture. This is 'literally' so, for, in an extraordinary act, he was to sell the library to the nation to form the basis of the Library of Congress. What would constitute wisdom for the future legislators of the people was what Jefferson himself had chosen to sell to them – an ideological equivalent of the Louisiana purchase.

But the route from the parlour to Jefferson's private domain is only one of the axes of the villa. In the public domain there is a progressive hierarchy to be followed from parlour to dining-room and thence to what Jefferson designated the 'most honourable' room in the 'suite', which is dedicated as a form of shrine to the heroes of the American revolution. From thence, at least in the hierarchy of the imagination, there is a further ascent, literal and metaphorical, to the dome room above, the most famous and most significant architectural icon of the villa. When the house was incorporated into the national currency (on the old two-dollar bill and the nickel), the façade of Monticello shown is that on which the dome rises above the portico. This is the western and garden front, and the house is seen, therefore, from the point of view of a visitor who has progressed through hall and parlour and acquired the status of some kind of resident, as much at home at Monticello as he (or she) is at home in America.

In country-house culture, the dining-room had a place of especial significance, but, as has been indicated, that signification varied between Gothic and classical tradition. In the Gothic order, dinner in hall had been the occasion when all the inhabitants of the house, or even all the people of the estate, were gathered under one roof. In fact, by a curious anachronism, it is a ritual still significant in the privileged colleges of Oxford and Cambridge in England. But, since tradition has preserved the ancient custom, it may be perceived that the communal ritual was not a democratic act within the collegiate community. As Oxbridge still shows, the distinction between high table and low, between senior common room and servants is jealously preserved. This is no Jeffersonian 'pell mell'. On the other hand, both fellows (and their 'Master') and servants are all members of the one household, and progression up the hierarchy, although difficult, is not impossible. The son of a servant, through hard work and scholarship, may aspire to Fellowship on high.

The classical tradition was more exclusive than the Gothic. The Socratic symposium provided the ideal model. The *triclinium* (three-sided couch) around the dining-table enclosed a different kind of space than the Gothic communal hall. The dining-table was an area where fine food and wine would stimulate fine discussion of matters of philosophy and art among an all-male gathering. The owner of the classical country house would gather about him friends chosen for their worth, not because of self-interest (this was the ideal promulgated by the poetry of Horace and Martial). There was no question of throwing open the house to the tenantry of the estate, because the estate was a slave economy. But in classical antiquity, progression up this hierarchy was not impossible for some. The practice of freeing favoured house-slaves was common, and educated freedmen were capable of progression even into the landed orders. Perhaps the most famous example was the poet Horace himself, who was the son of a freed slave. His small Sabine farm, given him for services to the Augustan regime, became the idealised basis of that literary tradition which underlies Jefferson's establishment of Monticello as a site of desire.

The dining-room at Monticello belongs to the classical tradition. The 'Gothic' has no part either in the iconography or practice of this American country house and the significant architectural signs clearly establish the distinction. Jefferson's entablature is derived from Fréart de Chambray's *Parallèle de l'Architecture antique avec la moderne* (1766). The 'parallel' with classical antiquity is iconographically and ideologically correct and the repeated motif of rosette and ox-skull is more than mere decoration. It declares that there is a relationship between the dining-room and some ancient temple of fertile sacrifice and celebration. It is an enunciation of the ritual signification of Jefferson's architectural space and its hierarchic importance. This is not merely a place to eat in, but, like a visit to a temple, part of a 'suite' of ritual and public acts. Therefore, as in the penetralia of a sacred temple, and in contradistinction to the 'hall' of Gothic tradition, the dining-space is exclusive. In Jefferson's hierarchy, the lower orders ultimately became invisible, for the room was serviced by dumb waiters from the subterranean quarters. Progression from below was, in Jefferson's view, impossible. In antiquity, freed slaves might ascend because they were white men like their masters, so he claimed. But the racially separate negro, even if the evidence for racial inferiority were false, would never integrate.

The elegance and intelligence of Jefferson's dinner-parties is well documented biographically. One instance may serve to illustrate the ideal. In April 1782 the Chevalier de Chastellux, an officer in Rochambeau's army and author of a treatise on public 'happiness' (*De la Félicité Publique*), dined at Monticello. He records that his own 'feelings and opinions' were in 'conformity' with those of his host:

> so perfect that not only our tastes were similar but our predilections also – those predilections or partialities which cold and methodical minds hold up to ridicule as mere 'enthusiasm,' but which men of spirit and feeling take pride in calling by this very name of 'enthusiasm.' I recall with pleasure that as we were conversing one evening over a 'bowl of punch,' after Mrs. Jefferson had retired, we happened to speak of the poetry of Ossian. It was a spark of electricity which passed rapidly from one to the other; we recalled the passages of those sublime poems which had particularly struck us, and we recited them for the benefit of my travelling companions.... Soon the book was called for, to share in our 'toasts': it was brought forth and placed beside the bowl of punch. And, before we realized it, book and bowl carried us far into the night. At other times, natural philosophy was the subject of our conversations, and at still others, politics or the arts, for no object has escaped Mr. Jefferson; and it seems indeed as though, ever since his youth, he has placed his mind, like his house, on a lofty height, whence he may contemplate the whole universe.[38]

This is a 'model' description of a dinner in the tradition of the classical symposium and has often been cited as an example of the culture of Jefferson at Monticello.

It was an all-male gathering. It was in keeping with classical tradition that the *servi* and also the womenfolk had been removed.

'Woman', however, as an ideal category, was to return. She was eventually (post-Paris) incorporated in the iconography of Jefferson's tableware. Soft paste porcelain statuettes of a naked Venus with Cupid, and a clothed (female) Hope with Cupid were to became part of the dining-room decoration. If the Wedgwood plaques of the dining-room fireplace are Jeffersonian, then Woman recurs also as Muse. The dining-room develops upon an idealised image already enunciated in the entrace hall where the visitor would have seen the sleeping Ariadne (or Cleopatra, as some believed). To the real presence in the villa of Woman as wife and mother – Mrs Jefferson, or Martha – one must add, therefore, another presence in the forms of art. Jefferson's choice of icons suggests a sensuality of taste here which recalls rather the world of Maria Cosway than the republican matron Martha with her 11 children in the schoolroom. The icons exist partly to arouse male sensuality, partly to sublimate that sensuality into art. But it is only in the forms of art that Woman participates in the symposium.

The 'classicism' of this symposium is 'romanticised' in Chastellux's discourse. But this romantic classicism, he claims, was in perfect conformity with the 'enthusiasm' of his host. The word 'enthusiasm' had formerly carried condemnatory connotations and in eighteenth-century usage had religious connotations (it was applied, for instance, to the excesses of revivalist evangelical movements like Methodism) but here it is used as an appropriate description of the sensibility of the rising revolutionary generation in America and France. 'It was a spark of electricity which passed rapidly from one to the other.' That image of an electrical spark relates the gathering to Franklin whose experiments in drawing down lightning to earth became iconised as a sign of that natural force which would, like a bolt from heaven, strike and destroy the tyrants of the earth. Its most famous representation in art was as yet in the future. In David's *Le Serment du Jeu de Paume*, as the united assembly pledge their lives and sacred honour to the revolution, at the same instant a great shaft of storm-engendered light bursts through the window above and the wind of change sweeps through the room. It is one of the greatest images of fascist art in the European tradition. But, as a 'sublime' force (to utilise Chastellux's vocabulary) lightning was associated with Terror. In Brown's *Wieland* it was this same elemental electrical force, out of control, which destroyed the philosopher in his classical temple on a hill. In the Frankenstein myth (created by the generation who knew of a real Terror), it is lightning drawn down from the sky which galvanises into life that Promethean Man, who is a monster. Chastellux's image of the electrical force of Jefferson's symposium, therefore, is enunciatory of a long romantic tradition.

In 1782 electrified enthusiasm demanded that Ossian should be the text called for by the revolutionary generation. (Since this symposium took place within a country house, the book was instantly available from the essential repository of western tradition: the library.) Ossian was a key text in romantic nationalism post-1776, and it has been already suggested that Macpherson's cultural incorporation of the defeated Celts into British nationalism parallels Jefferson's placing of the Indians within the emergent American nation. But that was not the primary function of the text here. Ossian's sublime and deeply melancholic epic of a past warrior caste provided the subject of a series of 'toasts'. If this had been a merely drunken male dinner (the antitype of the symposium) it might have been the absent women who would be the subject of sexual 'toasts'. But in the ideal world of Monticello, as Chastellux recalls it, the men pledged themselves to imitate the heroic life of ancient epic heroes: to war, to honour and, although death is inevitable, to fame among future generations of men. This is what the ideal archetype demanded, for the epic traditionally provided models of conduct for gentlemen, 'fashioned in perfect discipline'. The genre was also claimed by traditional criticism to be encyclopedic, and from Ossian the discourse moved out thus to embrace natural philosophy, politics and the arts. So too, like the epic, the mind of Chastellux's host embraced an entire culture in its scope, and Monticello was the objective correlative of Jefferson: 'he has placed his mind, like his house, on a lofty height, whence he may contemplate the whole universe'.

This is one of those 'spots of time' which might be interpreted iconologically as a summation of the ideal order which Monticello embodied. It resembles that other famous 'spot of time' in 1789, when the leaders of the liberal revolution translated from America to France gathered round Jefferson's table to catch the electric spark from the New World. Not every meal is like that, but this was the ideal to which Man aspired. This is why the dining-room has a special place in the hierarchy of space at Monticello, or the 'high' table in an Oxbridge College. That 'height' at Monticello is both literal and metaphorical. The icon is intensely romanticised and self-consciously constructed by Chastellux. In the dining-room at

Monticello the officers of the revolutionary army became part of a field of force with the 'sage' who was a Founding Father of a new nation. But there is also an irony about this spot of time which none of the participants seem to have grasped. (Part of the romanticism of Monticello is that Jefferson is oblivious of irony.) Ossian, the favoured text, and one of Jefferson's best-loved poems, is about the passing away of an aristocracy. The epic tragedy concerns a caste, dedicated to honour and to war, which has lost its historic *raison d'être*. The officers of the army of the *ancien régime* in toasting Ossian were toasting their own demise.

But the 'suite' at Monticello seems to suggest, on the other hand, that old epic has acquired new significance. The progression takes one from the dining-room to 'the most honourable' room (which is also, in practical use, a domestic tearoom) (Plate 11). This is dedicated to four great men of the revolutionary nation whose busts adorn the walls: George Washington, Benjamin Franklin, the Marquis de La Fayette and John Paul Jones. These are the modern equivalent of ancient epic heroes. The progression of the classical orders though-out the house reaches its climax in the composite consuls which carry the busts. The motif of sacrifice – in the ox-skulls of the dining-room – is removed. There are only rosettes on the frieze, and the triple bay-window commands a prospect out over the garden to the circumambient world of Nature beyond. What is domestically a mere 'tearoom' has been made iconographically a shrine. If Monticello were an ironic house, some play of wit might be provoked by the juxtaposition of national heroes and a genteel Virginian 'tea-party' (compared with the Bostonian kind!) Out of war has come this kind of domestic peace. But that kind of irony would be unusual for Jefferson. A simpler explanation of the symbiosis of national shrine with domestic tearoom is the practical difficulty of crowding different functions into limited space at Monticello.

Of the four heroes, Washington, warrior and statesman, and Franklin, natural philosopher and statesman, are obvious and commonplace nationalist choices. A new nation needs heroes who define its best characteristics and on whose model self-identity may be formed. The function of La Fayette in the pantheon is equally obvious. He is both a supranational unifying symbol, and a sign of the internationalisation of the revolution. The addition of Jones, however, is more problematic. His addition to the American pantheon tilts the balance towards a celebration of the *Blut und Eisen* of the war against Britain, beaten at sea as well as on the land. The iconisation of the dare-devil and renegade Jones suggests that Jefferson, the admirer of Ossian, had an imaginative taste for violence. It did not trouble him that Jones had learnt his seamanship, and toughened his spirit, by trading in slaves.

This kind of ideal pantheon is not uncommon in country-house tradition. The obvious 'parallel' (to utilise de Chambray's word) is at Stowe, which Jefferson and Adams had visited in 1786. It is a parallel, of course, with a marked difference, for Viscount Cobham's palace at Stowe was built as an expression of dynastic, even Timonesque, pride. It is so magniloquent that the motif of the pantheon, which Monticello, as a whole, imitates in domestic form, is incorporated merely as one room at Stowe: the Marble Saloon, whose frieze depicts a Roman triumph with 280 human figures and 14 sacrificial animals celebrating the dynasty of the Temples. The modest structure of Monticello (modest by comparison) might easily be lost within the suites at Stowe, as, indeed the original country house on Cobham's site had already been ingested by the time of Adam's and Jefferson's visit in 1786. By comparison, therefore, the combination of national shrine and domestic tearoom at Monticello, although an odd symbiosis, establishes a marked contrast between the aristocracy of the monarchical-aristocratical system in Europe, and the domesticity of the aristocracy of virtue in the United States of America.

There is no need to elaborate that obvious distinction. But in the garden at Stowe there exists an iconographical schema which parallels 'the most honourable' room at Monticello in ideological intention. On a small hill at Stowe in a region of natural landscape there stands a circular temple (Plate 12). Like 'the most honourable' room at Monticello, it is dedicated to four figures who contemplate each other within, enclosed, as it were, in the circle of their own perfection. They are Epaminondas, Homer, Lycurgus and Socrates, representing the greatest patriot general, the greatest poet, the greatest lawgiver (and founder of a nation), and the greatest philosopher of classical antiquity. *Mutatis mutandis*, in the circle of self-contemplating heroes at Monticello, Washington embodies the virtues of both Epaminondas and Lycurgus, and Franklin, as natural philosopher, is the new-world equivalent of Socrates. That Jones stands in place of Homer may reinforce the point already made: that Jefferson's pantheon emphasises the element of violence in the making of the new world. But the simple parallel between the temple of Ancient Virtue at Stowe and Monticello is that the new world has revived the virtues of the old. What had died in Greece is now living at Monticello.

But the temple at Stowe forms part of a widening, and deeply ironic, schema in an extensive region called 'the Elysian Fields'. Separated from the temple by a stream (known as the Styx), there is a Shrine dedicated to British Worthies divided into two wings: one, emphasising the contemplative life, commemorates Alexander Pope, Sir Thomas Gresham, Inigo Jones, John Milton, William Shakespeare, Sir Isaac Newton, Sir Francis Bacon; the other wing (the active life) commemorates King Alfred, Edward Prince of Wales, Queen Elizabeth, William III, Sir Walter Raleigh, Sir Francis Drake, John Hampden and the merchant, Sir John Barnard. On the summit of the shrine, Mercury, emerging from a pyramid, waits to carry their souls across the Styx to join the Ancients on the other side. Lines from the *Aeneid* remind the reader how in the Elysian fields are found patriots, poets and inventors of the useful arts (but a reference by Virgil to chaste priests is omitted). Thus, just as at Monticello, the argument is that the best of classical antiquity is reincorporated in the renaissance of an aristocracy of virtue.

But there are no living Britons in the Elysian Fields. On the contrary, living 'Modern Virtue' was represented by a heap of ruins displaying a headless bust. There are more perplexing ironies yet. Concealed behind the Shrine of British Worthies there is a bitterly satirical comment on the nature of human virtue and of praise. The longest inscription within the complex is devoted to the celebration of one who, it is written, followed Nature, respected the laws, and who was a perfect philosopher, faithful friend and loving husband: 'Reader, this stone is guiltless of Flattery; for he, to whom it was inscribed, was not a Man, but a———.' The stone, in fact, commemorates a dog. One may ask, if this stone is guiltless of flattery, which stones in the Fields might be guilty? Further off behind the shrine, on a higher hill even than that of ancient virtue, stands a Gothic building. Iconographically, the change of architectural form indicates a change of ideology. This temple is dedicated to Liberty. The implication is clear. Not even the greatest men of classical culture achieved that freedom enjoyed by the barbarous Goths who destroyed their ancient Elysium. The iconographic contrasts are deliberately planted in architecture and inscription, and are disturbing.

The signification of the national iconography at Monticello changes in this context. Four of the dead British Worthies from the

Shrine in the Elysian Fields at Stowe are incorporated into Jefferson's domestic schema. The triad Bacon, Newton and Locke, from the contemplative wing of the Shrine, have their portraits (specially commissioned by Jefferson) displayed in the common-room of the parlour. In a famous exchange with Hamilton, Jefferson had declared them to be the greatest men who ever lived (Hamilton preferred Julius Caesar – maker of an empire). Sir Walter Raleigh also reappears in the same room, forming part of Jefferson's collection of discoverers of America. But in the hierarchy of Monticello no Briton, of course, can achieve that national greatness which makes Washington an Epaminondas and Lycurgus (or Alfred), and Franklin the American Socrates (or Newton, or Bacon, or Locke). Nationalism, therefore, is the most important factor in Jefferson's hierarchy. From a national point of view, therefore, John Paul Jones is a good parallel for the pirate Sir Francis Drake at Stowe (the scourge of imperial Spain as Jones was the scourge of imperial Britain). La Fayette might have been flattered to have replaced the Black Prince, the hammer of France, as a national Worthy. But since La Fayette was still living, progress into Jefferson's American pantheon was swifter than in the Elysian Fields at Stowe. National self-congratulation at Monticello has no place for the ruins of a contemporary Temple of Modern Virtue with its headless bust. That kind of self-critique belonged across the Atlantic divide.

Thus, the self-doubt, the ironic complexity, and the raw satire of the Elysian Fields at Stowe is utterly foreign to Monticello. The divide between the two iconic spaces raises questions about the nature of symbolic history itself. By what tropes do you construct the ideal narrative? At Stowe, there are two major modes of representing the order of things: cultural relativity in the presentation of architectural form; and ironic interrelation between modes of iconic discourse. These are not resolved. On the contrary, the diverse architectural forms – ancient and modern, classic and Gothic – carry a variety of inscriptions ranging across a plenitude of discourses. The genres range from epic (in Virgil) to satire (in the Temple of Modern Virtue) and even to burlesque in the only sincere stone in the garden, dedicated to a dog. The meanings given to history are relative to one's position in time and space, and dependent on which discourse is chosen among many to give signification to things. To knowingly construct some form of coherence in sign or word must be to choose irony, therefore, as the only honest mode of discourse. If so, it is appropriate to ask whether even the four ancient worthies, turned inward into their own shrine, belong to anything which might be construed as real history. In their self-contemplation they become a kind of Platonic idea beyond space/time and existent essentially only as figments of an idealising imagination. As Congreve (who has his own monument at Stowe) wrote of the garden:

> ... Virtue now is neither more or less,
> And Vice is only Varied in the Dress.
> Believe it, Men have ever been the same,
> And all the Golden Age is but a Dream.
> (*Of Improving the Present Time*, 79–82)

Congreve's own monument depicted a monkey (Mankind) contemplating itself in the mirror of its own vanity. But, then, Congreve's world-weary cynicism at the dream of virtue is only one way of putting things. It has no more authority than any other.

But Monticello does not function in that way. The 'suite' of public rooms are not counterpointed, but are conceived as a progressive, idealistic ascent. If there is irony it is not inherent in the iconographic mode, but rather in the recalcitrance of things to be sublimated by Monticello's high, romantic nationalist sublime. This is most clearly revealed by the dome-room (Plate 13) which is the ultimate ideal icon at Monticello and is both beyond and (metaphorically and in fact) higher than 'the most honourable' room. The dome, like Yeats's 'Byzantium', is above 'the fury and the mire' of human history. Progression through the 'suite' of the villa is, therefore, a movement out of time towards an abstract classical ideal expressed in pure form. The dome, moreover, is the most Jeffersonian of those icons by which one, as it were, recognises the nation. On the Capitol (repeatedly cloned in other capitols) it marks that common space where the representatives of 'we, the people' meet beneath the sign of God's heaven. That space is now dedicated as the holiest place of the nation, for it is the repository of the most significant signs of the founding of the nation. Had Jefferson's plan for the White House been adopted, the President's villa would also have been domed. To which one may add the Rotunda of the University of Virginia. In this scheme, the national *fons et origo* is Monticello to which Presidential residence, the seat of government and the seat of learning all pay an act of architectural homage. The Jefferson Memorial on the Mall at Washington closes the loop, for its allusion to the Pantheon returns Monticello to its classical original (Plate 14).

Seen from the garden front at Monticello, the dome defines the place of the parlour as the iconic centre of the house – that common-room in which all the functions of the household meet. From here, unlike the entrance front, one is aware of an hierarchy of ascent, although the means of ascent is obscure (a 'progress' through the villa will not have revealed the staircases). Seen thus from below it appears that the dome must function as some kind of panoptic belvedere. The windows provide the point of vantage for that 'comprehensive and equal eye' of which Washington spoke in his Inaugural. If Jefferson's mind, like his villa, is set on a great height, here is the place in the order of things in which the mind arises above even the villa itself. One escapes, through Monticello, to something above and beyond. Although from beneath one cannot see the oculus which provides an equal and central illumination for the dome, yet the allusion to the Pantheon is so clear that one knows that God's light will be streaming in from above. The mind's eye perceives God's eye.

Jefferson's famous letter of love to Maria Cosway (12 October 1786) provides his own gloss. He celebrates

> our own dear Monticello, where...nature [has] spread so rich a mantle under the eye[:] mountains, forests, rocks, rivers. With what majesty do we ride above the storms! How sublime to look down into the workhouse of nature, to see her clouds, hail, snow, rain, thunder, all fabricated at our feet! And the glorious Sun, when rising as if out of a distant water, just gilding the tops of the mountains, and giving life to all nature!

He was thinking of national subjects for Maria Cosway as a land-scape painter: the sublime Niagara, the passage of the Potomac, the Virginian natural bridge. But the domestic landscape here – 'our own dear Monticello', he writes, incorporating her into the villa – subsists in this poetic vision above the regions of cloud, snow, rain and thunder – the tumults of the natural sublime – and in the enlightening beams of the life-giving sun. This effusion (of the 'heart') places Jefferson himself in the position of a demi-god look-ing down on the inchoate tumult of the creation. The classical affinities are with that passage in Lucretius in which the Epicurean sage gazes with philosophical tranquillity upon those storms which signify the perturbations of the unphilosophical mind (*De Rerum Natura*, II, 1*f*.) The wise man applies his own Monroe doctrine of the mind to the disturbances of the world. But there is also a strongly neo-Augustan element to the writing. Jefferson is a kind of sun-king. This Augustan tradition links Jefferson's letter to that dawn-sequence in *Tom Jones* where the wise patriarch Allworthy and the sun rise together to survey the well-kept estate of Paradise Hall.[39] Fielding then lifts the mind from man's estate to Nature's God as the eye moves to contemplate the mountains, sea and sky which close the distant prospect. Compared with an English Whig estate, Jefferson's American scene suggests something of the raw and terrible power of the divine in the process of creation. Compared with the Epicurean philosopher in 'the pursuit of happiness', Jefferson constructs himself as a man not so much retreating from the tumult of affairs as being above them.

This was written before the dome was built, but it reveals the visionary purpose. The famous 'head and heart' letter to Maria Cosway is unusual for Jefferson, however, for two reasons. It provides one of the few glimpses of passionate and idealising sensuality in Jefferson's nature. Maria Cosway has acted upon him as some form of Muse. The passionate 'heart' in the letter provides a link, therefore, to those other manifestations of sexuality existing only in icons in the villa – the sleeping Ariadne/Cleopatra in the hall, or Venus and Cupid upon the dining-table. But the letter is unusual also because it is a rare example in Jefferson's work of a sustained and deliberately unresolved irony. The debate between 'heart' (which speaks about 'our own dear Monticello') and head, which seeks to restrain the enthusiasm of the passions, is, as it were, a perpetual conflict within the human psyche. The other major divisions in Jefferson's symbolic history are political: the eternal divide between Whig and Tory, the conflict between inalienable rights and the demands of national unity. But the head-and-heart letter is personal rather than political and more autobiographical than the *Autobiography*. In Jefferson's 'heart' Maria Cosway has replaced his former wife or present daughters at Monticello, joining Jupiter as Juno in the dome-room in Epicurean happiness out of the conflicts of the mundane world. Which fantasy the 'head' denies.

But irony, unresolved, may also become inchoate. The dome, as conceived by Jefferson's imagination before it was built, or as seen now by the visitor from the garden below, appears to signify some form of panoptic and universal vision. The founder of the nation is next to God. But when approached from within the villa, the vision disintegrates before a recalcitrant actuality. Indeed, few Americans ever get inside the dome. The room is not shown on the yellow schoolbus tour of the house. One of the reasons is that the room is so difficult of access – it is too dangerous to go there. It is necessary to make the ascent by two of the ladder-like stairways (which Jefferson did not use) (Plate 15). Even when the villa was serviced by slaves, no purpose could be found for the dome. It remained, therefore, a purely visionary idea, and in practice degenerated into a mere loft – the lumber-hole for the detritus of a house.

Albeit, if the ascent is accomplished, on first sight the dome emerges as one of the most beautiful spaces in the villa, elegant in form, flooded with light. It might be claimed that although Jefferson never worked out in practice how to achieve the ascent to ideal reality, the ideal is unimpaired. But, on closer inspection, even as a belvedere the room is perverse. It has not been raised far enough above the line of the roof, so that some of the windows, instead of looking outwards merely turn inward into the roof space. These introspective lights are currently filled with mirrors, so that instead of perceiving Nature, visitors receive back only a reflection of themselves (as if one were shut within the dome, as if within the inner imagination). If one crosses the room and steps out of the double doors the other side (which match the entrance), instead of entering upon some wider prospect or nobler room, one merely tumbles downwards into a hole within the roof itself. *Du sublime au ridicule il n'y a qu'un pas.* As an icon the dome-room undoes itself, the visionary prospect outside conflicting with some form of psychic derangement within which is self-reflexive, introspective, leading into an empty, downward space.

This is utterly different from the ironic relativities of the Elysian Fields at Stowe. This kind of derangement is far closer to the icons of psychological and cultural *angst* represented, for instance, by another of the European icons which shaped Jefferson's architectural imagination: the column-house in the Désert de Retz (the location of one of Jefferson's romantic perambulations with Maria Cosway). The formal 'influence' of the geometry of the column-house has long been recognised on Jefferson (especially the introduction of oval rooms within a circular form in the Pantheon of the University of Virginia). But the iconography of the Désert has been neglected. As an icon, the column-house expressed a tragic and romantic irony. It is the hub of an Elysian circuit-walk which encompasses, within the ideal world of the garden, an encyclopedia of allusions to architectural culture both in the west and east. The column, if it had been completed, would signify the 'orders' of architecture representative of a universal Order. Since the column stands in isolation, it is also a triumphal signifier. It should, therefore, be surmounted by some figure of epic grandeur. But, instead, the giant column is snapped short. It is a ruin left by some departed civilisation greater in stature than the modern world, and lost to the moderns. The bottom of the column is now a mere domestic dwelling, recalling the houses Piranesi depicts incongruously constructed among the ruins of Rome. Inside the house a tightly spiralling staircase leads upwards into nothing. As in Jefferson's dome-room, mirrors instead of windows function in places to turn the imaginative eye back on itself within. Like the Temple of Modern Virtue at Stowe, the column-house in the Désert is a signifier of the ultimate impossibility of realising imagined perfection. It might also be seen as a indication of the self-awareness of the *ancien régime* of its own imminent demise. In that respect it is the architectural parallel to Rochambeau's officers reading the tragic epic of Ossian around Jefferson's dinner-table.[40]

The sublime dome at Monticello which turns out to be a lumber-room leading only to a downward void has affinities with the column-house. But this is through misachievement, not iconographic irony or tragic self-awareness. Monticello, as a simulacrum of an ideal national culture, does not get it quite right. But then, how could it? Jefferson, just as much as the new nation, is seeking not only to unite plurality into one, but to make that one a perfect ideal. Some form of irony might sustain diversity at least in imaginative form, but the drive for coherence – one folk, one (father)land, one icon – is in direct conflict with the inchoate nature of things. The apparent public progress through the villa from hall to parlour to dining-room to 'most honourable room' to dome, in its pretended unity only serves, ultimately, to emphasise the immense fractures within the culture. Up in the dome-room the black spaces below the level of culture have become invisible to the sublime eye of the Founding Father and sage of Monticello. Here are no racial or political conflicts. We are above the *Sturm und Drang* of things. But once get up into the dome, the supreme signifier of the house and national culture, one finds it to be no more than a beautiful, but empty and useless excrescence. That is not the intention. But that is the effect.

Or, perhaps, after all, there is an awareness in Jefferson that the ideal national culture of Monticello is inchoate. 'Things fall apart, the centre cannot hold.' There is in Jefferson, ultimately, a revulsion against Monticello itself as a failed ideal. Stated thus bluntly the assertion may seem merely perverse, for an anthology might be made of Jefferson's reiterated declarations of love for his 'dear' Monticello, of his desire to turn away from the world and to return to that home he ruined himself to build. But such statements, of course, are two-thousand-year-old, post-Augustan, commonplaces. They are, thus, the appropriate discourse to sustain an ideal public image of a man, who in another characterisation might be seen as an absentee landlord, slave-dealer, ruthless party politician, and (although ostensibly some form of democrat) at heart an admirer of the sophisticated culture of the *ancien régime* in Paris. Of course it was the domestic American farmer, the national type, that Jefferson must be as a model for the folk. But at Monticello, for long parts of the day, Jefferson totally excluded family, friends and farm by retreating into a private space within the villa. But that was not sufficient. Insouciant of impending bankruptcy, he abandoned Monticello, and the upkeep of his estate, to build the retreat of Poplar Forest – a house, in fact, centred solely upon himself, revolving in its daily routine only around himself. One of the grand-daughters sent to Poplar Forest to 'enliven it for him' explained the reason for his retreat:

> The crowd at Monticello of friends and strangers, of stationary or ever-varying guests, the coming and going, the incessant calls upon his own time and attention, the want of leisure that such a state of things entailed as a necessary consequence, the bustle and hurry of an almost perpetual round of company, wearied and harassed him in the end, whatever pleasure he may have taken, and it was some-times great, in the society and conversation of his guests.[41]

A Roman gentleman, like Pliny, possessed villas to which he could retreat even from the villa, but one cannot imagine 'Georgic' Washington retreating from Mount Vernon. The improvement of the estate, he knew, was the essential source of his independent wealth. But Jefferson, having spent a long life in public declaring his desire to return home to Monticello, when he came home found distasteful 'the incessant calls upon his own time and attention'. He got out of it.

This is ostensibly biographical matter, and the reasons for Jefferson's retreat from utopia-become-dystopia are open to psychological speculation. But the retreat from the press of things at Monticello may be read iconographically also. The ways in which the culture within the villa 'wearied and harassed' Jefferson have a relation to the formation of national culture in society outside. One way of interpreting the nature of the 'democratic' revolution in America (and the design of Monticello is ostensibly democratic) is to see the new nation as challenging and demolishing the old hierarchical structures of the monarchical aristocratical system. Indeed, the attack on the monarchical aristocratical system is the centre of Jefferson's paradoxical position in history as an aristocratical Jacobin. If that is so, then the entire culture of the country-house order comes into question, and thus Monticello is not a signifier of what the nation might aspire to (Jefferson's purpose in the use of the house as a public theatre), but a sign of what the nation should reject (and the civil war is only a few decades away). If one detects incoherence within the culture of Monticello itself that incoherence may not be mere Jeffersonian eccentricity. The public theatre of the villa shows the unsustainable competition between cultures within the revolutionary nation itself.

One way in which this cultural competition manifests itself is in the total, ultimately overwhelming, superfluity of artefacts which inundate the ostensibly 'democratic' space of what is in practice the *piano nobile* of the villa. Consider, as one example, the signifiers which form a running subtext round the wall of 'the most honourable' room competing for attention against the four sublime busts in their place of honour. In addition to Washington, Franklin, La Fayette and Jones, there are Tiberius (in bronze) and Captain Lewis (a print), Nero (a bronze) and General Clinton (a miniature), Otho (a bronze) and J. W. Eppes (a miniature), Louis XVI (a medal), General Gates (a miniature), and so on. (Nero *and* Washington in the *locus* of Honour!) Or – to return to the common-room of the parlour – why, (if there is any reason at all) is the emperor Napoleon, whom Jefferson detested, paired with Emperor Alexander whom Jefferson admired, but who, as passionate Christian mystic, was the founder of the detested Holy Alliance? If Monticello is a container which represents what constitutes 'culture' for the new nation, the cup runs over.

Tant pis for the system-making iconographer. There is a ready counter to the argument that there is competitive incoherence in the villa. It is that Monticello is merely a house where Jefferson gathers together the artefacts collected in a long life. It would be absurd to argue that all things should be organised to promulgate a unified ideology. Of course. But, nonetheless, the multiplicity of things, when brought together, constitute a culture, and things will jostle together, willynilly. Since this is unavoidably so, what, accordingly, might the overcrowding of things tell of the compromises, tensions, even contradictions in Jefferson's cultural theatre – the *locus* of self-display?

One crucial instance may suffice iconologically. (Otherwise there could be no end to examples.) After Jefferson left Paris in 1789 he was presented by Louis XVI with a 'miniature picture of the king set in brilliants'. Since American Ambassadors were not permitted to receive gifts from foreign monarchs without the consent of Congress, the gift produced one of Jefferson's characteristic exercises in secrecy. Unbeknown to Congress, William Short sold the 'brilliants' for him to defray his expenses, but Jefferson kept the picture. Later he received an engraving of Louis XVI 'ROI DES FRANÇAIS, RESTAURATEUR DE LA LIBERTÉ' by Charles-Clément Bervic, a gift from the king brought to the United States by Jean Baptiste Ternant. This image (or the earlier gift) was displayed in the parlour of Monticello, listed in the catalogue of paintings as 'a present from the King to Th.J.' and set next to an engraving of Napoleon Bonaparte. But had not Jefferson once declared it to be outrageous that even the mere 'forms' of the monarchical aristocratical system had been adopted by the administration of George Washington? Yet now there is no suggestion of irony in the display in the central commonroom at Monticello of a Bourbon monarch as the restorer of liberty (nor any apparent self-awareness that secretly selling a precious frame but keeping a monarchical image might be a betrayal of selfintegrity). Can one, by contrast, imagine Byron bestowing a place of honour, or any place whatsoever, on any of the Bourbons? One would not necessarily attach iconographical signification to such things if Monticello were merely any old plantation 'home'. But it is Mr. Jefferson's home – a place set on a high hill, like his mind. It is an expression of a cultural ideal, and of an immense self-confidence in that ideal as a national role-model. That things do not cohere in a cultural ideal would not surprise those (sharing the sensibility of Congreve) for whom the Golden Age is always a dream (classical or American). But when, for whatever reason, an ideal order, as it were, ploughs into the inchoate multiplicity of things, how do you move to a solution in which idealism does not dissolve into irony?

Jefferson's attempted solution was withdrawal – a getting away from the inchoate pressure of things and people in the villa, either to his private apartments or to Poplar Forest. But there is also an iconic 'withdrawal' in the creation of alternative and simpler models of symbolic architecture. The 'cloning' of Monticello in Jefferson's late architectural projects develops as a form of rejection of complexity for an ideal simplicity. The campus of the University of Virginia and the hermitage (or Petit Trianon) of Poplar Forest, are places of strictly limited access and function. Both redefine Monticello. In the University, the Pantheon stands to the 'academical village' round the Lawn as the country house used to stand to the organic community of the estate in the old world. It is that 'village' which is glaringly absent at Monticello itself, as it is from the whole of Virginian plantation culture. (One need only set the slave-village of Mulberry Row against the idealisation of a very different America in Timothy Dwight's *Greenfield Hill*.) Hence the need to create another kind of village round the Lawn directly under the prospect of another kind of Monticello, and where iconographic form and cultural purpose might unify. The slave-quarters of Monticello, concealed beneath the inverted *cour d'honneur*, have vanished round the democratical and republican village green (the Lawn), removing at once one of the greatest and most blackly disturbing paradoxes of Monticello – the single-storeyed villa which conceals no less than four hierarchical levels of society. A further simplification of things is embodied in the Pantheon. This is iconographically a derivative from the dome-room of Monticello, but is now made both accessible and functional. The dome at the University was to serve as a planetarium, providing, thus, a God-like perspective for each young American who ascended there; and the drum of the dome was to incorporate the university library, whole and complete in the perfect form of a circle: *e pluribus unum*. Except, of course, that the planetarium was never built, and the perfect, circular form of the secular temple proved utterly inadequate to house the library. Once again the container could not contain.

The iconography of Poplar Forest was simpler yet, for, as a hermitage, it is centred entirely upon Jefferson in retreat, deep into the primeval forest, back to the origins of the nation in the wilderness and back into the traditions of the sacred grove and the Germanic forest as the *locus* of liberty. Here he shut himself away in the imaginary world of his books, and here his needs, and his alone, determined the routine of the house. *Hoc erat in votis*, as the classical ideal had it, but now, in that tradition, Poplar Forest is rather some kind of romantic excrescence. Here the sage walks in the twilight in the garden 'with the owls and bats' for company (so those admiring servants, his granddaughters, tell the story). Rather than signifying the culture of the ancient villa, Poplar Forest resembles Samuel Palmer's or Yeats's lonely tower. But not Thoreau's Walden pond. If Jefferson's distaste for Monticello and withdrawal suggest the exhaustion of the old ideal, it is not replaced by an alternative. He can only think in terms of the very villa culture which overwhelmed him with the press of things as it also bankrupted him by demanding more from his estates than even the free land of America could give.

The need to redefine Monticello, and to withdraw from the problems of Monticello, is indicative of the stress within the cultural ideal Jefferson was seeking to embody for the nation. The traditional, hierarchical culture of the ruling classes in Europe has been, in some way, cobbled on to an emergent (and undefined) culture. The incoherence, the need continually to try to rewrite the inherited icons, is, ultimately, a form of self-contradiction rather than irony. That should not be taken to mean that there was, or is, some formal structure, or ideology expressed through form, which happily brings us ('we, the people') into some kind of unity of being and into that 'Truth' which Jefferson believed could be separated from 'Error'. Nor is there a dialectic, Blakean or Hegelian, by which Monticello might be progressively restructured to serve some 'progressive' end. That is practically absurd. The villa, like any other work of art, is what it is, to be understood in terms of its own formal structures and interrelations. Monticello, thus, as national *Kunstwerk*, has been interpreted here as a kind of mythic structure in the sense that Northrop Frye described myth: as the projection of a vision of human fulfilment, and of the obstacles that stand in the way of that fulfilment. If it were a poem, it would be somewhere between an epic (about the foundation of a new nation, told through a 'master' narrative) and a romance (something fabulous and belonging to the world of dreams). One might suggest also that the epic turns into tragedy, for the story of Monticello is a tale of the ruin of an ideal house, an American Castle Rackrent or Big House of Inver. Between the vision of fulfilment and the obstacles that stand in the way, there is, of course, always contradiction. Or, put another way, there is always a way of telling things – 'diction' which may run *contra* to the way the artist wishes the work of art to be interpreted. How did other voices interpret the villa on its high hill?

5

Writing Monticello

> A house divided against itself cannot stand.
>> Abraham Lincoln, 17 June 1858

Since 'the earth belongs to the living', the past cannot be entailed upon futurity. There is only the Heraclitean flux. Even if it were universally accepted that architectural conventions derive from the permanent forms of Nature and Nature's God (Jefferson's neoPalladian belief) the very concepts 'Nature' and 'God' are subjective, subject to fundamental contestation, and may even be mutually contradictory. Any attempt to 'fix' the meaning of Monticello as an icon defining the culture of the emergent American nation, therefore, cannot establish the definitive and originary Jeffersonian meaning for the villa. There can be no definitive parameters for the multiplicity of interpretations which might be derived from the infinite permutations of the plurality of things and points of view which constitute Monticello and the history of Monticello. All that has been offered in the preceding 'reading' of the villa is one way in: through the English country-house tradition in transpontine translation and in process of indefinite mutation. That historical process, it has been claimed, is that in which Whig philosophy transforms in some way into an undefined (because undefinable) romantic nationalism. The making of Monticello is, thus, a kind of iconographic signifier like the momentary beating of the butterfly's wings in Chaos Theory. There is some kind of connection between this small spot of time and place on a remote Virginian hillside and the subsequent Atlantic tempest of the *Sturm und Drang* of nationalist revolution throughout the European world. But what that relationship is, ultimately, is too complex to be definitively understood.

In that process the emergence of what might be called a 'discourse' of Monticello comes late. By 'discourse' in this context is meant the creation of a web of interrelated texts which control the matrices of interpetation through which the villa is seen and understood. Such a 'discourse' was readily available in villa culture of the ancients, and its variants in the English country-house tradition, and

159

Monticello came out of these as a butterfly out of a chrysalis. Yet Monticello itself did not generate any definitive body of interpretative textuality in Jefferson's lifetime, nor, arguably, until the originary work of Fiske Kimball in the twentieth century. A simple comparison with the 'discourse' of the English country house may illustrate. By the time Jefferson visited the house and gardens at Stowe with John Adams in 1786, Benton Seeley had already produced his authoritative guide: *A Description of the Gardens of Lord Viscount Cobham, at Stow in Buckinghamshire* (1744). This was itself derived from Daniel Defoe's and Samuel Richardson's *A Tour thro' the Whole Island of Great Britain* (version of 1742). Seeley, moreover, to lend status to his guide, quoted on his title page one of the most distinguished panegyrists of Stowe, Alexander Pope. But this was only a small part of a matrix of interrelated texts. They included works by other canonical writers, such as Wiliam Congreve's *Of Improving the Present Time* (1728) and James Thomson's *The Seasons* (*Autumn*, 1744). But equally significant is the fact that the discourse (and ideology) of Stowe was so strongly established that it could readily absorb and turn to didactic use the kind of adverse criticism (of useless ostentation) dialogically voiced in William Gilpin's *A Dialogue upon the Gardens . . . at Stow* (1748). An assured and stabilised 'meaning' for the complex imagery of the garden, therefore, had been swiftly established, and Jefferson on his visit was following a well-trodden itinerary guided (in his case) by Thomas Whately's *Observations on Modern Gardening* (1770).

Although Monticello, from an early period, became part of an American itinerary, it did not acquire that kind of authoritative discourse. There were, of course, self-produced texts by Jefferson which laid down the basis from which such a discourse eventually might be generated. There is, for instance, his personal catalogue of pictures – but compare with Jefferson's ms. the status in England of *Aedes Walpolianae: or a description of the collection of paintings at Houghton Hall* (1752)[1] or Joseph Heely's picture-guide in his *Letters on the Beauties of Hagley* (1777). There is also the transitory catalogue of his library – 'transitory' because the books were sold for the practical purpose of staving off bankruptcy, and with the ideological aim of establishing the basis of national culture for the Library of Congress. But no itinerant visitor to Monticello came, as Jefferson did to houses in England, knowing from authoritative and generally available sources what was to be seen (although many had predetermined ideas of what they would find). Hence the many lists which visitors were compelled to draw up for themselves of what was to be seen in the villa: witness Lavasseur's account of his visit with La Fayette in 1824.[2] These lists were often merely compendia. (They may serve as a salutary warning to iconographers, for later scholarship often constructs meanings to which contemporaries were oblivious. The Seymours, for instance, saw at Monticello an unintelligible 'profusion' of merely 'ornamental' statuary, pictures and curiosities.)[3] Baron de Montlezun's account of Jefferson's collection of the *beaux arts* is a well-known example and important because the Baron belonged to Jefferson's culture and he was on a tour of Presidential homes which took in Madison's Montpelier and Monroe's Highlands. His letter could be the basis of a guidebook, such is the detail, but it is a guidebook which is overwhelmed by the multiplicity of things:

> The portraits of Washington, La Fayette, Adams, Franklin, Walter Raleigh, Amerigo Vespucci, Columbus, Bacon, Locke, Newton, etc., etc... the colossal bust of Mr. Jefferson by [Ceracchi]. It is supported on a broken column, the pedestal of which has for ornament the representation of the twelve tribes of Israel and the twelve signs of the zodiac.... The collection of pictures is precious: among others one sees the Ascension by Poussin, the Holy Family by Raphael, the Flagellation of Christ by Rubens.... The natural history curios are very numerous: they consist of mammoth bones, horns, antlers or tusks of various animals, a head of a mountain goat, petrifactions, crystallisations, minerals, shells, etc.[4]

Those 'etcs.' reduce iconography merely to a neutral list of things.

The reasons why this is so may be merely fortuitous. American culture did not produce a country-house literature in Jefferson's lifetime; but, then, Monticello did not exist in any kind of completed form until 1809. It had long resembled a building-site, like the national capital itself, and was, by 1809, in any case, already lapsing into decay and was subject, as always, to extended periods of absence by its master. After 1826 the estate, and the contents of the villa, were swept away by the disaster of Jefferson's Castle Rackrent-like bankruptcy. The loss by the South of the Civil War (war between the States) was then not only to expose the plantation house to the depredations of the victorious enemy, but also made the southern villa the signifier of southern slavery. In that ambience the useless and insignificant structure of Monticello was only preserved by a Jew (Uriah Levy) who admired Jefferson as a champion of religious liberty. Jefferson's own family, meantime, having sold Monticello, had swiftly abandoned the discomfort and disrepair of Poplar Forest. Its programmatic function for Jefferson in retirement made it an impractical house for anyone else to live in. These are mundane considerations, but against this background Monticello was not likely to easily acquire the kind of significations with which it is now invested.

Against this kind of historical fluidity around Monticello as icon, one might set the fixed point of the Jefferson Memorial in Washington, DC. The Mall, on which it stands, is the iconographical centre of the nation, derived from Le Nôtre's great western vista at Versailles. There the Sun-King sought to express the permanent, natural and divine order of his regime in a formal landscape, and through an elaborate interrelation of architectural ornament. (Like the Lawn of the University of Virginia, the vista at Versailles was given no fixed termination, extending indefinitely into the landscape as the regime extended indefinitely in territory and time.) In English Whig iconography the most obvious 'rewriting' of the landscape of Versailles is the vista from the garden-front of Stowe (Versailles translated as a form of English 'liberty'). Subsequently, in the Mall, Versailles blends with Stowe, as English 'liberty' is now 'republicanised' by the American nation. In this context, the Jefferson Memorial (a domed temple rising above an expanse of water) has become the grandiloquent nationalist redefinition of Viscount Cobham's Temple of Ancient Virtue at Stowe. But, since the architects of the Memorial were learned men, there may be wider allusions yet to the originary tradition. A closer parallel to the Memorial even than the temple at Stowe is the Pantheon *redivivus* in Henry Hoare's emblematic garden at Stourhead. The central deity of this Pantheon is the hero Hercules, allegorised as a type of civic virtue. But, in the national capital, Washington, DC, the gigantic figure of a real American hero, Jefferson, has replaced myth with history. Centred beneath the dome, like George Washington in the rotunda at Richmond, the real Jefferson has taken on the role of the universal figure of Vitruvian Man, the measure of the order of architecture and of the divine cosmos. The dedication of this religious place at a time of war fought for world hegemony in the 1940s would make the Memorial also the ultimate and definitive signifier of what Jefferson called 'the empire for liberty'. The conflicts of the world will be ended by the victory of the Jeffersonian *novus ordo seclorum.* The United States will become the national model for the United Nations of the world. It is a *Weltordnung* to which the later Vietnam memorial was to add a darker, Virgilian, afternote. For the new order has met resistance. *Quae regio in terris nostri non plena laboris?*[5] The official discourse of Jeffersonianism is inscribed (like the discourse of the Temple of Ancient Virtue at Stowe) in tablets of stone in four inscriptions on civic and religious liberty drawn from the Declaration of Independence, the Virginia Statute for Religious Freedom, from the *Notes on the State of Virginia* (attacking the institution of slavery) and from the letter to Samuel Kercheval from Monticello (12 July 1816) on the progressive amelioration of the law and constitution. These are gathered under a classic Whig rubric of the doctrine of 'resistance': 'I have sworn upon the altar of God eternal hostility against every form of tyranny over the mind of man.' The inscription abruptly divides the world into the divinely appointed people of liberty and the lackeys of tyranny. This light and darkness is separated in 'eternal hostility'. It is this dichotomy which Jefferson himself had enunciated to Adams as the universal political and psychic struggle between 'Whig' and 'Tory', but now raised to a level of religious principle on which the universal order is founded. (See pp. 23–4 above.) The utterance has its roots in Miltonic tradition; it is also, self-evidently, part of the koine of post-Miltonic romanticism. (See pp. 22–5 above) Here it becomes, ultimately, a declaration of national mission.

It is remarkable that Jefferson, who was condemned by some in his age as an 'atheist' (that is, a Socinian for whom the laws of Nature and the idea of a Creator are one) is so religiously inspired that he invokes God in four of the five inscriptions, and on nine occasions as 'God', 'Creator', 'Holy Author', the maker of 'Divine Providence' and the inspiration of 'sacred honour'. There is, thus, in the discourse of the Memorial, a strong element of religious mysticism involved with the foundation of the nation. These are the American Mosaic tablets of stone. In one instance, the passage on slavery, Jefferson's public views (his private opinions were alarmist) are grossly misrepresented by selective editing of a kind no objective scholar could accept. His commitment to *apartheid* and his doubts about the place of the negro in the chain of being are written out of the text. This is a religiously corrected and politically corrected Jefferson. New England puritanism has, as it were, made the Virginian plantation holder a pilgrim father. The only allusion to Monticello is in the use of the Pantheon as the architectural signifier. The same form historically provides the basis for Jefferson's rural villa and the Memorial temple in the Mall, although the most obvious allusion is to the Rotunda of the University of Virginia. Jefferson is reduced (and it is a fair reduction) to an architect of one architectural form only. At the same time the icon is given a reductive ideology. There is an attempt to give the essential meaning of Jefferson, as it were, in five resonant soundbites. Monticello, by comparison, is a remote and domestic signifier which represents not the creator of the model order of the national culture, but merely the private man.

A discourse of Monticello emerged in process of history somewhere between the transient state of Monticello in Jefferson's lifetime (as a building-site for forty years, or as a colonial plantation ruined by extravagance) and the nationalised essential Jefferson of the Memorial on the Mall. An appropriate point of entry into that historical process is through the words of the originary pioneer of Jeffersonian architectural studies, Fiske Kimball. Writing in the *Journal of the American Institute of Architects* in 1924 (as Jefferson's reputation rose dolphin-like above the party and civil conflicts of the nineteenth century) Kimball sought to define the meaning of Jeffersonian architecture.[6] For him the key to understanding was in the idea of 'Nature'. (It is, significantly, a favoured Jeffersonian word which was to be later written out of the religious vocabulary of the Jefferson Memorial for it carried too much of the associations of Deism for a Christian nation.) But for Kimball, 'Nature' is the norm to which diversity returns, and he uses his key word with full awareness of its romantic connotations. In grounding his architecture in Nature, Jefferson, Kimball wrote, 'began as a thorough romantic':

> To us, heirs of the romanticism of which he was the American pioneer, there is nothing strange in this, but in his day it was wholly new, even in Europe. From his boyhood home in the watered valley, his spirit yearned toward the heights, with that profound reverence for nature to which he once gave expression at a prospect in the Alpes Maritimes: 'Fall down and worship ...you never saw, nor will ever see such another.'

The commonplaces of European Romanticism – Nature, the Alps, the worship of natural sublimity – blend in Kimball's account with nationalist ideology as Jefferson becomes an American 'pioneer' in discovering the new frontier of sensibility. The Wordsworthian child, in his valley home, 'dreamed of creating' in the American 'wilderness' another order of being on a mountain top. It was Jefferson, in the new world, who, as Kimball represents him, discovered romanticism for Europe.

But Kimball, in romanticising Jefferson, faced what was (for an architectural historian) a 'paradox'. Although Jefferson began as a pioneer of romanticism, yet, Kimball's account continues, the architectural form Jefferson chose was classical and neoPalladian. Since Palladio claimed that architecture is the imitator of Nature, this might seem an obvious way to resolve the romantic/classic 'paradox'. But it is a resolution with which Kimball is not entirely at ease. Kimball's problem is that Jefferson, who is an 'apostle of individualism', nonetheless chose 'as his first master of architecture, Palladio, who passes as the chief representative of dogmatic authority'. The reason why this is so is that Jefferson so much feared the 'anarchy' to which freedom might 'degenerate', that he accepted in its place 'dogmatic authority' to provide stability and order. One extreme ('anarchy') implies the other ('dogma'). But if that is a 'paradox' for an American historian, this conflict between freedom and authority, from a European perspective, might be said to be part of the whole dilemma of romantic history. The romantic dream of unfettered individual 'freedom' (of which Jefferson was the 'apostle'), as it developed in practice, provoked extreme forms of authoritarian reaction. 'Anarchy' and 'tyranny' are commonplace antitheses in the Koine of romanticism (witness Shelley's *The Masque of Anarchy*). But there was a tyranny of the Left as well as of the Right, and often the two are difficult to tell apart. Jacobinism (of which Jefferson was accused) and Bonapartism, Marxist Socialism and National Socialism are all forms of dogmatic authoritarianism spawned by the dialectic of the romantic era.

No one understood Jeffersonian architecture better than Kimball. But if the key to understanding Jefferson's choice of form is the romantic divide between anarchy and order, then there exists a profound *Zerissenheit* in the ideology of Jeffersonian architecture. On the side of order Kimball recognises the argument that what was 'natural' possesses 'authority'. This is one of the fundamental tenets of the neoPalladian and Whig country-house tradition which Jeffersonian national culture rewrites. In that tradition, the material signifier of order (the country house) is represented as natural in form and setting, and thus normative because formally mirroring Nature's God. But, as Kimball recognises, on the other hand, in the romantic epoch, that tradition had changed into something 'wholly new'. There is now a yearning after what had been hitherto inexpressible. It is something which Jefferson could only dream of creating as he launched himself as a pioneer of the spirit into what was literally and metaphorically a new world. The risk, in such a leap, is that the 'pioneer' crosses some unexplored frontier which leads into 'anarchy'. Or, put another way, beyond the frontier there is the great American 'wilderness'. The heart of the matter is whether 'Nature' is representative of God's order, or signifies an ultimate disorder beyond culture.

This romantic *Zerissenheit* in Jefferson is an intrinsic part of his own perception of 'Nature'. It may be seen in the interrelationship between two of the key signifiers in the Monticello landscape: the pyramid, and the 'looming' of the natural landscape in which Jefferson's imagination discovered or created the icon of the pyramid. (See pp. 85–7 and 119–21 above.) On the one hand, there is the originary national sign of the divine order of architecture and of the permanence of the nation thus signified; on the other, there is the actual experience of the Heraclitean flux of things and of the unreliability of human organs of perception. In iconographical terms, the pyramid might be said to belong to the kind of world order represented by the 'classic' art of Nicholas Poussin, and the 'looming' of the Virginian landscape to the 'romantic' instability of the watercolours of J. M. W. Turner. Jefferson, when conducting visitors on the itinerary of the estate, himself drew attention to the paradox. Francis Hall, on his visit of 1817, records that Jefferson explained to him the signification of the 'Egyptian pyramid', but that he pointed out to him also its 'most singular property' for 'on different occasions it looms, or alters its appearance, becoming sometimes cylindrical, sometimes square, and sometimes assuming the form of an inverted cone'.[7] Hall's choice of words indicates that besides listening to Jefferson, he had been reading the *Notes on the State of Virginia* as an authority and that the uncertainties of Jefferson's fragmentary text – 'the measure of a shadow' – were become part of his own interpretative discourse. Subsequently, the romanticisation of the historical process develops further the instability of things, as may be seen in another rewriting (in 1858) of the originary passage from the *Notes on the State of Virginia* in Randall's *Life* of Jefferson:

> To one unacquainted with these optical illusions, they bring unutterable amazement. It is as if he had stepped into a land of

enchantment, where, according to the superstitions of past ages, necromancers or genii were sporting with the forms and consistency of the solid globe. And what must have been the emotions of the former Indian inhabitant – the wild and roving Tuscarora, whose hunting-grounds embraced this region – as he paused, startled in the morning chase, to witness these tremendous transfigurations of the most massive and immobile objects in nature.[8]

For Randall, what should be a permanent form in Nature, 'massive and immobile', is subject to 'transfiguration'. His nineteenth-century scientific positivism knows that these illusions are merely 'optical', but what Randall emphasises here is the relativity of historical interpretation which the scene evokes. His mind invokes the whole span of human history as he sees through the eyes of the primitive savage, now only a 'former inhabitant', then passes through the superstitious mysticism of the European dark ages to emerge into his own self-aware post-Enlightenment romanticism. To which self-awareness one must add now our own view upon Randall himself. If all observers of the natural scene perceive the same phenomena, their place in history and their culture constantly changes the signification of what is seen.

This iconic instability is symptomatic of the difficulty of establishing an assured discourse of Monticello. Which is not to say that there was no attempt to establish a point of view. Just as Jefferson built a 'Grecian temple' in his grounds to direct the eye towards the pyramid, so the villa itself in its location and in its 'suite' of rooms sought to construct an authoritative meaning. There is ample evidence that from the time of the earliest visitors there did develop a kind of Jefferson-approved and reiterated ideology. In its simplest form (and it is often very simple) it emerges as a kind of crude Wordsworthianism. The 'sage of Monticello' (a bizarre, archaic and otherworldly formulation) is wise because he lives close to Nature. He who dwells upon a high mountain is sublime. It is a representation which dates from at least the time of the Chevalier de Chastellux (1782) whose idealisation of the Jeffersonian romantic symposium has already been cited (pp. 141–4 above). The house, wrote de Chastellux, 'shines alone in this secluded spot', and he linked house and host at once to Nature (as a philosophical norm): 'Nature so contrived it, that a Sage and a man of taste should find on his own estate the spot where he might best study and enjoy Her.'[9] This is Monticello as Jefferson would wish it to be seen. Few visitors, for instance, responded more readily to the charm of the 'man on the hill' than Margaret Smith in 1809:[10]

> When I crossed the Ravanna, a wild and romantic little river, which flows at the foot of the mountain, my heart beat – I thought I had entered, as it were the threshold of his dwelling.... At last we reached the summit, and I shall never forget the emotion which the first view of this sublime scenery excited....

So, from the sublimity of this wild and romantic natural landscape, she comes to the master of the prospect:

> I looked upon him, as he walked the top of this mountain, as a being elevated above the mass of mankind, as much in character as he was in local situation.

When Jefferson, all too aware of the neglect of his estate occasioned by his absenteeism and his worsening finances, apologised for the 'wilderness' his visitors saw around them, Margaret Smith overwhelmed his modesty by celebrating him as a patriarch 'in the midst of his children and grandchildren':

> But you have returned and the wilderness shall blossom like the rose and you, I hope, will long sit beneath your own vine and your own fig tree.

Thus, fanned by female panegyric, Jefferson opened the *sanctum sanctorum* of his library to her, and then, whirling her on a ride round and round the mountain (which filled her with a far from sublime terror), he expatiated on 'all his plans for improvement, where the roads, the walks, the seats, the little temples were to be placed'. He still envisaged, therefore, adding more to the iconography of his villa in the sublime wilderness. In vain.

This kind of adulation of the romantic sublime was part of the mystique of Monticello. The 'steep, savage hill' which retarded George Ticknor's ascent, was none the less an 'ascent to Paradise' through the 'ancient forest' (the sign and refuge of the romantic *Urvolk*). For Benjamin Rush, the mountain was 'Olympus', or a 'Mecca' for the American pilgrim; a 'fountain in the desert' for Lieutenant Francis Hall; 'the up-hill path to fame' for the Seymours. On the hill at Monticello one might dwell, wrote John H. B. Latrobe, 'in the silence and solitude of its lofty summit, above the contentions and meannesses of his fellow men and gaze down upon this world which they inhabit, having his mind elevated by its glorious perfection to his Creator and Judge'. The 'noble oaks', although blasted by hurricanes and decaying from age, became natural correlatives to the godlike quality of the ancient hero of Monticello, and Wirt's famous eulogy to the dead Jefferson was ultimately to pile Pelion on Ossa by transforming the sublime philosopher and patriot on his mountain into a signifier of the nation itself:

> From this summit, the Philosopher was wont to enjoy that spectacle, among the sublimest of Nature's operations, the looming of the distant mountains; and to watch the motions of the planets, and the greater revolution of the celestial sphere. From this summit, too, the patriot could look down, with uninterrupted vision, upon the wide expanse of the world around, for which he considered himself born; and upward, to the open and vaulted Heavens, which he seemed to approach, as if to keep him continually in mind of his high responsibility.[11]

In Keatsian phrase, James Silk Buckingham, quoting Wirt in his own account of Monticello, could do no more than assent to the 'truth and beauty' of this apotheosis.[12]

This is, as it were, the approved ideology of Monticello, even though it lacks the canonical authority which comes from the coincidence of great writers, or the establishment, even, of the official discourse of a guide (although Wirt's eulogy, which praises Jefferson room by room through Monticello, comes close to a kind of panegyrical guide). But, by comparison with the discourse of Stowe (used here as a benchmark) these romantic fictions about Monticello are remarkably imprecise and mystical. Their emphasis is on the separation from the everyday world of the man on the mountain – 'as immoveable as the mountain on which he dwells' (as the Seymours praised him). The wilderness and the difficult ascent to Jefferson are correlatives for *his* distance and *his* elevation. Thus, when Wirt writes that the dead Jefferson 'considered himself born' from 'the world', the implication of the rhetoric is that Jefferson was not of our world. Heaven seems Jefferson's natural element. This distance from common humanity, this ascent and apotheosis has a strong romantic element. In so far as it mythologises Jefferson, it suggests a continuity in symbolism between the new world and the old religious sublime with which the *ancien régime* in Europe invested itself. The symbolic order is rewritten, but its basis remains the same. In the palaces of Europe the enfilade of state rooms led to the great man. In the new world the enfilade now finds its equivalent in the difficult progression of the visitor through the American wilderness; the ceremonial staircase of the old order has been replaced by the ascent of the mountain; the old Augustan or Apolline imagery is replaced by the natural 'paradise', 'temple' and 'vaulted heaven' of romantic panegyric. It might be claimed by American patriotism that this naturalising of hierarchy represents the truly spontaneous praise of the folk, compared with the false adulation bestowed on the monarchical aristocratical system in Europe. But the cult of personality was not discouraged by the man on the mountain. On the contrary, it is an essential part of his own discrimination between the visionary ideal of his America, and that other America of vicious class and ideological division beyond the *cordon sanitaire* of the hurricane-torn forest of ancient oaks. As early as 1782 he had represented himself to de Chastellux as 'a Philosopher, retired from the world and public business, because he loves the world only insofar as he can feel that he is useful, and because the temper of his fellow citizens is not as yet prepared either to face the truth or to suffer contradiction'.[13] Thereafter this became the approved discourse of Monticello. On the mountain one finds truth and Jefferson. Beyond, there is 'contradiction'.

The degree of abstract detachment here is necessary because the materiality of things will not sustain this romantic idealism. Jefferson's apology to Margaret Smith for the rack and ruin of the estate relates to intrusive, real-world problems, and nothing is more symptomatic of that 'whirligig' quality in Jefferson which his enemies criticised, than the virtually bankrupt Jefferson rushing through the wilderness expatiating to her on his plans for yet more building (which plans were to include Poplar Forest). His *ancien régime* French furniture was threadbare; a flood swept away the estate mill on which he had expended a small fortune; the exigencies of the unstable agricultural market and the crazy Virginian economy of promissory notes would have undermined even a serious attempt to retrench and reform. But there was never any serious attempt to restrain his hunger of the architectural imagination. The end of the road was to be the desperate appeal to the nation to save the sage by purchasing Monticello in a national lottery. It was a bizarre attempt to link the purity of republican virtue to the independent greed of the capitalist economy, and failed. The idea of the 'sage' contemplating 'Nature' from his lofty mountain can only be sustained, therefore, at a level of abstraction which has no eye for the contradictory materiality of the landscape. But the problem was that visitors could not escape the materiality of the wilderness. To reach Monticello involved a long, perplexing and strenuous journey across terrain in places little removed from its primeval state, and even the estate, by Jefferson's neglect, Mrs Seymour noted, was returning to 'the wilderness and solitude'. It was a solitude from which the original inhabitants had somehow disappeared, for the only signs of aboriginal culture were the artefacts preserved in the museum of the villa. But the presence of numerous negroes, and 'mongrel negroes' (as La Rochefoucauld-Liancourt noted) provoked frequent comment. There was only one source of the 'mongrels'. They were the product of the prostitution of black slave women to white property-owners. The approach to the villa was by way of the 'outhouses' of the slaves, better at Monticello than elsewhere, as Margaret Smith's apology records, 'but to an eye unaccustomed to such sights, they appear poor and their cabins form a most unpleasant contrast with the place that rises so near them'. The indigent poor increased 'in population more rapidly than the white', Jefferson told Augustus Foster, and his conversation with Foster shows that his opinions on negro improvidence and intellectual inadequacy had not improved since the *Notes on Virginia*. Nor had his fear of civil war and mutual genocide lessened. In a remarkable outburst to the Quaker Isaac Briggs at the time of 'the Missouri question' he exclaimed that nothing had been accomplished towards 'improving the condition of this poor, afflicted, degraded race'. Instead, 'our land' (meaning the land of the whites) was moving rapidly towards 'the horrors of civil war, embittered by local jealousies and mutual recriminations. Bloodshed, rapine and cruelty will soon roam at large, will desolate our once happy land and turn the fruitful field into a howling wilderness.'[14] From Nature as a cultural norm, expressed by the form of Monticello, one has here imaginatively degenerated to the originary wilderness itself – not the divine *paradeisos* but a place of horror, rapine and cruelty. To return to Fiske Kimball's romantic designation, it is a place of 'anarchy'.

To the degraded negroes and mongrels, the second British war added indigent whites, riddled with typhus and ague, discharged without pay and unable to buy food – so Francis Gray noted in 1815. The Duke of Saxe-Weiner-Eisenal's account of a visit ten years later is abruptly divided between a romantic discourse which teaches him to admire 'the prospect on the mountains' and an estate-owner's practicality which makes him note the desolation of a countryside where, Monticello apart, there are only 'miserable log houses'. Some, like de Chastellux, became lost among the tracks of this desolate countryside (despite possessing an eye instructed for military exigencies). Others, like La Rochefoucauld-Liancourt, observed the exhaustion of the very soil of Virginia upon which the country-house order depended. This is the Virginia of John Taylor's *Arator* (1813). 'The hardy sons of the forest' had once converted 'a wilderness into a paradise,' Taylor wrote, but corrupted now by rack-renting overseers, the corruptions of capitalism and bad management of the estate, the 'terrible facts' of the situation were tearing the people from their 'natal spot'. 'They view it with horror, and flee from it,' so that 'emigration, and not improvement' will lead 'to an ultimate recoil from this exhausted resource, to an exhausted country.'[15]

Thus, for those visitors who were disenchanted, the long, steep climb up to Monticello was not an ascent of the high hill of Truth but a final sign of Jefferson's disregard for those unpleasant realities in the state of Virginia which he chose to overlook in the pursuit of indefinite prospects. The sceptical George Ticknor did not discover a 'sage' at the top of the hill in 1815, but was reminded rather of Henry Fielding's eccentric recluse, the 'Man of the Mountain'. He judged Jefferson to be only a 'notional philosopher', 'curious' in those notions, 'extraordinary' in character and so bizarre in his dress (in his imitation of Franklin as a homespun American icon) that were he wise he might be laughed out of his eccentricity. The British diplomat, Augustus John Foster, in 1807 thought of Jefferson as a kind of transpontine German romantic (and, like Ticknor, noted the affectation of Jefferson's contempt for dress). But, the diplomat noted, the Germanic dreamer was, paradoxically, also a ruthless politician:

In conversation…he was visionary and loved to dream, eyes open, or, as the Germans say, 'zu schwärmen', and it must be owned that America is the paradise for 'Schwärmers', futurity there offering a wide frame for all that the imagination can put into it. If he lived, however, on illusions and mystic philanthropical plans for the benefit of mankind in the country, or in his bed, he was not the less awake or active in taking measures to ensure the triumph of himself and his party at the capital of the Union....[16]

Samuel Whitcomb found him 'rapid, varying, volatile' in converse, a view which fits too with that headlong descent of the mountain with Margaret Smith as he expatiated on his visionary schemes. This is Jefferson as Irving's William the Testy, a Laputan philosopher whose mind is filled by 'perpetual whirlwinds and tornadoes'. Perhaps most remarkable of all is Foster's account of meeting a naked-footed boy in the drawing room. This may have been mere chance, but Foster at once goes on to establish Jefferson as a kind of new-world Blake. He 'would, I dare say, if he could have ventured it without ridicule, have been for a still greater degree of nakedness, so fond was he of leaving nature as unconfined as possible in all her works'. Jefferson's romanticism, if left to itself, is on the frontier of running wild.

Not all the anecdotes can be relied on. The very orientation of Monticello spins round the compass between different accounts, and the print of a British horseshoe in the hall seen by one visitor has as much substance as the billiard table in the dome-room seen by another. But there is an immense gap between the 'sage' of Monticello of the approved ideology and the slovenly, Blakean eccentric twirling on his notorious 'whirligig' chair, who was to be overwhelmed eventually by the collapse of his own and the Virginian economy. Is the landscape he contemplates from his mountain-top Nature as a philosophical norm, or the 'howling wilderness' threatening the end of civilisation as Jefferson understands it?

But, like the new nation, Monticello was never an achieved and fixed thing. It was first a projection upon futurity by Jefferson's imagination, then a project in decay. No less than three decades into the scheme Anna Thornton in 1802 was invited to examine Jefferson's 'plan' for the villa – now to be completed 'next summer'. It was a timetable she was (correctly) unable to accept, for, 'he has altered his plan so frequently, pulled down and rebuilt, that in many parts without side it looks like a house going to decay from the length of time that it has been erected'. Despite Jefferson's great expenditure, this 'whimsical and droll' house is 'a place you wou'd rather look at now and then than live at. Mr. J. has been 27 years engaged in improving the place, but he has pulled down and built up again so often, that nothing is compleated, nor do I think ever will be.'[17] All accounts of Jefferson as an architect quote his statement that 'architecture is my delight, and putting up and pulling down, one of my favourite amusements'. This is exactly what Anna Thornton describes, but rather than praising Jefferson for his architectural ambition, she indicates instead the fundamental instability of a project conceived in this way. It decays even in the erection. But read as a symbolic (rather than practical) statement, Jefferson's passion for 'putting up and pulling down' suggests there is a radical disruption in him between (in Kimball's terms) a desire for the 'classic' permanence implicit in achieved architectural form and a 'romantic' imagination which, committed to revolution as the only permanent phenomenon ('the earth belongs to the living'), can never rest with that completed form – indeed, can bring nothing to completion.

Accordingly, the lovingly restored house known to visitors today never existed as it is now seen. The disordered villa as it then was is the objective correlative for the Protean Jefferson seen by his contemporaries. What was conceptually ripened was physically always tending to rot. For Edward Thornton in 1802 Monticello was already a house in 'a state of commencement of decay'; for John Dix (c. 1820) 'the dwelling...like its illustrious occupant is fast tottering to decay'. The fine *ancien régime* furniture had become battered (by generations of children and visitors), the terraces were rotten, the estate mill swept away. By the end of his life Jefferson was merely hanging on to the estate in bankruptcy. After his death accounts of the overwhelming dilapidation of things are so frequent that it would be tedious to multiply examples. But the Reverend Stephen Higginson Tyng's account of the decay even of Jefferson's commemorative obelisk may serve as a marker of the end of that process. The ruined obelisk for Tyng, writing in 1840, was not a subject for regret, but, rather, an icon of everything that was wrong with Jefferson and his culture:

the battered, defaced, and broken stone, appeared but an illustration of the character of him whom it commemorates, as it now appears in the eyes of men, while the desolation around would exhibit the ruin and darkness he would have spread upon the world abroad. It was a suitable commemoration of the man who set himself against the Lord of hosts.[18]

This is a comment upon the one icon at Monticello which Jefferson inscribed. Unlike the obelisk at Chiswick, which Jefferson had referred to as 'useless', the obelisk at Monticello recorded for posterity the three great achievements of his life for which he wished to be remembered: the Declaration of Independence, the Virginia Statute for Religious Freedom, and his fathering of the University of Virginia. It is a highly specific icon, therefore, even if not 'fixed' by the inscription, for one can never break the silence of the omitted reference to the Presidency. But the decay even of that sign (16 years only after Jefferson's death), the defacement of the inscription and the utter denial by the Reverend Tyng of everything that Jefferson claimed for himself constitute one of the clearest examples of the transitory nature of even the most apparently 'fixed' iconography. For Tyng, Jefferson is an American Ozymandias:

> Round the decay
> Of that colossal wreck, boundless and bare,
> The lone and level sands stretch far away.

Tyng's condemnation of one of the most crucial signifiers at Monticello might not seem the obvious termination of a study of Jefferson and the romantic nation. It is a denial of the essential claims by Jefferson for the value of his life. A patriotic conclusion should be, rather, the celebration of the patriot himself as a national icon: the figure to emerge in the twentieth century as the canonical father of American architecture; canonised architecturally and textually in the Memorial in Washington, DC. Compare with Tyng the conclusion of Merrill D. Peterson's Viking edition of Jefferson (a provocatively Anglo-Saxon title for a series). For Peterson, this 'essential' collection of Jefferson's writings ends with the famous letter to Roger Weightman from Monticello, 24 June 1826. In the letter (written for posterity) Jefferson celebrates that among the living there yet remain 'the remnant of that host of worthies' of 1776 who by taking up 'the sword' for 'our country' had sent forth 'the signal of arousing men to burst the chains under which monkish ignorance and superstition had persuaded them to bind themselves'. Peterson's essential Jefferson establishes himself by his last words as the national figurehead of La Fayette's visit to Monticello in 1824 where these essays began. He is an American worthy, a nationalist who is a celebrant of an armed, revolutionary and romantic revolt.

This is not an American icon to be commemorated by a stone 'battered, defaced, and broken' – which is Tyng's signifier of his essential Jefferson. But to deny Tyng's image of this other Jefferson, whose home at Monticello represents everything that had failed in Jeffersonian culture, and to return instead to the flag-waving celebration of 1824 would be to deny the very indefiniteness, the sense of continual change, the 'looming' of the Jeffersonian landscape. Neither the letter for posterity to Weightman, nor Tyng upon Jefferson, can constitute a termination, for the icon is made only to be broken, then reconstituted again. There is only the process of what Renan called the daily plebiscite which constitutes a 'nation'. How do 'we' (whoever 'we' are) imagine the nation? By what signs do 'we' constitute it, or recognise it? To this imaginative process of cultural formation and re-formation there can be no end, only the 'indefiniteness' of that symbolic landscape which Jefferson saw (in the University of Virginia) as the architectural sign of universal enquiry. All of us should be free to make that enquiry. Each generation may seek to separate what each of us hold to be 'Truth' from 'Error'. That, at least, might be claimed as a a truly Jeffersonian principle to be extracted from the complexities of history. But, in the words of a late romantic ironist, 'the truth is never pure, and rarely simple'.

Notes

1 The Pilgrimage to Monticello

1. Cited by E. J. Hobsbawm, *The Age of Revolution: Europe 1789–1848* (London: Sphere Books, 1973/1962) p. 164.
2. The best account of the iconography of La Fayette's tour of the United States is S. J. Idzerda, A. C. Loveland, M. H. Miller, *Lafayette, Hero of Two Worlds: The Art and Pageantry of His Farewell Tour of America, 1824–1825* (Hanover and London: the Queen's Museum, 1989). There is a substantial bibliography. There are good illustrations also in M. Klamkin, *The Return of Lafayette 1824–1825* (New York: Charles Scribner's Sons, 1975). Contemporary accounts are reprinted in E. E. Brandon, *Lafayette, Guest of the Nation: a Contemporary Account of the Triumphal Tour of General Lafayette through the United States in 1824–1825, as Reported by the Local Newspapers*, 3 vols (Oxford, Ohio: Oxford Historical Press, 1950–57). Also useful is J. B. Nolan, *Lafayette in America Day by Day* (Baltimore: Johns Hopkins University Press, 1934). I have drawn particularly on the contemporary newspaper (and other) material reprinted in 'General La Fayette's Visit to Monticello and the University' in *The Virginia University Magazine*, IV, 3 (December, 1859) 113–25; Auguste Levasseur, *Lafayette in America, in 1824 and 1825*, translated from the French (2 vols, 1829), and Jane Blair, Cary Smith, 'The Carysbrook Memoir', Wilson Miles Cary Memorial Collection (University of Virginia Ac. No. 1378) pp. 55–62. These have been supplemented by the newspapers on file at the International Center for Jefferson Studies, Charlottesville. For analysis of the influence of La Fayette's tour on forming national consciousness in the USA, see F. Somkin, *Unquiet Eagle: Memory and Desire in the Idea of American Freedom, 1815–1860* (Ithaca: Cornell University Press, 1967) and L. Kramer, *Lafayette in Two Worlds: Public Cultures and Personal Identities in an Age of Revolution* (Chapel Hill and London: University of North Carolina Press, 1996).
3. Intense emotion was an expected part of public symbolism, cf. La Fayette at the tomb of Washington: 'gazing intently on the receptacle of departed greatness [La Fayette] fervently pressed his lips to the door of the vault, while tears filled the furrows in [his] cheeks. The key was now applied to the lock – the door flew open, and discovered the coffins, strewed with flowers and evergreens. The general descended the steps, and kissed the leaden cells...then retired in an excess of feeling which language is too poor to describe.' *Niles' Weekly Register*, cited in Idzerda, op. cit. n. 2, p. 79.
4. S. Balaye (ed.), *De L'Allemagne*, 2 vols (Paris: Garnier-Flammarion, 1968) I, 81.
5. Levasseur provides an account both of the iconography he found of significance in the villa of 'the sage of Monticello', and of the

conversations of Jefferson and La Fayette. He was particularly aware of the gradation of the orders of architecture in the villa and of the importance given to the busts of Franklin, John Paul Jones, La Fayette and Washington. He also paid close attention to what he called the 'museum' in the hall, and to the relics of the Indian chief Tecumseh (see pp. 132–5 below). Conversation in the villa returned repeatedly to the issue of slavery. The French visitors were unconvinced by the southern slaveholders who argued that the negroes were 'an inferior species of men' whose liberty would be injurious, both to the whites (who would be threatened by 'the greatest misfortunes') and also to the negroes whose ignorance would lead them to idleness and 'excess'. La Fayette argued for repatriation of the negroes to Liberia. Another account of the visit is provided by Cary Smith (op. cit. n. 2) who, from a woman's point of view, recounts the problems of a house full of French-speaking guests in a mainly Anglophone society.

6.   P. Scott, *Temple of Liberty: Building the Capitol for a New Nation* (New York: Oxford University Press, 1995) p. 3.

7.   The Greek nationalist rising was a not uncommon theme of the tour. 'Greece regenerated' was toasted in Philadelphia, and at Mobile a triumphal arch incorporated a Greek flag with the flags of Mexico and the South American republics. The Harvard College Phi Beta Kappa Society toasted *'The sons of classic Greece* – whose ancestors shed an imperishable lustre on the military and literary world, now bravely contending against fearful odds for independence; may they find among their natives a Washington, and among their allies a Lafayette, to lead them on to victory, to glory, and a *free government!'* It is probable that Byron's decision to fit out his own ship for Greece (the *Bolivar*) was inspired by La Fayette's famous declaration in the war of 1776 'I will fit out and equip a vessel at my own expense.' More generally, see E. M. Earle, 'American Interest in the Greek Cause, 1821–1827, *AHR*, XXXIII (1927) 44–63 and S. A. Larrabee, *Hellas Observed: the American Experience of Greece, 1775–1865* (New York: New York University Press, 1957).

8.   S. Schama, *Citizens: a Chronicle of the French Revolution* (London: Viking Penguin, 1989) pp. 500–13 on 'Sacred Spaces'. Accounts of the Fête estimate that 150 000 citizens spontaneously created for the celebration the arena with its great triumphal arch and 'Altar of the Fatherland'. Helen Maria Williams enthused at the 'sublime spectacle' of old men, women and children crowding around the procession. The climax was La Fayette's administration to the federalists of the oath which instituted a week of festivity.

9.   People not free were less welcome. The *Virginia Herald* carried a notice during La Fayette's progress to Fredericksburg that 'All coloured people are warned they are not to appear.' La Fayette's sympathy for the cause of emancipation and for the Indians was a constant source of embarrassment, as was his willingness to travel on the Lord's Day.

10.   I am indebted to E. Kedourie, *Nationalism* (London: Hutchinson, rev. edn, 1961) who cites Turgot: 'It is only through turmoil and

destruction that nations expand'; Fichte's definition of 'a true and proper war – a war of subjugation', which leads to advances in civilisation; and Herder, 'Only amid storms can the noble plant flourish' – 'the seed' 'when irrigated with blood seldom fails to shoot up to an unfading flower'. Bismarck's phrase *Blut und Eisen* (from Max von Schendorf) occurs in a speech to the Prussian House of Deputies, 1886, asking that the executive be given 'the strongest possible military power'. In which context one may place Jefferson's assertion that republican revolution was 'worth rivers of blood, and years of desolation' (to John Adams, 4 September 1823).

11. For the evolution of Independence Day as a national celebration, see Somkin (op. cit. n. 2) and L. Travers, *Celebrating the Fourth: Independence Day and the Rites of Nationalism in the Early Republic* (Amherst: University of Massachusetts Press, 1997). Typical of the millennial mysticism of the orations is John Quincy Adams in 1837: 'Is it not that, in the chain of human events, the birth-day of the nation is indissolubly linked with the birth-day of the Saviour... and gave to the world the first irrevocable pledge of the fulfillment of the prophecies, announced directly from Heaven at the birth of the Saviour....' (Somkins, p. 204). For millennialism in American culture, see (among others) L. Baritz, *City on a Hill: A History of Ideas and Myths in America* (New York: Wiley, 1964); E. L. Tuveson, *Redeemer Nation: the Idea of America's Millennial Role* (Chicago: University of Chicago Press, 1968); E. A. Smith (ed.), *The Religion of the Republic* (Philadelphia: Fortress Press, 1971); C. Strout, *The New Heavens and New Earth: Political Religion in America* (New York: Harper & Row, 1974); S. Bercovitch, 'The Typology of America's Mission', *AQ* 30 (1976) 135–55; N. O. Hatch, *The Sacred Cause of Liberty: Republican Thought and the Millennium in Revolutionary New England* (New Haven: Yale University Press, 1977) R. H. Bloch, *Visionary Republic: Millennial Themes in American Thought, 1756–1800* (Cambridge: Cambridge University Press, 1985); and see also Looby, op. cit. n. 30, p. 225, n. 21.

12. Cited by H. Honour, *The European Vision of America* (Cleveland, Ohio: Cleveland Museum of Art, 1975) p. 220.

13. Jefferson wrote in his *Autobiography* that it was a time of 'enormities which demoralized the nations of the world, and destroyed, and is yet to destroy, millions and millions of its inhabitants. There are three epochs in history, signalized by the total extinction of national morality. The first was of the successors of Alexander, not omitting himself: The next, the successors of the first Caesar: The third, our own age.' Crimes, cruelties and evils passed from France 'to Europe, and finally America'. A. A Lipscomb and A. E. Bergh (eds), *The Writings of Thomas Jefferson.* (20 vols, Washington, DC: Thomas Jefferson Memorial Association, 1903) cited hereafter as *Writings*, I. 152 and 150.

14. *Writings*, I, 156.

15. *Writings*, I, 158.

16. *On Nationality* (Oxford: Clarendon Press, 1995).

17. *Metahistory: the Historical Imagination in Nineteenth-Century Europe* (Baltimore: Johns Hopkins University Press, 1973).

18. *The Enlightenment in America* ((New York, Oxford University Press, 1976). See also A. Koch (ed.), *The American Enlightenment: the Shaping of American Experience and a Free Society* (New York: Braziller, 1965); H. S. Commager, *Jefferson, Nationalism, and the Enlightenment* (New York: Braziller, 1975) and *The Empire of Reason: How Europe Imagined and America Realized the Enlightenment* (London: Weidenfeld and Nicholson, 1978); J. R. Pope, 'Enlightenment and the Politics of American Nationalism' in R. Porter and M. Teich (eds), *The Enlightenment in National Context* (Cambridge: Cambridge University Press, 1981) pp. 192–214; R. A. Ferguson, 'The American Enlightenment, 1750–1820' in S. Bercovitch and C. R. Patell (eds), *The Cambridge History of American Literature* (Cambridge: Cambridge University Press, 1994) pp. 347–537.

19. H. Kohn, *The Idea of Nationalism* (New York: Macmillan, 1944).

20. *Individualism and Nationalism in American Ideology* (Cambridge, Mass.: Harvard University Press, 1964); *Nationalism: Five Roads to Modernity* (Cambridge, Mass: Harvard University Press, 1992).

21. Kramer, op. cit. n. 2.

22. Thomas Paine, *Common Sense* (ed.), I. Kramnick (Harmondsworth, Pelican, 1996), pp. 65 & 97; Rousseau, 'Considerations' ch. 4, 'Education'.

23. *The Radicalism of the American Revolution* (New York: Alfred A. Knopf, 1992) p. 222. J. P. Greene states that, with the exception of 'a few dissenters, most historians have agreed ... nationalism was a result, not a cause, of America's war for "national liberation" in 1775–83.' *Imperatives, Behaviours and Identities: Essays in Early American Cultural History* (Charlottesville and London: University Press of Virginia, 1992) p. 290. The word 'invented' is taken from G. Wills, *Inventing America: Jefferson's Declaration of Independence* (New York: Doubleday, 1978). See also J. M. Murrin, ' "A Roof Without Walls": The Dilemma of American National Identity' in R. Beeman *et al.* (eds), *Beyond Confederation: Origins of the Constitution and American National Identity* (Chapel Hill: University of North Carolina Press, 1987) pp. 333–48; P. C. Hoffer, 'The Constitutional Crisis and the Rise of a Nationalistic View of History in America, 1786–1788', *New York History* 52 (1971) 305–23; L. Banning, 'Republican Ideology and the Triumph of the Constitution, 1789 to 1793' *WMQ* 3, XXXI (1974) 167–88. In orientating myself in relation to the immense literature on the revolution I have found particularly useful P. S. Onuf, 'Reflections on the Founding: Constitutional Historiography in Bicentennial Perspective', *WMQ* 3, XLVI (1989) 341–75 and C. Gordon, 'Crafting a Useable Past: Consensus, Ideology, and Historians of the American Revolution', ibid, 671–95; J. Appleby, 'A Different Kind of Independence: The Postwar Restructuring of the Historical Study of Early America', *WMQ*, 3, L (1993) 245–67; E. Countryman, 'Indians, the Colonial Order, and the Social Significance of the American Revolution', *WMQ* 3, LIII (1996) 342–62 and *Americans: a Collision of Histories* (London: I. B. Tauris, 1997).

24. 'An Oration on the Political Situation of the United States of America in the Year 1789' in *The Miscellaneous Works of David Humphreys*, 1804, p. 342.

25. See J. M. Smith (ed.), *The Republic of Letters: the Correspondence between Thomas Jefferson and James Madison, 1776–1826*, (New York and London: W. W. Norton & Company, 1995) p. 1760.

26. Arieli, op. cit. n. 20, p. 289, quoting Emerson.

27. Adolf Hitler, declaring war on the USA.

28. See *Greenfield Hill*, (1794) which forecasts the coming of 'a new Messiah' who will bring 'the renovating morn' to Europe and Asia: 'One blood, one kindred, reach from sea to sea;/One language spread; one tide of manners run;/One scheme of science, and of morals one;/And GOD's own Word the structure and the base;/One faith extend, one worship, and one praise' (VII, 656–60); and Joel Barlow *The Columbiad*, X (1807) which envisions the 'Assimilation and final union of all languages' and 'a general Congress of all nations' formed on the example of the USA. Dwight's *The Conquest of Canaan* (1785) declares that mankind's 'blissful Eden' will be recovered by the American people, first in the new world 'by heaven design'd/The last retreat for poor, oppress'd mankind'; then in the extension of the American 'empire from sea to sea' until finally 'one vast household' unites the enlightened globe (I, 755–8; V, 184; X, 481–2). David Humphreys, writing in the same tradition, is the first writer I know to see the United States as a future world policeman opposed to the development of socialist ideas, see *A Poem on the Future Glory of the United States of America* and the 'Address to the People of the United States of America' prefacing *A Poem to the Industry of the United States of America* in his *Miscellaneous Works* (1804). Romantic nationalism, thus, assimilates 'enlightened' cosmopolitanism so that the nation cloned becomes the model to be imitated by the rest of humanity. The relationship of this vein of nationalist millennianism to Romano-British sources is examined by W. C. Dowling, *Poetry and Ideology in Revolutionary Connecticut* (Athens & London: University of Georgia Press, 1990) and the relationship between nationalism, imperialism and cosmopolitanism by A. Pagden, *Lords of the World: Ideologies of Empire in Spain, Britain, and France, c. 1500–c. 1800* (New Haven: Yale University Press, 1995).

29. Quotations from the preface to the 'new edition' of 1794 commenting on the edition of 1789.

30. See Noah Webster, *Dissertations on the English Language, with Notes, Historical and Critical* (1789) and Walter Channing, 'Essay on American Language and Literature', *North American Review*, I (September 1815) 307–14. For the politics of American English see D. Simpson, *The Politics of American English, 1776–1850* (Oxford: Oxford University Press, 1986). For the history of the rise of literary/cultural nationalism, see B. T. Spencer, *The Quest for Nationality: an American Literary Campaign* (Syracuse, New York: Syracuse University Press, 1957); R. B. Nye, *The Cultural Life of the New Nation* (London: Hamish Hamilton, 1960); K. Silverman, *A Cultural History of the American Revolution* (New York: Thomas Y. Cromwell & Co., 1976); L. Ziff, *Literary Democracy: the Declaration of Cultural Independence in America* (Harmondsworth: Penguin, 1982); T. Gustafson, *Representative Words: Politics, Literature, and*

the American Language, 1776–1865 (Cambridge: Cambridge University Press, 1992); M. P. Kramer, *Imagining Language in America: From the Revolution to the Civil War* (Princeton: Princeton University Press, 1992) and C. Looby, *Voicing America: Language, Literary Form, and the Origins of the United States* (Chicago and London: Chicago University Press, 1996). The issue of language has been fundamentally reopened by W. C. Spengemann, *A New World of Words: Redefining Early American Literature* (New Haven: Yale University Press, 1994).

31. Smith, op. cit. n. 25 has a good introductory discussion of Jefferson's passionately binary rhetoric.

32. I am indebted to L. K. Kerber, *Federalists in Dissent: Imagery and Ideology in Jeffersonian America* (Ithaca: Cornell University Press, 1970); R. K. Matthews, *The Radical Politics of Thomas Jefferson: a Revisionist View* (Lawrence: University Press of Kansas, 1984); R. J. Twomey, *Jacobins and Jeffersonians: Anglo-American Radicalism in the United States, 1790–1820* (New York: Garland, 1989) and S. Elkins and E. McKitrick, *The Age of Federalism* (Oxford and New York: Oxford University Press, 1993).

33. Ed. I. Kramnick (Harmondsworth: Penguin, 1976) p. 122.

34. Cited in W. H. Pierson, *American Buildings and their Architects: the Colonial and Neoclassical Styles* (Oxford and New York: Oxford University Press, 1986/1970) p. 212.

35. Ibid. pp. 286–7.

36. Jefferson's involvement with the development of Washington, DC, is documented in S. K. Padover (ed.), *Thomas Jefferson and the National Capital ... 1783–1818* (Washington, DC: United States Printing Office, 1946) and P. F. Norton, 'Thomas Jefferson and the Planning of the National Capital' in W. H. Adams (ed.), *Jefferson and the Arts: an Extended View*, (Washington, DC: National Gallery of Art, 1976) pp. 187–232. The iconography of the Capitol is examined by Scott, op. cit. n. 6 and V. G. Fryd, *Art and Empire: The Politics of Ethnicity in the U.S. Capitol, 1815–1860* (New Haven: Yale University Press, 1992). For the history of the inception of the national capital, see K. R. Bowling, *The Creation of Washington, D.C.: The Idea and Location of the American Capital* (Fairfax: George Mason University Press, 1991); R. Longstreth (ed.), *The Mall in Washington, 1791–1991* (Washington, DC: National Gallery of Art, 1991); W. Seale, *The President's House*, (Washington, DC: White House Historical Association, 1986).

37. *Writings*, I, 382.

38. *Landscape and Written Expression in Revolutionary America: the World Turned Upside Down* (Cambridge: Cambridge University Press, 1988). He argues that the experience of 'the west' could not be encompassed by the kind of discourse the expedition had learnt from Jefferson, and that experience of the American heart of darkness profoundly destabilised Lewis. See also J. Seelye, 'Beyond the Shining Mountains: the Lewis and Clarke Expedition as an Enlightenment Epic', *Virginia Quarterly Review* 63 (1987) 36–53. For less contentious accounts, see D. Jackson, *Thomas Jefferson & the Stony Mountains: Exploring the West from Monticello* (Urbana: University of Illinois Press, 1981);

S. E. Ambrose, *Undaunted Courage: Meriwether Lewis, Thomas Jefferson, and the Opening of the American West* (New York: Simon and Schuster, 1996).

39. The literature is immense. On nationalism generally I have been particularly influenced by B. Anderson, *Imagined Communities: Reflections on the Origin and Spread of Nationalism* (London: Verso, 1983); Sir Isaiah Berlin, *Vico and Herder: Two Studies in the History of Ideas* (London: Hogarth Press, 1976); H. K. Bhabha (ed.), *Nation and Narration* (London: Routledge, 1990); E. Gellner, *Nations and Nationalism* (Oxford: Basil Blackwell, 1983); Greenfield, op. cit. n. 20; E. J. Hobsbawm, *Nations and Nationalism since 1780: Programme, Myth, Reality* (Cambridge: Cambridge University Press, 1990); J. Hutchinson and A D. Smith, *Nationalism* (Oxford & New York: Oxford University Press, 1994); E. Kamenka (ed.), *Nationalism: the Nature and Evolution of an Idea* (London: Edward Arnold, 1976); E. Kedourie, *Nationalism* (London: Hutchinson, 1960); Kohn, op. cit. n. 19; D. Miller, *On Nationality* (Oxford: Clarendon Press, 1995); V. Newey and A. Thompson (eds), *Literature and Nationalism* (Liverpool: Liverpool University Press, 1991); B. Shafer, *Nationalism: Myth and Reality*, and *Faces of Nationalism: New Realities and Old Myths* (New York: Harcourt, Brace, 1955 and 1972); H. Seton-Watson, *Nations and States: an Enquiry into the Origins of Nations and the Politics of Nationalism* (London: Methuen, 1977); A. D. Smith, *Theories of Nationalism* (London and New York: Holmes and Meier, 2nd edn, 1983) and *The Ethnic Origins of Nations* (Oxford: Basil Blackwell, 1986) and 'The Myth of the "Modern Nation" and the Myths of Nations', *Ethnic and Racial Studies* 11 (1988) 1–26. For general accounts of the rise of American nationalism I have drawn on H. Kohn, *American Nationalism* (Westport: Greenwood Press, 1957); E. M. Burns, *The American Idea of Mission: Concepts of National Purpose and Destiny* (New Brunswick, NJ: Rutgers University Press, 1957); M. Savelle, 'Nationalism and Other Loyalties in the American Revolution', *AHR* LXVII (1962) 901–23; Arieli, op. cit. n. 20; G. Dangerfield, *The Awakening of American Nationalism 1815–1828* (New York: Harper and Row, 1965); D. Boorstin, *The Americans: the National Experience* (New York: Vintage Books, 1965); R. K. Ketcham, *From Colony to Country: the Revolution in American Thought, 1750–1820* (New York: Macmillan, 1975); S. Thernstrom (ed.), *The Harvard Encyclopedia of American Ethnic Groups* (Cambridge, Mass.: Belknap, Harvard University Press, 1980); P. Miller, *Nature's Nation* (Cambridge, Mass.: Belknap, Harvard University Press, 1967); A. M. Schlesinger Jr, *The Disuniting of America* (New York: W. W. Norton, 1992).

40. Johann Gottlieb Fichte's *Addresses to the German Nation* (1808) may serve as a key example of such self-definition, with obvious parallels to the development of nationalism in the United States. Fichte perceives that the emergence of the German nation will inaugurate 'a new world...a new epoch of history' based on the separation of the originary people from the contamination of alien culture (for him the Romano-French tradition, for Jeffersonian America, the *ancien régime* in Europe). Fundamental in the defining tradition of the people is

Lutheran religion and the language; and the 'natural' boundaries of the nation are coterminous with the spread of the language. (So, in the United States, the Christian religion and the English language are coterminous with the spread of 'the empire for liberty'.) Equally important is the creation by the poetic imagination of the appropriate symbols for the nation, and national recognition of 'our future heroes, sages, lawgivers, and saviours of mankind'. (Compare the Capitol in Washington, DC.) There is in the creation of this 'race of men' a 'providence' and a 'divine plan', and thus the fate of all mankind depends upon Germania: 'If you go under, all humanity goes under with you, without hope of any future restoration.' The parallels to the manifest destiny of America as the last, best or only hope of the world are self-evident. I stress, however, that 'romantic nationalism' is too variable to be reduced to any theoretical template.

41. Volney was on John Adams's list of Frenchmen to be deported as undesirable aliens. For his critique of the United States see the prefatory material to *A View of the Soil and Climate of the United States of America* (1804). His projected history of the States would have represented 'the people' as 'a mere medley of adventurers from all parts of Europe' bent on 'imperial aggrandizement', depraved in manners and corrupt in principles by events of the 1790s. Chance, not Providence, guides their affairs, and their 'vanity' leads them to claim that the 'nation is the wisest and most enlightened upon earth'. For the disillusioning experience of some European radicals in the USA, see M. Durey, *Transatlantic Radicals and the Early American Republic* (Lawrence: University of Kansas Press, 1997).

42. Op. cit. n. 2.

43. J. S. Ackerman, *The Villa: Form and Ideology of Country Houses* (London: Thames and Hudson, 1990); W. H. Adams, *Jefferson's Monticello* (New York: Abbeville Press, 1983) with extensive bibliography, and see Chapter 4 below. An important, radical, challenge to the interpretation of Monticello through past history is B. L. Pickens, 'Mr. Jefferson as Revolutionary Architect', *JSAH* 34 (1975) 257–79.

44. P. B. Shelley, preface to *The Revolt of Islam*.

45. For biographical knowledge, I am principally indebted to the six volumes of D. Malone, *Jefferson and His Time* (Boston: Little, Brown and Company, 1948–81); M. D. Peterson, *Thomas Jefferson and the New Nation* (New York: Oxford University Press, 1970); F. M. Brodie, *Thomas Jefferson: an Intimate History* (New York: W. W. Norton & Company, 1974); C. C. O'Brien, *The Long Affair: Thomas Jefferson and the French Revolution* (Chicago: Chicago University Press, 1996) and J. J. Ellis, *American Sphinx: the Character of Thomas Jefferson* (New York: Alfred A. Knopf, 1997). Peterson's *The Jeffersonian Image in the American Mind* (New York: Oxford University Press, 1960) is the best survey of Jefferson's changing reputation. For recent adverse judgements of Jefferson see L. W. Levy, *Jefferson and Civil Liberties: the Darker Side* (Cambridge, Mass.: Harvard University Press, 1963) and the survey article by Gordon S. Wood, 'The Trials and Tribulations of Thomas Jefferson', in P. S. Onuf (ed.), *Jeffersonian Legacies* (Charlottesville:

University of Virginia Press, 1993) pp. 395–417, and, for the darkening judgement of Jefferson and racism, P. Finkelman, 'Jefferson and Slavery: "Treason Against the Hopes of the World" ', pp. 181–221 (see also Chapter 3 below). The standard bibliographies are F. Shuffelton, *Thomas Jefferson: a Comprehensive Annotated Bibliography of Writings About Him 1826–1980* and *Thomas Jefferson, 1981–1990: an Annotated Bibliography* (New York: Garland, 1983 and 1992). See also M. D. Peterson (ed.), *Thomas Jefferson: a Reference Biography* (New York: Charles Scribner's Sons, 1986). Current scholarship on Jefferson is brilliantly reviewed by P. S. Onuf, 'The Scholar's Jefferson', *WMQ* 3, L (1993) 671–99.

2 Jefferson Seals the Revolution

1. Cited in R. S. Patterson and R. Dougall (eds), *The Eagle and the Shield: a History of the Great Seal of the United States* (Washington, DC: Department of State, 1976) p. 553.
2. For the history of the Seal I am indebted to Patterson and Dougall, op. cit. n. 1. See also F. H. Sommer, 'Emblem and Device: the Origin of the Great Seal of the United States', *Art Quarterly* 24 (1961) 57–76. The relation of the Seal to the creation of national identity is discussed by J. Fliegelman, *Declaring Independence: Jefferson, Natural Language, and the Culture of Performance* (Stanford: Stanford University Press, 1993) pp. 160–4. See also S. Hamilton, ' "The Earliest Device of the Colonies" and Some Other Early Devices', *Princeton University Library Chronicle* 10 (1941) 117–23 and P. M. Isaacson, *The American Eagle* (New York: New York Graphic Society, 1975).
3. For the Whig origins of the revolution, see especially B. Bailyn, *The Ideological Origins of the American Revolution* (Cambridge, Mass.: Belknap, Harvard University Press, 1967) and J. G. A. Pocock, *The Machiavellian Moment: Florentine Political Thought and the Atlantic Tradition* (Princeton: Princeton University Press, 1975). See also F. McDonald, *Novus Ordo Seclorum: the Intellectual Origins of the Constitution* (Lawrence: University Press of Kansas, 1985) and M. White, *The Philosophy of the American Revolution* (New York: Oxford University Press, 1978). I am also heavily indebted to G. S. Wood, *The Creation of the American Republic, 1776–1787* (Chapel Hill: University of North Carolina Press, 1969). For the spread of revolutionary ideas in Europe, see R. R. Palmer, *The Age of Democratic Revolution* (2 vols, Princeton: Princeton University Press, 1959, 1964). For other interpretations of the ideological, economic, racial and gendered forces at work in the revolution, see the review articles cited in Ch. 1, n. 23.
4. Early signifiers of the colonies are analysed by L. C. Olson, *Emblems of American Community in the Revolutionary Era* (Washington, DC: Smithsonian Institution Press, 1991). The principal emblems were the snake, the Indian and the child.
5. The Seal and the flag were combined in Pierre Charles L'Enfant's pediment for the double-storey Doric portico of Federal Hall

(c. 1788–89) in New York. The armigerous eagle of the Seal rose in a sun-burst amid billowing clouds; four relief panels displayed clusters of 13 arrows as symbolic *fasces* bound with olive wreaths; 13 metopes were ornamented with the 13 stars of the States, and for Washington's inauguration, 30 April 1789, L'Enfant added a red and white festoon. For fuller discussion of the iconography and its relation to French national symbolism, see P. Scott, *Temple of Liberty: Building the Capitol for a New Nation* (New York: Oxford University Press, 1995) p. 3.

6. *Fame and the Founding Fathers* (New York: Norton, 1974).

7. Patterson and Dougall, op. cit. n. 1, p. 11.

8. Sommer, op. cit. n. 2, argues that the committee neglected the Renaissance tradition that an *impresa* should contain no human figures and carry an enigmatic motto in a foreign language, both of which requirements are met by the present Seal.

9. Jefferson's ambivalence about the sign may be seen in *Notes on the State of Virginia*, Query 13 where the *fasces* and 'heavy-handed ... aristocracy' are seen as related: 'Those who assume the right of giving away the reins of government ... must be sure that the herd, whom they hand on to the rods and hatchet of the dictator, will lay their necks on the block when he shall nod to them.'

10. For historical archetypes for Washington see Gary Wills, *Cincinnatus: George Washington and the Enlightenment* (London: Robert Hale, 1984). Sommer, op. cit. n. 2, p. 74 cites L'Enfant's design for a medal for the Society of the Cincinnati: 'The Principal Figure to be Cincinnatus, three Senators presenting him with a Sword and other military Ensigns; on a field in the background, his wife standing at the door of their cottage, near it a plough and instruments of husbandry; round the whole, OMNIA RELIQUIT SERVARE REMPUBLICAM. On the reverse: Sun rising – a city with open gates and vessels entering the port. Fame crowning Cincinnatus with a wreath inscribed *Virtutis Praemium*, – below, Hands supporting a heart, with the motto ESTO PERPETUA – round the whole, SOCIETAS CINCIN-NATORUM, INSTITUTA A.D. 1783.'

11. See W. Schleiner, 'The Infant Hercules: Franklin's Design for a Medal Commemorating American Liberty', *E-CS* 10 (1976–77), 235–44; Olson, op. cit. n. 4, pp. 189–92; Scott, op. cit. ch. 1 n. 6, pp. 12–14; W. H. Adams (ed.), *The Eye of Thomas Jefferson* (Washington, DC: National Gallery of Art, 1976) item 177. Hercules is joined with another signifier used on the Seal, the pyramid, in Robert Edge Pine's 'Allegory of America' (1778) where he presents Liberty to an American altar of Peace. He is linked with the *fasces* in Luigi Persico's allegorical scheme the 'Genius of America' for the Capitol (1825). John Quincy Adams's objection to the figure may mark a threshold of rejection of an emblem too learned for popular culture and, as Scott suggests, perhaps too savage. None of the authorities cited make the commonplace association in classical antiquity of Hercules with Cato Uticensis and the Stoic opposition to the Caesars (kingship). But the oppositional motif would have been known to Jefferson, who proposed the motto *Rex est qui regem non habet* as an alternative to Franklin's 'Rebellion to

Tyrants is Obedience to God' for the arms of the State of Virginia; see D. Malone, *Jefferson and His Time* (6 vols, Boston: Little Brown and Company, 1948–81) I, 242, n. 14.

12. L. H. Cohen (ed.), *The History of the American Revolution* (Indianapolis: Liberty Fund, 1990) I, 28.

13. Quotations from R. B. Nye, *The Cultural Life of the New Nation, 1770–1830* (London: Hamish Hamilton, 1960) p. 18.

14. G. S. Wood, *The Radicalism of the American Revolution* (New York: Alfred A. Knopf, 1992) pp. 365f. citing, among others, John and Samuel Adams, Benjamin Franklin, David Ramsay, Benjamin Rush, 'even Jefferson' (p. 367). But such disillusionment is commonplace in European romanticism after the apparent failure of the ideals of revolutionary republican virtue. For the republican ideology of early historians of the American revolution, see R. E. Shalhope, 'Towards a Republican Synthesis: the Emergence of an Understanding of Republicanism in American Historiography', *WMQ* 3 XXIX (1972) 49–80 and 'Republicanism and Early American Historiography', ibid. XXXIX (1982) 334–56; A. H. Shaffer, *The Politics of History: Writing the History of the American Revolution* (Chicago: Precedent, 1975); L. H. Cohen, *The Revolutionary Histories: Contemporary Narratives of the American Revolution* (Ithaca: Cornell University Press, 1980) and 'Creating a Useable Future: the Revolutionary Historians and the National Past' in J. P. Greene (ed.), *The American Revolution: Its Character and Limits* (New York: New York University Press, 1987) pp. 309–30; L. K. Kerber, 'The Republican Ideology of the Revolutionary Generation' *AQ* 37 (1985) 474–95.

15. The American icon of Minerva/Liberty is an importation from Europe during the romantic period: witness Benjamin Latrobe's designs for the Capitol, Giuseppe Ceracchi's 'Minerva as the Patroness of American Liberty (1792) placed behind the Speaker's chair in Philadelphia's Congress Hall, or Auguste Bartholdi's statue for New York to mark the hundredth anniversary of the Declaration of Independence. The difficulties in finding a 'native American' icon are obvious, although Walt Disney's 'politically correct' (and 'mulatto') Indian princess Pocahontas is a sign for our times. For Pocahontas, see R. S. Tilton, *Pocahontas: the Evolution of an American Narrative* (Cambridge: Cambridge University Press, 1994) and *Pocahontas: Her Life and Legend* (ed.), W. M. S. Rasmussen and R. S. Tilton (Richmond: Virginia Historical Society, 1994). See also E. M. Fleming, 'The American Image as Indian Princess, 1768–1783', *Winterthur Portfolio* 2 (1965) 65–81 and 'From Indian Princess to Greek Goddess: the American Image, 1783–1815', *Winterthur Portfolio* 3 (1967) 37–66.

16. Likewise, Washington's 'Augustan' Inauguration procession celebrated the 'mighty chief' as 'the defender' of revolutionary motherhood and their daughters. See Ramsay, op. cit. n. 12, II, 659f. For a gendered reading of Virtue at this time, see R. H. Bloch, 'The Gendered Meanings of Virtue in Revolutionary America', *Signs* 13 (1987) 37–58; and, generally, L. K. Kerber, *Women of the Republic: Intellect and Ideology in Revolutionary America* (Chapel Hill: University of North

Carolina Press, 1980) and A. Parker (ed.), *Nationalism and Sexualities* (New York: Routledge, 1992).

17. See S. Schama, *Landscape and Memory* (London: HarperCollins, 1995) ch. 2, '*Der Holzweg*: the Track Through the Woods'.

18. The letter to James Monroe, 24 November 1801, hints at both continents as future *Lebensraum* without racial intermixture. He envisions the settlement of 'the whole northern, if not the southern continent, with a people speaking the same language, governed in similar forms, and by similar laws; nor can we contemplate with satisfaction either blot or mixture on that surface'.

19. The icon had been established as early as 1789 when Madame de Tessé gave Jefferson 'a broken green-marble column' decorated with the signs of the Zodiac and of the ten lost tribes of Israel, inscribed (in Latin) 'To the Supreme Ruler of the Universe; under whose watchful care the liberties of North America were finally achieved, and under whose tutelage the name of Thomas Jefferson will descend forever blessed to posterity.' See S. R. Stein, *The Worlds of Thomas Jefferson at Monticello* (New York: Harry N. Abrams, 1993) pp. 22 and 69. The place of the column in the iconographic scheme of Monticello is discussed in Chapter 4 below. On the USA as the new Israel, see M. I. Lowance, *The Language of Canaan: Metaphor and Symbol in New England from the Puritans to the Transcendentalists* (Cambridge, Mass: Harvard University Press, 1980). For a radical rewriting of the myth from a slave position, see Phillis Wheatley's letter to the Rev. Samson Occom, 11 February 1774, casting the whites in the role of Egyptians and the blacks as the enslaved chosen people of God.

20. Ramsay records that to the colonists 'their country was looked upon as a waste, which was open to the occupancy and use of other nations' and that America, 'the asylum of liberty', was 'no more than a barren wilderness, inhabited only by savage men and beasts'. Ramsay, op. cit. n. 12, I, 15 and 63. The conjunction of 'savages' with 'beasts' dehumanises the Indians.

21. See Linda Colley, *Britons: Forging the Nation, 1707–1837* (New Haven: Yale University Press, 1992) and for a review article (with extensive bibliography) of the interrelationship between the development of nationalisms in Britain and the United States, see T. H. Breen, 'Ideology and Nationalism on the Eve of the American Revolution: Revisions *Once More* in Need of Revising', *JAH* 84 (1997) 13–39.

22. See M. E. Deutsch, 'E Pluribus Unum', *The Classical Journal* 18 (1922–23) 387–407.

23. Cited in Y. Arieli, *Individualism and Nationalism in American Ideology* (Cambridge, Mass: Harvard University Press, 1964) p. 301.

24. For Freemasonry and the revolution, see S. C. Bullock, 'The Revolutionary Transformation of American Freemasonry, 1752–1792', *WMQ* 3 XLVII (1990) 347–69: 'The ideals of the Revolution... appeared to be closely related to the developing Ancient fraternity and its social constituency – indeed, so intimately related that many post-Revolutionary Americans came to see Masonry as an archetype of the republican society based on the virtue and talent they were attempting to

build', p. 368. Also idem, 'A Pure and Sublime System: the Appeal of Post-Revolutionary Freemasonry', *Journal of the Early Republic* 9 (1989), 359–73 and *Revolutionary Brotherhood: Freemasonry and the Transformation of the American Social Order, 1730–1840* (Chapel Hill: University of North Carolina Press, 1996). See also Scott, op. cit. n. 5, pp. 11 and 18.

25. *Aeneid* VI, 853–5: 'These will be your arts, O Roman! Impose the custom of peace, pardon the subdued, subdue the recalcitrant by war.' The passage foretells how the Romans will establish their sway over lands more widespread than even Hercules travelled in his labours. Sommer, op. cit. n. 2, p. 72f. notes the transfer of the Roman eagle to the Holy Roman Empire, and its use as the personal device of Charles V: *Aquilam semper insigne fuisse alicuius imperii ... Atque nunc etiam Imperatores Romani felici auspicio eam gestant ... tam pacem, quam bellum repraesentans*. The 1782 Seal committee would be aware both of the imperial connotations and of the 'war and peace' signification. Wood, op. cit. n. 14, p. 215f. idealistically suggests that the founding fathers would prefer Juba's Whig reinterpretation of Virgil in Addison's *Cato* I, iv: 'A Roman soul is bent on higher views ... /To make man mild, and sociable to man;/To cultivate the wild, licentious savage/With wisdom, discipline, and liberal arts....' But in my opinion, Juba's speech is an idealised version of 'the white man's burden' of British imperialism rather than a description of the racial and religious imperatives of American *Westpolitik*.

26. The phrase glosses the common icon of the colonies as a divided snake, derived from Franklin's device published in the *Pennsylvania Gazette*, 9 May 1754.

3 Kennst du das Land? *Notes on the State of Virginia*

1. Cited in G. Clark (ed.), *The American Landscape: Literary Sources and Documents* (3 vols, East Sussex: Helm Information, 1993) I. 27.

2. *Voyage en Amérique*, cited by H. Honour, *The European Vision of America* (Cleveland, Ohio: Cleveland Museum of Art, 1975) item 264.

3. David Ramsay, *The History of the American Revolution* (ed.), L. H. Cohen (Indianapolis: Liberty Fund, 1990) I, 13.

4. 'Names of cities, islands, rivers, new settlements & co.,/These must assimilate in sentiment and/in sound, to something organic in the place, or identical/with it ...' in Clark, op. cit. n. 1, p. 44.

5. Ibid, pp. 42–3.

6. For early iconography and ideas of America, see E. O'Gorman, *The Invention of America: an Enquiry into the Historical Nature of the New World and the Meaning of its History* (Bloomington: Indiana University Press, 1961); H. M. Jones, *O Strange New World* (London: Chatto and Windus, 1965); H. Honour, *The New Golden Land: European Images of America from the Discoveries to the Present Time* (London: Allen Lane, 1976); J. P. Green, *The Intellectual Construction of America: Exceptionalism and Identity from 1492 to 1800* (Chapel Hill: University of North Carolina Press, 1993); A.R. Pagden, *European Encounters with the New World:*

from Renaissance to Romanticism (New Haven: Yale University Press, 1993).

7. *Travels* (ed.), M. Van Doren (New York: Dover, 1955) pp. 130 and 183. 'The Indians make war against, kill, and destroy their own species, and their motives spring from the same erroneous source as they do in all other nations of mankind; that is,...ambition ....or revenge...or, lastly, to extend the borders and boundaries of their territories. But I cannot find, upon the strictest inquiry, that their bloody contests at this day are marked with deeper stains of inhumanity or savage cruelty, than what may be observed amongst the most civilized nations....'

8. Clark, op. cit. n. 1, provides an excellent introduction to the literature of 'place' in the United States and an extensive bibliography of primary and secondary sources. Particularly close to part of my argument here are C. Looby, 'The Constitution of Nature: Taxonomy as Politics in Jefferson, Peale and Bartram', *EAL* 22 (1987) 252–73; P. Semonin, ' "Nature's Nation": Natural History as Nationalism in the New Republic', *Northwest Review* 30 (1992) 6–41 and P. Regis, *Describing Early America: Bartram, Jefferson, Crèvecoeur, and the Rhetoric of Natural History* (De Kalb: Northern Illinois University Press, 1992) and J. H. Richards, 'Revolution, Domestic Life, and the End of "Common Mercy" in Crèvecoeur's "Landscapes" ', *WMQ*, 3, LV (1998) 281–96. More generally, see P. Brook, *The Pursuit of Wilderness* (Boston: Houghton Mifflin, 1971); P. Conrad, *Imagining America* (London: Routledge and Kegan Paul, 1980); W. H. Goetzmann, *Exploration and Empire: The Explorer and the Scientist in the Winning of the American West* (New York, Vintage Books, 1972); Honour, op. cit. n. 2 and 6; H. Huth, *Nature and the American: Three Centuries of Changing Attitudes* (Berkeley and Los Angeles: University of California Press, 1957); L. Marx, *The Machine in the Garden: Technology and the Pastoral Ideal in America* (New York: Oxford University Press, 1964); D. Miller, *Dark Eden: The Swamp in Nineteenth Century American Culture* (New York: Cambridge University Press, 1989) and (ed.), *American Iconology: New Approaches to Nineteenth-Century Art and Literature* (New Haven: Yale University Press, 1993); P. Miller, *Errand into the Wilderness* (Cambridge, Mass.: Belknap, Harvard University Press, 1976); R. Nash, *Wilderness and the American Mind* (New Haven: Yale University Press, 1967); R. Slotkin, *Regeneration Through Violence: the Mythology of the Frontier, 1600–1860* (Middletown, Conn: Wesleyan University Press, 1973); H. N. Smith, *Virgin Land: the American West as Symbol and Myth* (Cambridge, Mass.: Harvard University Press, 1950).

9. Op. cit. n. 7, pp. 284 and 287.

10. E. Elliott (ed.), *Wieland* (Oxford and New York: Oxford University Press, 1994) p. 11.

11. John Rastell, *An Interlude of the Four Elements* in Honour, op. cit. n. 2, p. 123.

12. Cited in S. Daniels, *Fields of Vision: Landscape Imagery and National Identity in England and the United States* (Cambridge: Polity Press, 1993) p. 158. Cole, however, is unusual among early landscape artists

in the United States in his pessimistic (Volneyan) view of history. See Daniels, pp. 146–73, 'Thomas Cole and the Course of Empire' and A. Miller, 'Thomas Cole and Jacksonian America: *The Course of Empire* as Political Allegory', *Prospects* 13 (1989) 65–92.

13. For an introduction to landscape painting in the United States, see B. Novak, *Nature and Culture: American Landscape and Painting 1825–1875* (rev. edn New York: Oxford University Press, 1995). There is an extensive bibliography. See also A. Boime, *The Magisterial Gaze: Manifest Destiny and American Landscape Painting c. 1830–1865* (Washington, DC: The Smithsonian Institution Press, 1991); G. G. Deak, *Picturing America, 1479–1899* (Princeton: Princeton University Press, 1988); F. Kelly, *Frederic E. Church and the National Landscape* (Washington, DC: The Smithsonian Institution Press, 1988); L. Marx, op. cit. n. 8 and *The American Revolution and the American Landscape* (Washington, DC: American Enterprise Institute for Public Policy Research, 1974); A. Miller, *The Empire of the Eye: Landscape Representation and American Cultural Politics 1825–75* (Ithaca: Cornell University Press, 1993) and 'Everywhere and Nowhere: the Making of the National Landscape', *ALH* 4 (1992) 207–29; W. J. T. Mitchell (ed.), *Landscape and Power* (Chicago: Chicago University Press, 1994); E. J. Nygren and B. Robertson (eds), *Views and Vision: American Landscape before 1830* (Washington, DC: The Corcoran Gallery of Art, 1986). A more general debt is due to the writings on English landscape painting by John Barrell and Ann Bermingham.

14. Edn cit. n. 10, p. 10.

15. To John Eliot and Jeremy Belknap op. cit. n.3, p. xvii. See also Hutchins, *Historical Narrative....*, pp. 92–4, who argues that whereas old empires were heterogeneous in character and language, and hence of short duration, the United States 'will be peopled by persons whose language and national character are the same, and the whole people, physically speaking, one' and thus break from the old cycle of imperial rise, decline and fall.

16. Many writers on the *Notes* have commented on the potentional tensions and disorder in the work; but there has been substantial agreement in principle that the *Notes* achieve some sort of harmonious resolution. L. Marx op. cit. n. 8 argues that the first seven queries control the reader's response and W. Scheck claims that the theme of chaos and order provides a 'beautiful' equilibrium equivalent to 'democracy' itself, 'Chaos and Imaginative Order in Thomas Jefferson's *Notes on the State of Virginia*', in J. A. Leo Lemay (ed.), *Essays in Early Virginian Literature Honoring Richard Beale Davis* (New York: Burt Franklin, 1977) pp. 221–34. Likewise R. A. Ferguson claims that natural and civil law resolve the disorderly tendencies in Jeffersonian Nature, '"Mysterious Obligation": Jefferson's *Notes on the State of Virginia*', *AL* 52 (1980) 381–406 and H. Hellenbrand sees Jefferson finding a path out of 'tumult' into 'harmony', 'Roads to Happiness: Rhetorical and Philosophical Design in Jefferson's *Notes on the State of Virginia*', *EAL* 20 (1985) 3–23. See also F. Ogburn Jr, 'Structure and Meaning in Thomas Jefferson's *Notes on the State of Virginia*', *EAL* 15

(1980) 141–50; C. Daufenbach, ' "The Eye Composes Itself": Text and Terrain in Jefferson's Virginia', in *Rewriting the South: History and Fiction* (ed.), L. Honnighausen *et al*. (Tubingen: Franke, 1993) pp. 99–111; G. A. Davy, 'Argumentation and Unified Structure in *Notes on the State of Virginia*', *E-CS* 26 (1993) 581–93; G. Tauber, '*Notes on the State of Virginia*: Thomas Jefferson's Unintentional Self-Portrait', ibid, pp. 635–48. Two important general essays pertinent to my argument are M. R. Breitweiser, 'Jefferson's Prospect', *Prospects* 10 (1985) 315–52 and L. P. Simpson, 'Land, Slaves, and Mind: the High Culture of the Jeffersonian South' in *Mind and the American Civil War* (Baton Rouge: Louisiana State University Press, 1989) pp. 1–32.

17. See C. L. Rossiter, *The American Quest 1790–1860: an Emerging Nation in Search of Identity, Unity, and Modernity* (New York: Harcourt Brace Jovanovitch, 1971).

18. Jefferson supplemented his interpretation with the 'observations' of his friend Charles Thomson, whose vocabulary underscores how 'this country must have suffered some violent convulsion, and that the face of it must have been changed from what it probably was centuries ago'. Thomson finds similar 'convulsion of nature' widespread, and 'hurried away by fancy' envisages Lake Erie inundating the States and the Atlantic surging to the Andes.

19. Op. cit. n. 3, I, 172.

20. Imlay, letter VII, shows how far romantic idealisation of the *Volk* might go. His Americans enjoy 'raptures of love and rational felicity' in their luxurious land, united in universal friendship and virtue. On the farm Youth sports on the green turf before the eyes of aged Nestors in 'uncontaminated felicity'. Woman gardens, arranges flowers, plays music and indulges all the delights of leisured socialising. 'Sincerity and politeness of manners [are] universal'. Load your covered wagon, Imlay advises, camp by the wayside and, escaped from the contamination of Europe, enjoy the 'simplicity' of Nature in the United States. This romantic and nationalistic idealisation of a mythic 'American farmer' is separable from the extended economic debate whether Jefferson was a reactionary conservative or a progressive liberal; but, from the extensive literature, see D. L. Wilson, 'The American Agricola: Jefferson's Agrarianism and the Classical Tradition', *SAQ* 80 (1981) 339–54 and 'The Fate of Jefferson's Farmer', *North Dakota Quarterly* 56 (1988) 23–34; on the conservative/liberal division, see J. Appleby, 'What is Still American in the Political Philosophy of Thomas Jefferson?', *WMQ* 3 XXXIX (1982) 287–309; and for an attempt to reconcile the conservative and liberal positions, see A. W. Foshee, 'Jeffersonian Political Economy and the Classical Tradition: Jefferson, Taylor, and the Agrarian Republic', *History of Political Economy* 17 (1985) 523–50.

21. The standard account of Jefferson and racial issues is J. C. Miller, *The Wolf by the Ears: Thomas Jefferson and Slavery* (Charlottesville and London: University Press of Virginia, 1991/1977) with extensive bibliography. There are good overviews of the issues of race and slavery by P. Finkelman (op. cit. ch. 1, n. 45) and *Slavery and the Founders: Race*

and Liberty in the Age of Jefferson (London: E. M. Sharpe, 1995) and D.B. Davis, 'Constructing Race: a Reflection', *WMQ*, 3, LIV (1997) 7–18. I have also drawn upon P. S. Onuf (ed.), *Jeffersonian Legacies* (Charlottesville: University Press of Virginia, 1993) and W. D. Jordan, *White Over Black: American Attitudes to the Negro, 1550–1812* (Chapel Hill, University of North Carolina Press, 1968) on the psychotic tendencies in Jefferson; L. P. Simpson, 'The Ferocity of Self: History and Consciousness in Southern Literature', *South Central Review* 1 (1984) 67–84 on the relation of 'self' to 'other' in Jefferson's account of his slaves; and F. Shuffelton (ed.), *A Mixed Race: Ethnicity in Early America* (New York: Oxford University Press, 1993) pp. 257–77 for Shuffelton's account of 'the failure of anthropological method' in Jefferson. Gilbert Imlay's contemporary attack (letter IX) on Jefferson is a powerful refutation of the *Notes*, and Fanny Kemble's journals provide the best account I know of the shock to a liberal conscience of passing from the ideology of American 'liberty' to the experience of slavery.

22. Op. cit. n. 3, I, 4.

23. His account for Démeunier goes on to complain that the colonists were 'perpetually harassed' by the Indians but without examining why the harassment occurred. It is an issue he skirts around in the *Notes* also where his unease at publishing material he considered dangerous led him to suppress his alternative account of the 'purchase' of Indian lands in Query XI: 'it is true that these purchases were sometimes made with the price in one hand and the sword in the other'.

24. The standard account of Jefferson's Indian policy remains B. W. Sheehan, *Seeds of Extinction: Jeffersonian Philanthropy and the American Indian* (Chapel Hill: University of North Carolina Press, 1973). See also R. F. Berkhofer, Jr, *The White Man's Indian: Images of the American Indian from Columbus to the Present* (New York: Vintage Books, 1978). Charles Thompson's 'observations' might have warned Jefferson of one of the difficulties in his preferred solution to the Indian problem: that they should become farmers. Thomson records 'this is what the Indians call making them women', i.e. the very basis of their cultural identity would be destroyed. A harsher view of the Indian problem than Jefferson's is provided by Williams, VII, whose detailed sociological account contains a scathing attack on the effects of white settlement. 'Wherever the Europeans have settled, misery, calamity, and destruction, have been entailed on the Indians. ... The vices we have taught them, the diseases we have spread among them, the intemperance they have learnt of us, and the destruction of their game ... [have given them] a contempt of our morals, a horrour at the knavery that has attended our commerce with them, and the constant advances we have made into their country, have filled their minds with prejudices against our arts and improvements.' Volney notes the extreme racial antipathy of the 'Anglo-Germans' to the Indian peoples, but grimly observes that the Anglo-Germans were the best fitted to survive in the interracial struggle (pp. 350–1). Belknap sees 'Providence' leading to the 'extirpation' or 'extinction' of

the Indians (p. 124). In relation both to the Indians and black slavery, Ramsay asked whether Columbus brought greater happiness or misery to the continent (op. cit. n. 3, I, 14).

25. The notorious case of the slave, Sally Hemings, the mulatto half-sister of Jefferson's wife, makes the issue of miscegenation a crucial matter at Monticello. She was either the long-term mistress of Jefferson after his wife's death, or he connived at her regular prostitution to some other white(s) in the family or on the estate.

26. I have been influenced by T. Todorov, *The Conquest of America: the Question of the Other*, translated by R. Howard (New York: Harper, 1984).

27. Colonel Barré in Ramsay, op. cit., n. 3, I, 55.

4 The Villa on a Hill

1. Cited by Elizabeth Bowen, *Bowen's Court* (London: Virago, 1984) pp. 208–9.

2. See L. Marx, *The Machine in the Garden: Technology and the Pastoral Ideal in America* (New York: Oxford University Press, 1964).

3. Horace, *Odes* III, xxix, 12: 'the smoke and the grandeur and the noise [of Rome]'.

4. For La Grange, see L. Kramer, *Lafayette in Two Worlds: Public Cultures and Personal Identities in an Age of Revolution* (Chapel Hill: University of North Carolina Press, 1996) ch. 4, passim.

5. To Phillip Mazzei, 24 April 1796.

6. For an extended account of the classical origins of villa culture and its relation to Monticello, see J. Ackerman, *The Villa: Form and Ideology of Country Houses* (London: Thames and Hudson, 1990) and K. Prothero, 'Monticello as Roman Villa: the Ancients, Architecture, and Jefferson', *Virginia Cavalcade* 39 (1989) 10–21. See also M. Kelsall, *The Great Good Place: the Country House and English Literature* (Hemel Hempstead: Harvester Wheatsheaf, 1993).

7. Cicero, *Pro Sestio*, xlv, 98: 'a peaceful life with honour' [which is most desirable to all healthy and good and well-off men].

8. II, xii.

9. Cited in R. G. Wilson (ed.), *Thomas Jefferson's Academical Village: the Creation of an Architectural Masterpiece* (Charlottesville: University Press of Virginia, 1995) p. 10. For the architectural history of the Lawn, see also P. Hogan, *The Lawn: a Guide to Jefferson's University* (Charlottesville: University Press of Virginia, 1987) and M. Brawne, *University of Virginia, the Lawn* (Charlottesville: University Press of Virginia, 1994). For the Rotunda, see W. B. O'Neal, *Jefferson's Buildings at the University of Virginia: the Rotunda* (Charlottesville: University of Virginia Press, 1960) and J. L. Vaughan and O. A. Gianniny, Jr, *Thomas Jefferson's Rotunda Restored, 1973–1976* (Charlottesville, University of Virginia Press, 1981). For a study of specific French influence, see L. S. Greenbaum, 'Thomas Jefferson, the Paris Hospitals, and the University of Virginia', *E-CS* 26 (1993) 607–26. Closest to my own

iconographical and cultural reading are G. Le Coat, 'Thomas Jefferson et l'architecture métaphorique: le "Village Académique" à l'Université de Virginie', *Revue d'art canadienne* 3 (1976) 8–34 and W. L. Creese, 'Jefferson's Charlottesville' in *The Crowning of the American Landscape: Eight Great Spaces and Their Buildings* (Princeton: Princeton University Press, 1985) pp. 9–45.

10.   *Notes on Virginia*, Query XV.
11.   Particularly revealing is the debate between Jefferson and Madison by letter, c. February 1825, on maintaining the university free from 'heresies' by 'previous prescription of texts'. See J. M. Smith (ed.), *The Republic of Letters: the Correspondence Between Thomas Jefferson and James Madison, 1776–1826* (3 vols, New York: W. W. Norton, 1995). See also A. Bestor, 'Thomas Jefferson and the Freedom of Books' in A. Bestor (ed.), *Three Presidents and Their Books* (Urbana: University of Illinois Press, 1955) pp. 1–44; L. W. Levy, *Jefferson and Civil Liberties: the Darker Side* (Cambridge, Mass.: Belknap, Harvard University Press, 1963); and D. L. Wilson, 'Jefferson vs. Hume', *WMQ* 3, XLVI (1989) 49–70. More generally, see R. J. Pudaloff, 'Education and the Constitution: Instituting American Culture' in R. B. and G. J. Browne (eds), *Laws of Our Fathers: Popular Culture and the U. S. Constitution* (Bowling Green: Bowling Green State University Popular Press, 1986) pp. 23–41 and H. Hellenbrand, *The Unfinished Revolution: Education and Politics in the Thought of Thomas Jefferson* (Newark: University of Delaware Press, 1990).
12.   Horace, *Satires*, II, vi, 60: 'O country home, when shall I look on you again…?' [and read the writings of the ancients, dine with my friends, and take my rest free from care?]
13.   Wilson, op. cit. n. 9, p. 90, n. 94.
14.   The hemisphere of the auditorium in Cabell Hall faces the Rotunda. The intervening wall carries a reproduction of Raphael's 'School of Athens' which, thus, stands between the audience and the Lawn as a kind of mystic presence. The dimensions of the hemisphere halve the circle of the Rotunda.
15.   Armand-Guy de Kersaint, cited from the exhibition catalogue, *Les Architectes de la Liberté 1789–1799* (Paris: Ecole nationale supérieure des Beaux-Arts, 1989) p. 328; Ledoux from the 'Ramée' edn (1847), p. xv of *L'architecture considérée sur le rapport de l'Art, des Mouers et de la Législation* (1804).
16.   Ledoux, ed. cit. n. 15, p. xiii.
17.   The best account of the Capitol remains F. Kimball, *The Capitol of Virginia* (Richmond, Va: Virginia State Library and Archives, revised edn, 1989). For a comprehensive survey of architectural theory and practice as it moves from the Enlightenment into the era of romantic nationalism, see A. Braham, *The Architecture of the French Enlightenment* (London: Thames and Hudson, 1980), with extensive general bibliography, which should be supplemented from the more specific discussion and bibliographical material in *Les Architectes de la Liberté 1789–99*, edn cit. n. 15. Particularly pertinent to my own discussion of heroic icons in architectural space is G. Le Coat,

'Thomas Jefferson and the Architecture of Immortality', *Laurels* 55 (1984) 41–54.

18. See p. 53 above.

19. Travelling notes for Mr. Rutledge and Mr. Shippen, 19 June 1788.

20. The primitive hut is described by Vitruvius. The second edition of M. A. Laugier's *Essai sur l'architecture* (1755) illustrates the hut as its frontispiece, stressing its natural origins by showing it constructed from four trees growing from the ground, above which a triangular wooden cruck forms the roof. See J. Rykwert, *On Adam's House in Paradise: the Idea of the Primitive Hut in Architectural History* (New York: Museum of Modern Art, 1972). The pavilions at each end of the Monticello terraces use the form of the 'hut', thus forming part of the historical schema Jefferson envisaged for the site.

21. See F. D. Nichols and R. E. Griswold, *Thomas Jefferson, Landscape Architect* (Charlottesville: University Press of Virginia, 1978); W. L. Beiswanger, 'Jefferson's Designs for Garden Structures at Monticello', *JSAH* 35 (1976) 310–12 and 'The Temple in the Garden: Thomas Jefferson's Vision of the Monticello Landscape' in R. P. Maccubin and P. Martin (eds), *British and American Gardens in the Eighteenth Century* (Williamsburg: Colonial Williamsburg Foundation, 1984) pp. 170–88; P. Martin, 'Landscape Gardening at Mount Vernon and Monticello' in *The Pleasure Gardens of Virginia: from Jamestown to Jefferson* (Princeton: Princeton University Press, 1991) pp. 134–64; R. J. Favretti, 'Thomas Jefferson's "Ferme Ornée" at Monticello', *Proceedings of the American Antiquarian Society* 103 (1993) 17–29; C. Daufenbach, 'Jefferson's Monticello and the Poetics of Landscape Gardening', *Soundings* 78 (1995) 399–415. More generally, see W. H. Adams (ed.), *The Eye of Thomas Jefferson* (Charlottesville: Thomas Jefferson Memorial Foundation, 1976); W. H. Adams, *Jefferson's Monticello* (New York: Abbeville Press, 1983); G. Waddell, 'The First Monticello', *JSAH* 46 (1987) 5–29; R. Isaac, 'The First Monticello', in P. S. Onuf (ed.), *Jeffersonian Legacies* (Charlottesville, University Press of Virginia, 1993) pp. 77–108; J. McLaughlin, *Jefferson and Monticello: the Biography of a Builder* (New York: Henry Holt, 1988).

22. H. S. Randall, *The Life of Thomas Jefferson* (1858), III, 338.

23. M. D. Peterson (ed.), *Visitors to Monticello* (Charlottesville: University Press of Virginia, 1989) pp. 74–9, 111–13.

24. 'Now, Penshurst, they that will proportion thee/With other edifices, when they see/Those proud, ambitious heaps, and nothing else,/May say, their lords have built, but thy lord dwells.' For an extended discussion of the place of the poem in country-house tradition, see Kelsall, op. cit. n. 6, ch. 4.

25. See C. A. Brown, 'Thomas Jefferson's Poplar Forest: the Mathematics of an Ideal Villa', *JGH* 10 (1990) 117–39 and S. A. Chambers, Jr, *Poplar Forest and Thomas Jefferson* (Poplar Forest: Corporation for Poplar Forest, 1993) which subsumes earlier studies.

26. The best account of Monticello in architectural context is still T. T. Waterman, *The Mansions of Virginia, 1706–1776* (Chapel Hill: University of North Carolina Press, 1945). More up to date, with extensive

bibliography, is C. E Brownell, *et al.* (eds), *The Making of Virginia Architecture* (Richmond: Virginia Museum of Fine Arts, 1992). See also M. Lane, *Architecture of the Old South: Virginia* (New York: Abbeville Press, 1984). The standard account of Jefferson's knowledge of French architecture is H. C. Rice, Jr, *Thomas Jefferson's Paris* (Princeton: Princeton University Press, 1976). Although it is a commonplace in architectural histories of Monticello to emphasise the French connection, in my view this is to mistake similarities of architectural 'grammar' for correspondences in 'language' and to accept Jefferson's anglophobia at face value. I have discussed the issue in detail, op. cit. n. 28.

27. See E. Dumbauld, 'Jefferson and Adams' English Garden Tour', in W. H. Adams (ed.), *Jefferson and the Arts: an Extended View* (Washington, DC: National Gallery of Art, 1976) pp. 137–57.

28. See M. Kelsall, 'Vitruvian Man and the Iconography of Opposition: Lord Burlington's Chiswick and Jefferson's Monticello', *BJE-CS* 18 (1995) 1–17.

29. *Aeneid* VI, 258: 'Keep hence, ye that are uninitiated...', proclaimed as Aeneas began his journey into the underworld; at Stourhead inscribed on the Temple of Flora at one of the entrances to the garden circuit.

30. For the significations of the Orders, see J. Onians, *Bearers of Meaning: the Classical Orders in Antiquity, the Middle Ages, and the Renaissance* (Princeton: Princeton University Press, 1988).

31. See Kelsall, op. cit. n. 6, ch. 15.

32. For information on the artefacts at Monticello I have drawn generally upon S. R. Stein, *The Worlds of Thomas Jefferson at Monticello* (New York: Harry N. Abrams, 1993) which subsumes previous studies. See also the special edition of *The Magazine Antiques* 144 (1 July, 1993) devoted to Monticello and J. H. Robinson, 'An American Cabinet of Curiosities: Thomas Jefferson's Indian Hall at Monticello', *Winterthur Portfolio* 30 (1995) 41–58. I have also drawn extensively on the specialised files on the house in the archive of the International Center for Jefferson Studies at Kenwood and Monticello.

33. See R. F. Dalzell, Jr, 'Constructing Independence: Monticello, Mount Vernon, and the Men Who Built Them', *E-CS* 26 (1993) 543–80; C. Hunt-Jones, *Dolley and the 'great little Madison'* (Washington, DC: American Institute of Architects Foundation, 1977); A. Koch, *Jefferson and Madison: the Great Collaboration* (New York: Knopf, 1950); and J. M. Smith (ed.), cit. n. 11. Given the close relationship between Jefferson and Madison, the redesign, furnishing and function of Montpelier is an important supplement to the iconography of Monticello. Like Monticello, Montpelier functioned both as a 'museum' to educate family and visitors in national culture and as a theatre for the ostentation of family wealth. The drawing-room displayed portraits of the first five Presidents of the United States, and of early discoverers of America; the sculpture gallery included busts of Washington, La Fayette, John Paul Jones, Jefferson and Adams; prints of the patriotic paintings by Trumbull were interspersed with classics of European

art. Like Jefferson, Madison also affected the role of an independent and philosophical farmer, rich in books but 'wearing pantaloons Patched at the knees'. By choosing the Tuscan portico for Montpelier he opted for a more rustic simplicity in the Orders than at Monticello (Jefferson subsequently chose Tuscan for Poplar Forest), and the circular Temple of Venus in the garden 'naturalised' the house by iconographic allusion to natural fertility in what visitors saw as a 'romantic' landscape. But, as at Monticello, there is the same paradoxical relationship between an ideology of virtuous republican simplicity and the 'luxury' of imperial culture. The place of honour in the dining-room was given to a portrait of Louis XVI; the simple Temple of Venus was copied from a *fabrique* at Versailles; and visitors commented on the 'Presidential splendour' of the Sèvres china (from the collection of Marie Antoinette), the French furniture, gilt mirrors, pier glasses and fine silver. The economic basis of the villa was dependent on slave labour, and Madison, like Jefferson, was opposed to the incorporation of free negroes in the American nation. He favoured expulsion to that African homeland called 'Liberia'.

34.   'Seek out your ancient mother', *Aeneid* III, 96. Aeneas, about to found a new state by force of arms, is commanded to establish it on the soil of the ancient Italian motherland. The race, thus, is immemorially related to the native earth.

35.   'Happy the man' who, free from the cares of business, dwells in independence on his own country estate, Horace, *Epodes*, II,1.

36.   See Randall, op. cit. n.22, III, 343 on the regularity of the régime, especially of silent reading, imposed upon Jefferson's (adoring) granddaughters at Poplar Forest.

37.   *Jefferson's Monticello*, see n. 21.

38.   Peterson (ed.), cit. n. 23, p. 13. For Jefferson and Ossian see P. J. de Gategno, ' "The Source of Daily and Exalted Pleasure": Jefferson Reads the Poems of Ossian' in H. Gaskill (ed.), *Ossian Revisited*, (Edinburgh: Edinburgh Press, 1991) pp. 94–104 and J. McClaughlin, 'Jefferson, Poe, and Ossian', *E-CS* 26 (1993) 627–34.

39.   The passage in Fielding is discussed in detail in relation to country-house tradition in Kelsall, op. cit. n 6, ch. 11.

40.   For the *Désert* see D. Ketcham, *Le Désert de Retz* (Cambridge, Mass: MIT Press, 1994) with full bibliography.

41.   Op. cit. n. 22, III, 342.

5 Writing Monticello

1.   There existed already Isaac Ware's *The plans, elevations and sections; chimney-pieces and ceilings of Houghton* (1735) and, in addition to the catalogue of paintings in *Aedes Walpolianae*, there were bound in 'A sermon on painting preached before the Earl of Orford at Houghton' (1732) and 'A journey to Houghton . . . a poem by the Rev. Mr. Whaley' with plates and plans (1752).

2.   See Chapter 1 n. 2.

3. *A Winter in Washington; or, Memoirs of the Seymour Family* (3 vols, 1824) III, 215–30.
4. 'A Frenchman Visits Albemarle, 1816' tr. and (ed.), J. M. Carrier and L. G. Moffatt, *Papers of the Albemarle County Historical Society* 4 (1943–44) 45–52, reprinted in M. D. Peterson (ed.), *Visitors to Monticello*, (Charlottesville: University Press of Virginia, 1989) 67–71 (cited hereafter as *Visitors*). Peterson provides an excellent selection of early accounts of Monticello, and short quotations without reference in my text are drawn from him. I have supplemented Peterson from the incomplete bibliography of early descriptions of the house by J. A. Bear, Jr, 'Accounts of Monticello: 1780–1878: a Selective Bibliography', *The Magazine of Albemarle County History* 21 (1962–63), 13–21.
5. *Aeneid* I, 460. 'What part of the earth is not filled with our [Herculean] labours?'
6. 'Monticello', *Journal of American Institute of Architects* 12 (1924) 175–81; *Visitors*, pp. 188–92.
7. *Visitors*, p. 75.
8. III, 339.
9. *Visitors*, p. 11.
10. *Visitors*, pp. 45–54, from whom the subsequent quotations are drawn.
11. *A Discourse on the Lives and Characters of Thomas Jefferson and John Adams ... Delivered, at the request of the Citizens of Washington, in the Hall of Representatives of the United States* (1826) p. 59.
12. *Visitors*, p. 133.
13. *Visitors*, p. 12.
14. *Visitors*, p. 90.
15. Ed. M. E. Bradford, Indianapolis, Liberty Classics, 1977, pp. 80, 96, 67.
16. *Visitors*, p. 42.
17. *Visitors*, pp. 34–5.
18. *Visitors*, p. 128.

Index

Note: References are to Jefferson, unless otherwise indicated

Adair, Douglass 48
Adams, Henry 15–16
Adams, John (1735–1826) 14–15,
  24, 163
  letters to 29–30, 89
  and Seal 45, 48–55 *passim*, 58, 59,
    117, 186
  visits England with Jefferson
    124–9, 134, 160
Adams, John Quincy (1767–1848)
  179
Adams, William Howard 138
Addison, Joseph 52, 189
American defined 19–20
Ames, Fisher 54
ancient world as inspiration 4, 6,
  42, 140, 145–6, 186, 189, 198
  and *Notes* 80, 81, 85, 91
  and Seal 52–3, 55
  and villas 108, 109, 112–13,
    117–18, 123–4, 126, 137, 153,
    162, 194
  see also Capitols; Palladio;
    Pantheon; villas
Anderson, Benedict 36
arches, triumphal 6
architecture 6, 33–4, 42, 51
  see also Capitols; Monticello;
    pyramid; University of
    Virginia; villas *and under*
    Britain *and* France
Arieli, Yehoshua 13
'aristocracy of virtue' 112–13
Aristotle 65

Bancroft, George 15
Barlow, Joel 18, 23, 59
Bartholdi, Auguste 187
Barton, William 64–5
Bartram, William: *Travels* 74–9,
  83–4, 88, 95, 103

Belknap, Jeremy 84, 193–4
Benjamin, Judah Philip 18, 43
Bervic, Charles Clément 155
Bill of Rights 26
birth of nation *see* Independence
black people *see* slaves
Blake, William 22–3, 99, 106
Bolingbroke, Lord 62, 109
Bonaparte, Napoleon 19, 23, 34,
  133, 134, 155
Boullée, Etienne-Louis 34, 115, 117
Boyle, Robert 84, 88
Briggs, Isaac 171
Britain 29
  architecture 106–8, 114, 117, 118,
    121, 124–31, 134–6, 145–8,
    151–2
  rebellions against *see* Wars
  suggested symbolization on
    Seal 46, 47, 51, 52, 60–2
Brown, Charles Brockden:
    Wieland 74, 79–84, 86, 104, 142
Buckingham, James Silk 169
Bullock, S.C. 188–9
Burlington, Lord 124
  house *see* Chiswick
Byron, George Gordon, Lord 2, 4,
  12

Cabell Hall 113, 195
Campbell, Colen 129
Capitols
  state 51, 81, 116, 195
  Washington 15, 34, 115, 131, 148,
    186
Carter's Grove 105
Carwin (daemon) 82, 87
Cary, Jane 40–1
Castell, Robert 109
Catlin, George 78
Cato Uticensis 52

200

Ceracchi, Giuseppe   187
Channing, Walter   20
Chateaubriand, François
    August   69, 97
Chiswick (Britain) *Plate 5*;   121, 125,
    127–9, 136
Christianity *see* religion
Cicero   108, 109
Cincinnatus   52, 112, 186
Civil War   20
Clark, William: inscribes tree
    69–73, 74
    see also Lewis and Clark
classical inspiration *see* ancient
    world
Claude Lorrain   80
Cobham, Lord, house of *see* Stowe
Cogwell, Joseph   15
Coke, Sir Edward   50
Coleridge, Samuel Taylor   78
Cole, Thomas   80–1, 190–1
Congreve, William   148, 155, 160
conquest, rights of   56–7
Conrad, Joseph   40, 98
Constant, Benjamin   108
Constitution, American   4, 26, 47
    see also Founding Fathers
Cooper, James Fenimore   9, 53, 80,
    97, 108, 134
Correa de Serra, Joseph   114
corruption *see* degeneration
Cosway, Maria   114, 118, 142, 151
    letter to   149, 150
country houses *see* villas
cultural history   40–1
    see also Monticello

Darwinism   39, 76, 104
David, Gerard   142
Dawley Farm   109
decay *see* degeneration
de Chambray, Fréart   140, 145
de Chastellux, chevalier   141,
    142–3, 167, 170, 172
Declaration of Independence   175
    in Jefferson Memorial   163
    and *Notes*   99
    and pilgrimage to Monticello   2,
        6, 7, 14–17, 25–7, 35, 37, 40

and Seal   58
de Crèvecoeur   19, 20, 93
Defoe, Daniel   160
degeneration and corruption   93–4,
    101
    of Monticello   153–4, 162, 174–5
Démeunier, Jean-Nicolas   97, 100,
    193
democracy   37–8, 40
Désert de Retz (France)   117, 118,
    151–2
de Staël, Madame   3, 12
de Tessé, Madame   132, 188
discourse of Monticello   159–76
Dix, John   174
dollar   63, 139
domes *Plate 2*;   127
    see also under Monticello
domesticity of Jefferson   137–9, 141,
    142, 168
Drake, Sir Francis   146, 147
Durand, Asher Brown   81
du Simitière, Pierre-Eugène: and
    Seal of United States   26, 45,
    47, 49–51, 54, 60–1, 62, 92
Dwight, Timothy   39, 54, 57, 58–9,
    88, 156

eagle   63, 64, 131
Ellis, Joseph J.   40
Emerson, Ralph Waldo   17, 38
England *see* Britain
Enlightenment   12, 13, 14, 46, 82–3
e pluribus unum   5, 51–2, 61, 63–8
    passim, 123
Europe   8, 29, 76
    suggested symbolization on
        Seal   46, 47, 51, 52, 59–62
    see also Britain; France; Germanic;
        Ireland
Everett, Edward   16–17, 18, 19
extermination *see* genocide; Terror
eye
    depicted   6, 52, 66, 99
    panoptic vision   85–8, 101

fasces/bundle of rods   50–1, 68, 116,
    131, 186
'fascism'   13, 14, 44

Federalism and Seal   49, 54, 64,
   65
fête   5, 47, 178, 179
   see also visits *under* La Fayette
Fichte, Johann Gottlieb   5, 16, 32,
   183–4
Fielding, Henry   150, 172
First Inaugural   30–2, 35
flag   5, 47, 63
Foster, Augustus John   171, 172–3
Founding Fathers   48, 54
   see also Franklin; Madison;
      Washington
France   14–15
   architecture   34, 107–8, 115–18,
      151–2, 162
   Revolution and Terror   23, 27–30,
      99–100, 104, 114
   rights of man   10
   suggested symbolization on
      Seal   46, 47, 52, 62
   see also La Fayette
Franklin, Benjamin   26
   bust in Monticello   132–3
   and lightning   48, 133, 142–3
   and Seal   45, 48–53 *passim*, 56–68
      passim, 91
freedom *see* liberty
Freemasonry   2, 3, 6, 58, 66, 121,
   188–9
Freneau, Philip   30
Frye, Northrop   157

Gallatin, Albert   15
gardens   118, 128, 134, 139, 160
   Monticello *Plate 1*;   106, 118–19,
      143
genocide/ethnic cleansing   60,
   61–2, 103–4
George III   23, 25, 57, 58
Germanic culture and thinkers   95,
   183–4
   and pilgrimage to Monticello   5,
      12, 15, 16, 18, 20, 32, 36
   and Seal   47, 55, 61
Gilmer, Francis W.   6
Gilpin, Henry D.   120
Gilpin, William   160
Golden Age   78–9

Goya, Francisco J. de   83, 98
Grange, La (France)   107–8, 115
Gray, Francis   172
Greeks *see* ancient world
Greenfield, Liah   13
Gurley, Rev. R.R.   100

Hagley (Britain)   134, 136, 160
Hall, Francis   120, 166, 168
Hamilton, Alexander   24, 35, 54,
   132, 147
Heckewelder, John   103
Heely, Joseph   160
Hemmings, Sally   194
Hengist and Horsa   55–7
heraldic scheme for Seal   51, 60–1,
   63
Hercules   80, 81, 117–18, 162, 186,
   189
   suggested for Seal   52–3, 55
Herder, Johann G. von   5, 12, 20, 36,
   95
Hermes Trismegistus   66, 121
Highlands/Ashlawn   110–11, 161
hills, significance of   86, 106–7,
   117–21, 127, 166, 168–9, 171
Hoare, Henry   118, 162
Holkham (Britain)   135, 136
Holmes, John   36, 94
'homeland' as written place   70–2
Horace   52, 108, 140, 198
Houdon, Jean-Antoine   51, 116
Houghton Hall (Britain)
   Plate 8;   129–30, 131, 160
Humphreys, David   14, 23
Hutchins, Thomas   84, 191

iconography *see* Jefferson
'imaginary community'   36
   see also romantic nationalism
Imlay, Gilbert   84, 192
Inauguration/Inaugurals   30–2, 35,
   88, 138, 187
Independence   45, 95
   Day   5, 179
   War of   2, 24–5, 27, 36, 180
   see also Declaration of
      Independence; liberty
Indians   39–40, 143, 178

individuals 96–7, 102–3, 132, 133,
     178
   and *Notes* 70, 73, 76–9, 94–7,
     103–4, 190
   and Seal 59–60, 187
   Ireland 37, 47, 59–60, 61, 125–6
Irving, Washington 173

Jackson, Jesse 11
Jacobinism 8, 15, 23, 165
Jefferson (father of Thomas) 85
Jefferson, J. Garland 31
Jefferson, Martha (wife) 137, 141,
     142
Jefferson, Thomas: iconography of
   Romanticism *see* architecture;
   Monticello; *Notes*; romantic
   nationalism; Seal of United
   States
Jefferson Memorial *Plate 14*; 22, 43,
     111, 148, 162–3
Jones, John Paul 144–5, 147, 154
Jonson, Ben 123–4, 130

Kames, Lord 56
Kedourie, E. 178–9
Kenwood (USA) 105, 107
Kercheval, Samuel 163
Kersaint, Armand-Guy de 115
Kimball, Fiske 160, 164–6, 171, 174
Kohn, Hans 12–13
'Koine' 4–5, 8, 12, 14, 108, 163
Kramer, Lloyd 7, 13

La Fayette, Marie Joseph, Marquis
     de 16, 19, 28, 35, 57, 66
   correspondence with 6–10, 90
   and La Grange 107–8, 115
   significance of 12, 13, 114
   visits America 1–11, 14, 16, 17,
     37, 40–1, 105, 106, 114–15, 117,
     135, 161, 175, 177–8
land 40–1
   see also Nature; *Notes*
landownership and power 49, 72
   see also Whigs
landscape painting 80–1, 109, 191
language
   common *see* 'Koine'

national 20–1, 38–9, 41, 92,
     181–2, 184
   and *Notes* 71, 74, 92
   and Seal 49, 61–2
   see also Latin
La Rochefoucauld, François, duc de
     114
Latin mottos 66, 186
   see also e pluribus unum
Latrobe, Benjamin 34, 187
Latrobe, John H.B. 168–9
law and order 58
   see also Seal of United States
Lawrence, D.H. 69, 70, 78
Ledoux, Claude-Nicolas 34, 115,
     116, 117
L'Enfant, Pierre Charles 34, 185–6
Le Nôtre, André 162
Leutze 16, 47
Levasseur, Auguste 2, 161, 177–8
Levy, Uriah 162
Lewis and Clark expedition
   (Meriwether Lewis and William
   Clark) 35, 69–73, 77, 182
Lewis, George W. 22
liberalism 7–8, 9–10, 13
liberty 3, 4, 5, 8, 13, 24, 26, 33
   goddess 54
   see also Independence
Library of Congress 139
Lincoln, Abraham 17, 32, 159
Lincoln, Levi 24, 96
Livy 91, 112
Logan 96–7, 102–3
looming 86–7, 104, 166–7, 169
Louisiana
   explored *see* Lewis and Clark
   as imaginary space 72
   purchase 16, 20, 35, 38, 58, 131,
     133

McKinley, William 45, 66
Madison, James 3, 7, 15, 24, 26, 114
   house *see* Montpelier
Malone, Dumas 43
Martial 108, 140
Masons *see* Freemasonry
master/slave symbiosis 100–2
May, Henry 12

Mazzei letter 28, 30
Melish, John 85
metahistory 11–12, 13, 16, 23
 see also romantic nationalism
Middleton, Conyers 109
millennialism 18, 23, 181
Miller, David 11
Milton, John/Miltonic eschatology
 22–3, 24, 25, 26, 28, 33, 88
 and *Notes* 106, 146, 163
miscegenation 95, 97, 98, 194
Monroe, James 15, 111, 188
Monticello *Plate 4*; 34, 42, 105–58,
 194–8
 abandoned and decaying 153–4,
 162, 174–5
 comparisons *see* architecture
 under Britain *and* France
 dining-room 139–44
 dome *Plate 13*; 4, 124, 128–9, 139,
 148–51, 152
 entrance front *Plate 6*
 garden *Plate 1*; 106, 118–19, 143
 hall *Plate 6*; 124, 125, 129,
 130–5, 136
 hill as pyramid 86, 119–21
 'Indian hall' 132–5, 171
 Jefferson's bedroom *Plate 10*;
 124, 137, 138–9
 library 135–6, 137, 138–9, 168
 and looming 86–7, 104, 166–7,
 169
 Pantheon 6, 119, 121
 parlour 124, 135, 136, 147
 plan of ground floor *Plate 9*
 staircases *Plate 15*; 125, 135, 151
 tearoom *Plate 11*; 144–5
 visits to *see* pilgrimage
 writing 159–76, 198–9
Montlezun, Baron de 161
Montpelier (USA) 107, 108, 110,
 134, 161, 197–8
Morgan, Lady 107–8
Morse, Jedidiah 20, 84
Moses 58, 66–7, 121
motto *see e pluribus unum*
mountains *see* hills
Mount Vernon (USA) 108, 109, 110,
 153

myth, ethical/necessary *see* fête

names of Seal committee members,
 significance of 49–50
Napoleon *see* Bonaparte
national anthem 47
nationalism *see* language; romantic
 nationalism
'natural bridge' 89–90, 121
Nature
 battles with 74–8, 104
 benign 73
 controlled *see* gardens
 Golden Age 78–9
 and Monticello 86, 119–21, 159,
 164, 166–8
 sublime 87–90
 violence of 87–90, 93–4, 104
 worship of 79–82
 see also hills; land; wilderness;
 Wordsworth
Nietzsche, Friedrich W. 5, 15
Notes on State of Virginia (Jefferson)
 42, 69–104, 166–7, 189–94
 Bartram's *Travels* compared with
 74–9, 83–4, 88, 95, 103
 and Jefferson Memorial 163
 Lewis and Clark expedition 35,
 69–73, 77, 182
 map 85
 Monticello and looming 86–7
 'Patowmac, passage of' 87–90,
 93–4
 people and race 90–104
 reluctance to publish 84–5
 Wieland compared with *see*
 Brown

Occom, Rev. Samson 188
optical illusion *see* looming
Ossian 96, 97, 141, 143, 145, 152
'Other', racial 98–102
 see also race

Paine, Thomas 13, 14, 18, 30, 31
 and Seal 57, 58
Palladio and Palladian villas 3, 109,
 110, 113, 126, 165
 Villa Rotunda (Vicenza) 121

see also Monticello
Pantheon
  Monticello 6, 119, 121
  Paris 115
  Rome 121–4, 163–4
  Stourhead 118, 162
  University of Virginia 2, 3–4, 156
'Patowmac' *see* Potomac
Patterson, Richard 49
Pearse, Padraic 15, 37, 42
Peebles, Lawson 35
Pendleton, Edmund 113
people (*Volk*) 5, 9, 18–20, 35, 40–1
  absent 90
  chosen 91–6
  and *Notes* 73, 83, 90–104, 191, 192
  and Seal 46–7
  and villas 112, 153
  see also e pluribus; race
Persico, Luigi 186
Peterson, Merrill D. 43, 175–6
Pierson, William H. 33
pilgrimage to Monticello 1–44,
  160–1, 166–76, 177–85, 199
  see also visits *under* La Fayette
Pine, Robert Edge 131, 186
place 69
  see also land; *Notes*
Plato and Platonic 22, 85, 112, 113
Pliny the younger 108, 137, 153
Pocahontas 97, 133, 187
poetry and poets 3, 22–3, 99, 106,
  123–4, 129, 160
  see also Blake; Milton; Pope;
    Shelley; Wordsworth
Pope, Alexander 108, 119, 129, 146,
  160
Poplar Forest (USA) 124, 153,
  156–7, 162, 170
portico *Plate 1*; 2, 4
Potomac, passage of 87–90, 93–4,
  149
Priestley, Joseph 31, 57, 111
private realm 124, 135–6, 137,
  138–9
  united with public 3–4
property *see* landownership
Providence 6, 16
  eye of 52, 99

public realm 124, 125, 129–36,
  138–44, 148
  united with private 3–4
pyramid
  at Monticello 86, 119–21, 131,
    166
  and Seal 45, 52, 66–7, 121, 186

race 39–40
  miscegenation 95, 97, 98, 194
  and *Notes* 94–5, 192–3
  purity 92–7, 100–2
  see also Indians; people; slaves
Raleigh, Sir Walter 146, 147
Ramsay, David 14, 53, 69, 84, 89,
  96, 188
Randall, Henry S. 119–20, 137,
  166–7
Randolph, Sarah N.: and
  family 97, 137
Reinheit see purity *under* race
religion 38–9, 82, 184
  and Seal 49–50, 57–8, 66–7
  tolerance 123, 163, 175
  and villas 121, 123, 132–3, 163,
    169–70
Renan, Ernest 19, 21, 22, 34
Republicanism and Seal 49, 54
revolution 2–3, 4, 9–10, 60–1
  see also liberty; romantic
    nationalism *and under* France
Richardson, Samuel 160
Riefenstahl, Leni 21, 22
rights 4, 10, 26, 46, 96, 99
  of conquest 56–7
  see also liberty
Robinson, William 103
Romans *see* ancient world
Romanticism *see* Jefferson
romantic nationalism 2–45 *passim*,
  164–5, 180, 181, 183
  and democracy 37–8, 40
  Irish 37
  symbolic order *see* dollar; flag;
    Seal
  unity, national 31–3
  see also cultural history; Jefferson;
    land; liberty; Nature; people
Roosevelt, Franklin D. 107

Rousseau, Jean-Jacques   12, 13, 14, 19, 99, 137
Rush, Benjamin   168

savages   82
    noble   78–9
    see also Indians
Scott, Sir Walter   96, 134
Seal of United States *Plate 2*;   42, 45–68, 99, 121, 131–2, 185–9
Second Inaugural   32
Seeley, Benton *Plate 12*;   160
Serlio, Sebastiano   121–3
sexuality   55, 101–2
Seymour family   161, 168, 169, 171
Shaftesbury, Anthony A.C.   50, 52, 53, 80, 117
Shays's rebellion   28
Shelley, Mary   82–3, 108
Shelley, Percy B.   7, 12, 23, 31, 32, 98, 102, 165
Short, William   27, 155
slaves   36, 39–40, 43, 163, 178, 198
    invisible   135, 141, 156
    master/slave symbiosis   100–2
    and *Notes*   71, 94–100, 192–3, 194
    and Seal   65, 67
    and villas   124, 135, 140, 141, 156, 161–2, 171–2, 178
Smith, Cary   178
Smith, Margaret   168, 170, 171, 173
Sommer, F.H.   186
Sprat, Thomas   84, 88
Stourhead (Britain)   118, 119, 128, 162
Stowe (Britain)   108, 117, 118, 136, 145–8, 151, 152, 160, 162, 169
sublime, Nature as   87–90

Tacitus   44, 55
Taylor, John   93, 172
Tecumseh   132, 133, 178
Ternant, Jean Baptiste   155
Terror, American   20, 27, 29
    see also Revolution *under* France
thirteen   51, 63, 186
Thomson, Charles   64–5, 192, 193
Thomson, James   160
Thoreau, Henry David   35, 157

Thornton, Anna and Edward   173–4
Ticknor, George   16, 168, 172
Toqueville, A. de   37–41, 94
Tories   24, 29, 31–2, 54, 125, 163
    see also Adams, John
Trumbull, John   15, 21, 40, 72, 131
Turgot, A.R.J.   5, 132–3
Turner, Frederick Jackson   17, 72
Turner, Joseph M.W.   80, 166
Twickenham villa   108, 119
Tyng, Rev. Stephen Higginson   174–6

unity *see e pluribus and under* romantic nationalism
University of Virginia *Plate 2*;   34, 35, 112–13, 148, 162, 164, 175
    Pantheon   2, 3–4, 156
Urvolk see Indians
Utopianism   76, 82–3, 114

Vernon, Admiral Edward   110
Versailles (France)   34, 162
Vespucci, Amerigo   70
villas   105–58
    see also Monticello; Palladio *and* architecture *under* Britain
Virgil   52, 66, 67, 91, 121, 122, 146, 189
Virginia
    map of   85
    Statute for Religious Freeom   163, 175
    see also Monticello; *Notes*
vision *see* eye
Vitruvius/Vitruvian   123, 124, 126
Volk see people
Volney, comte de   38, 39, 84, 120, 184, 193

Walpole, Sir Robert: house *see* Houghton
Wars
    of 1812   15, 171–2
    of Independence   2, 24–5, 27, 36, 180
Washington, George   21, 28, 35, 52, 66, 155
    birthday   47

'Farewell Address' 18–19, 20
house *see* Mount Vernon
as iconological sign 42–3
obelisk 43
statues of 51, 70, 116, 162
tomb of 1, 5, 6, 177
see also Inauguration
Washington (city) 182
Capitol 15, 34, 115, 131, 148, 186
Mall 34, 42
White House 34, 148
Watson, General 107
Weightman, Roger 46, 175, 176
'West' *see* wilderness
Whately, Thomas 126, 160
Wheatley, Phillis 188
Whigs 24, 30, 31–2, 163
architecture *see under* Britain
and Seal 46, 49, 58, 185
and villas 109–11, 114, 115, 118,
125–30, 133, 162, 165
see also liberalism; Monticello
Whitcomb, Samuel 173
White, Hayden 11
White House 34, 148
white male supremacy 112–13, 125
see also race; women

Whitman, Walt 71, 73
wilderness 59–60, 62, 67, 73, 188
expeditions to *see* Bartram; Lewis
and Clark; *Notes*
and Monticello 166, 170–2
and Seal 58–60, 68
see also Nature
Williams, Helen Maria 178
Williams, Samuel 84, 193
Willis's Mountain 86, 119–21
Wilson, Richard 109
Wilson, Robert Woodrow 61
women 43, 54–5, 142
Wood, Gordon 14, 54
Wordsworth, William 23, 32, 72, 85,
86, 167
and American wilderness 164–5
and cult of cottage 108
'deep abiding place' 73
as spiritual socialist 90
see also Nature
written place
'homeland' as 70–2
Monticello as 159–76, 198–9

yeomanry *see* people
Young, Arthur 105, 125